Asian Canada Is Burning

Studies in Critical Social Sciences Book Series

Haymarket Books is proud to be working with Brill Academic Publishers (www.brill.nl) to republish the *Studies in Critical Social Sciences* book series in paperback editions. This peer-reviewed book series offers insights into our current reality by exploring the content and consequences of power relationships under capitalism, and by considering the spaces of opposition and resistance to these changes that have been defining our new age. Our full catalog of *SCSS* volumes can be viewed at https://www.haymarketbooks.org/series_collections/4-studies-in-critical-social-sciences.

Asian Canada Is Burning

Theories, Methods, Pedagogies, and Praxes

Edited by
Rose Ann Torres, Ian Liujia Tian
and Coly Chau

Haymarket Books
Chicago, IL

First published in 2025 by Brill Academic Publishers, The Netherlands

Published in paperback in 2026 by
Haymarket Books
P.O. Box 180165
Chicago, IL 60618
773-583-7884
www.haymarketbooks.org

ISBN: 979-8-88890-784-9

Distributed to the trade in the US through Consortium Book Sales and Distribution (www.cbsd.com) and internationally through Ingram Publisher Services International (www.ingramcontent.com).

This book was published with the generous support of Lannan Foundation, Wallace Action Fund, and the Marguerite Casey Foundation.

Cover design by Jamie Kerry and Ragina Johnson.

Printed in the United States.

Library of Congress Cataloging-in-Publication data is available.

Contents

Acknowledgements IX
Notes on Contributors X

1 Introduction 1
Ian Liujia Tian, Coly Chau and Rose Ann Torres

PART 1
Situating Asia(ns) beyond Settler Canadian Nationalism

2 Tearing Down Walls: Rethinking White Domesticity in the Context of Cultural Domicide 17
Shelly Ikebuchi

3 Unpacking the Festival of Diwali in Canada: Where have Rama, Sita, and Lakshman Gone? 30
Rajni Mala Khelawan

4 Seeking Pappy's Approval 42
Krystal Kavita Jagoo

5 Vulnerable Resisters: Decolonizing Voices of Asian Migrants in a Settler Colonial and Religious Context 45
Hyejung Jessie Yum

6 Unboxing Our Narrative of Space and Place: An Unsettling Dance of (Un)Belonging 58
Jose Miguel Esteban

PART 2
Gender, Sexuality and Other Intimacies

7 The Bee 73
Elisha Lim

8 Labour, Intimacy and Diaspora: Queer Asian Studies in Canada 88
Ian Liujia Tian

9 The Past in the Present: An Encounter between Gay Asians of Toronto and New Ho Queen 97
Samuel Yoon

10 Love Intersections: Queer Sensibilities and Relationality in Art and Cultural Production 109
David Ng and Jen Sungshine

11 Emergent Asian-Canadian Feminisms: Insights from Young Filipina/x Feminist Scholar-Organizers 125
Monica Batac, Julia Baladad, Psalmae Tesalona, Chloe Rodriguez and France Clare Stohner

PART 3
Building Solidarities

12 The Butterfly Effect: Asian Massage Parlour and Sex Workers and Historical Chinese Laundries Fighting By-Laws and Organizing Towards Justice 147
Coly Chau and Elene Lam

13 Asian Canadian Workers Organizing: The Making of the Asian Canadian Labour Alliance 159
Anna Liu

14 A Love Letter to Asian Canadian Studies: On Ethical Solidarities and Decolonial Futures 178
Janey Lew

15 Dumpster Fires, Burning Affects 190
Malissa Phung

16 Internationalist Solidarity: Palestinian Liberation, BDS, and the Struggle against Normalization 202
Boycott, Divest and Sanction Toronto

17 Conclusion: Asian Futurism as Living Labour 213
Ian Liujia Tian

Index 217

Acknowledgements

Collectively, we thank the contributors and editors! It is a dream comes true to make a book of Asian Canadian studies that feature new, emerging, radical, and activist voices. Dr. Rose Ann Torres would like to thank her family for their love, patience, and understanding during the making of this book. This book is dedicated to her husband, Dr. Dionisio Nyaga and their her children, Waywaya, Samuel, and Simon. She also wants to thank her co-editors, all the contributors, and Brill publishing.

Ian Liujia Tian wants to thank friends, mentors, and comrades who have journeyed together. Jamie Magnusson, Shana Ye, and Jesook Song have been great sources of inspiration, critique, and feminist care. Rose and Coly, thank you for staying and shaping this book together! Vedanth Govi, Sabra Rezaei, Yasmine Abdelhadi, Aida Parnia, Riu Liu, Idil Abdillahi, Gary Kinsman, Desmond Cole, Beverly Bain, Ran Deng, Sherry Ostappvitch, Aytak Dibavar, Grayson Lee, Mengzhu Fu showed me how to practice and live our politics. I want to thank everyone from No Pride in Policing and Chinese Feminist Toronto, whom I will not name for confidentiality. My friends who helped make Toronto my home: Vinnie and Liam, all the love to you two. Lastly, I would not be able to have a sense of belonging if it is not for my partner Arash Ghiassi and his parents, Amir and Nastaran, who take me in as their family member, although my family cannot do the same. Arash, this book is for you as much as it is for me and the field of Asian Canadian Studies.

Coly Chau would like to thank Rose and Ian. Rose, thank you for your warmth, humour and for bringing Ian and I into this project. Ian, thank you for your brilliance and tenacity in keeping us on track. Thank you to the many political and community spaces that have given me a home grounded in the realities, as well as possibilities for solidarity and liberation. Thank you to those who love and care for me. Fiona, Tharmila, Hibah, Kimberly, Kathleen, Rain, and countless others who have shared times of joy and creativity. Kam Siu, Chit Man, Jessie, Leon, dad, sister, my entire family, and ancestors. Jeffrey, thank you for bearing the endless amounts of time I have been too busy working on "book stuff", for the depths of support and endless laughs. Regent and Wendy, my whole entire heart, thank you for the unwavering love. Thank you to our contributors, to those who were "almost" contributors, and to all the scholars, activists, artists and communities that this collection is indebted to. Thank you Brill for allowing us to be in conversation with and within Asian Canadian Studies.

Notes on Contributors

Julia Baladad

was the Program Assistant and Logistics Coordinator for the main organizing team of the Pinay Power II Conference. Raised in the north suburbs of Chicago, Julia is the eldest daughter of three and a self-proclaimed sudoku master. At the time of writing, Julia was completing her final year of a Bachelor of Arts at McGill University. Currently, she is obtaining her paralegal certificate and plans to work within the immigration field, hoping to continue in work that is grounded in community and care.

Monica Anne Batac

is currently a Lecturer at University of Manitoba's Faculty of Social Work and completing her PhD in Social Work at McGill University. She is a critical qualitative researcher, community practitioner, and educator. Her interdisciplinary research program focuses on community capacity-building and mobilizing with Filipino community members, groups, and organizations in Canada. Monica is a co-founder and co-organizer of the Filipino Canadian Social and Community Workers Network.

Coly Chau

has a Master of Education in Social Justice Education from the Ontario Institute for Studies in Education, University of Toronto. Her research interests include race, gender, sexuality, migration, anti-colonial thought and spirituality. Coly is interested in the unearthing and reclamation of knowledges for the purposes of imagining and working toward decolonial and liberatory futures. They are often working, organizing and learning in their communities. Coly acknowledges and offers respect to the Dish With One Spoon territories and the Coast Salish territories, and their original stewards, on whose land she continues to learn from/on.

Jose Miguel (Miggy) Esteban

is a dance/movement artist and educator based in Tkaronto/Toronto. Miggy's artistic work develops improvisational practices of navigating mad and queer routes to embody Filipinx remembering and belonging. Currently a PhD candidate at the Department of Social Justice Education, OISE/University of Toronto, Miggy's research and teaching is oriented through disability studies, black studies, and dance/performance studies. Influenced by disability arts and culture, black radical traditions, indigenous storytelling, and queer performance, Miggy's dissertation project engages in embodied practices of improvisation to re-interpret curriculum as a choreographic site for inspiring pedagogies of/through dance.

Shelly Ikebuchi
holds a Master and PhD in sociology (UBC), as well as a Master of Educational Technology (UBC). She currently teaches in the Department of Sociology at Okanagan College in Kelowna, British Columbia which is on the unceded territory of the Sylix Okanagan Peoples. Shelly's research focuses on Japanese and Chinese Canadian histories. More recently her research has included more contemporary concerns such as accessibility issues in the use of educational technologies.

Krystal Kavita Jagoo
holds a Bachelor of Arts degree in Sociology and a Master of Social Work degree. As a fat queer disabled Indo-Trinidadian woman and settler on Turtle Island, she remains intent on anti-oppressive practice given social work's ongoing complicity with the problematic status quo, which is why she first taught "Justice and the Poor: Issues of Race, Class, and Gender" at Nipissing University in 2012 and worked as a Wellness Counselor and Coordinator for the University of Toronto in 2018 before transitioning into the role of Accessibility Advisor, which she held until December 2021, when forced out by rampant inherently ableist white supremacist workplace harassment. Her essay, "Inclusive Reproductive Justice" was published in Volume 2 of the Reproductive Justice Briefing Book: A Primer on Reproductive Justice and Social Change. Jagoo's commitment to equity can be seen from her arts programming, which includes offerings like Sustainable Resistance for BIPOC Folx, BIPOC Disability Justice (Un)Learning Journeys, Navigating Grief in BIPOC Solidarity, etc. With over 100 publications in 2021, her writing includes both reported work and essays but mostly illuminates the reality of oppression. Thanks to Ontario Arts Council and Toronto Arts Council grants, she is working on her essay collection, "They Colonized Even My Tongue."

Rajni Mala Khelawan
is an Indo-Fijian Canadian novelist and researcher. Her two novels are *Kalyana* (2016) and *The End of the Dark and Stormy Night* (2008). In 2024, her first children's book, *I am a Hindu*, was published by Saunders Book Company for Canadian schools and public libraries. She holds a Master of Arts Degree from the University of Toronto where she studied gender and ritual among Fijian Hindu Women under the SSHRC grant. Khelawan's areas of academic research includes South Asian religions; indentured history and colonization;

and transnational and diaspora studies. Currently, she lives in Toronto, and is working on completing her next novel under the Canada Council for the Arts grant, which she won in 2022. To learn more about her and her work, visit her website: www.rajnimalakhelawan.com.

Elene Lam
is the founder and Executive Director of Butterfly (Asian and Migrant Sex Workers Support Network) and the Migrant Sex Workers Project. She has been involved in both the gender and sex work movements, as well as migrant and labour activism for almost 20 years.

Anna Liu
is a union organizer and activist based in Tkaronto/Toronto. She is an active member of the Asian Canadian Labour Alliance (ACLA), a group committed to anti-racism, advancing equity in the labour movement, and fostering solidarity between labour and racialized communities. Anna holds an MA in Labour Studies from McMaster University and has authored several publications on the Canadian labour movement.

Janey Lew
is an educator, scholar, and writer living, playing, and loving on the unceded Coast Salish territories of Halkomelem speaking peoples. Janey is a Senior Strategist at the Centre for Teaching, Learning, and Technology at the University of British Columbia, where she supports faculty development and strategic educational initiatives for Indigenous engagement and anti-racist pedagogies. Janey holds a PhD in Ethnic Studies from the University of California, Berkeley and previously taught at UBC, SFU, Capilano University, Douglas College, and UC Berkeley.

Elisha Lim
is an Assistant Professor of the Technological Humanities at York University. Lim researches the intersection of social media, theology and critical race theory, and is currently working on a book called Pious about the rise in distorted identity politics, from ethnic fraud and polarizing populism to hyperbolic corporate solidarity statements. Lim has also produced numerous award winning queer and transgender films, comic strips, and a graphic novel, and is working on their forthcoming book 8 Dreams About You.

David Ng
is an interdisciplinary artist, filmmaker, activist, and academic. He is the Co-Artistic Director of Love Intersections, a media arts collective of queer artists

of colour with a mandate to share intersectional stories through art. He is a Research Associate for Hello Cool World Media, and he is the project lead for Cultivating Kin, which is an initiative to decolonize the Canadian art system by putting Indigenous arts practices at the centre, through the leadership of Indigenous artists, supported by artists of colour. David has been a filmmaker for 22 years, and his films have screened internationally at over 60 film festivals. He is currently a PhD candidate at the Social Justice Institute at the University of British Columbia. He holds a Master of Social Sciences degree from the African Gender Institute at the University of Cape Town.

Malissa Phung
is a Professor in the Faculty of Humanities & Social Sciences at Sheridan College. She is currently working on turning her PhD dissertation into a book manuscript on the settler colonial and racial politics of commemorating Chinese labour in Canada. Her next book project, Making Kinship, focuses on Indigenous and Asian relations in North American history and cultural production through the framework of kinship and indebtedness.

Chloe Rodriguez
is currently based in Tkaronto/Toronto and works for the Ecological Farmers Association of Ontario, where she advocates for accessible food systems and climate resilient agriculture. At the time of writing the co-authored chapter for this text, Chloe was in her third year of an undergraduate degree in English: Cultural Studies at McGill University. In her first year of university, Chloe joined Pinay Power II as a communications assistant and artist. This experience was formative for her, and continues to inspire her work and community practices today. Chloe has also continued her artistic practice, and her work is sustained by the emotional, ecological, and cultural bridges between plural spaces/identities.

France Clare Stohner
is a mental health counsellor and community organizer. She cares for her community by being on the Advisory Council for Kabangka and as Executive Director of Centre Kapwa, a non-profit organization supporting the leadership and mental health of Filipino/a/x-Canadians. France is also a coordinator for Super Inday Art, a program bringing art initiatives to incarcerated women at the Iloilo City District Jail on Panay Island. Passionate about youth, she has worked in post-secondary education mental health and wellness, and on campus sexual violence prevention and response. She serves on the Canadian Race Relations Foundation's Coalition Against Anti-Asian Racism Canada.

Jen Sungshine
is a queer Taiwanese-Canadian interdisciplinary artist, community facilitator, and cultural producer based in Vancouver, BC. She is the Co-Artistic Director of Love Intersections, a media arts collective producing intergenerational + intersectional QTBIPOC stories through documentary film and artwork. Her works include "Yellow Peril: Queer Destiny", winner of the Gerry Brunet Memorial Award for best BC Short; and "The House of 9 Dragons", an oral history exhibit in Chinatown. She curates public programming at The Polygon Gallery, and co-produces Hot Pot Talks, CURRENT: Feminist Electronic Art Symposium, and Seize the Means (of Production) Video Co-op. www.jensungshine.com.

Psalmae Tesalona
Indebted to years spent community organizing both around and within academia, Psalm Tesalona now works in the tech industry in Tkaronto/Toronto, doing entirely unrelated things as she focuses on taking care of her loved ones. In the semester following the Pinay Power II conference, Psalm left McGill University to pursue a Criminology & Sociology-legal Studies Degree at the University of Toronto to deepen her understanding of how collective care and disability justice inform abolitionist and transformative justice movements. Come what may, unsure of what the road ahead looks like for her work, her hopes, goals and politics remain the same – that there may be universal access, love and liberation for all.

Ian Liujia Tian
is an Assistant Professor of Global Equity Studies in the Department of Women's Studies at Mount Saint Vincent University, Kjipuktuk. Their research focuses broadly on the political economy of gender and sexuality in transnational contexts. They situate their research in queer Marxism, queer/trans of color critique, transnational feminism, and Asian Canadian/Asian studies.

BDS Toronto
is a collective of Palestinian activists and their allies working for the freedom of the Palestinian peoples.

Rose Ann Torres
PhD, is the Director and Assistant Professor in the School of Social Work at Algoma University. Dr. Torres pioneered the development of a Master of Social Work at Algoma University. She is the principal investigator of the SSHRC Insight Development Grants research project entitled "Examining Access to Mental Health Care Service: The Impact of COVID-19 on Filipino Health Care Workers

in Northern Ontario" and co-principal investigator of the SSHRC Institutional Grants project titled "Effects of COVID-19 on Teaching and Learning: Stories of Indigenous and Black and Asian Faculty Members and Students at Algoma University". Dr. Torres currently serves as an Advisory Board Member for Sault College and First Nations Technical Institute. She has been instrumental in establishing pathways and partnerships with local and international universities and colleges. She also co-edited of the following books: *Critical Reflexive Research Methodologies: Interdisciplinary Approach*; *Outside and In-Between: Theorizing Asian Canadian Exclusion and the Challenges of Identity Formation*; *Critical Research Methodologies: Ethics and Responsibilities*; *Transversing and Translocating Spiritualities: An Epistemological, Theoretical, and Pedagogical Conversations*; and "*Engaging Aboriginal Perspective in Education*".

Samuel Yoon
is a PhD Candidate at the Women and Gender studies Institute, in collaboration with Sexual Diversity Studies, at the University of Toronto. His dissertation examines the intersection of queerness and violence in Asian/American visual and performance culture. Outside of academia, Sam has been a performer and dancer in Toronto's queer of color spaces, performing and participating in New Ho Queen and Toronto's Kiki Ballroom scene.

Hyejung Jessie Yum
holds a PhD from the University of Toronto and is currently a faculty member in the Department of Theological Studies at Concordia University in Montréal. Her research and teaching focus on decolonization, intersectionality, and religion. Born and raised in Seoul, with time spent in Los Angeles and Toronto, she is now based in Montréal. These diverse experiences have ignited her passion for promoting equity and understanding across different cultures and walks of life.

CHAPTER 1

Introduction

Ian Liujia Tian, Coly Chau and Rose Ann Torres

The world we are living in is perhaps drastically different from the world we first discussed the idea of an Asian Canadian studies collection in early 2019. Yet in many ways, our pressing political and social issues remain the same, if not requiring more attention. COVID-19 revealed the underlying racial, gender and class disparities in Canada. In Toronto, Ontario, for example, poor, Indigenous, Black and racialized neighborhoods are three times more likely to get in contract with the deadly virus than middle-class and white communities (Cheung 2020). For communities with disabilities, challenges and inequities of access were further emphasized and made evident. For those incarcerated by the state, we saw heightened calls for abolition as outbreaks occured within prisons and detention centres. For those unhoused, we saw urgent calls to provide basic incomes and necessities, as police across cities globally simultaneously targeted, attacked and destroyed encampments. For migrant workers or those with precarious migration status, we saw the continued disparities in access to supports and basic necessities, further revealing their produced disposability.

For those of us who identify or are seen as East and Southeast Asians, COVID-19 rendered visible to the wider public our conditional belonging and permanent outsider status (Lowe 1996). The various strains of COVID-19 and global restrictions further rendered those who identify or are seen as South Asian, or Brown and Black as inadmissible or as carriers of variants. The ongoing violent attacks on women, children and elders are manifestations of systemic anti-Asian and Islamophobic racisms that harbor in Canada's immigration policies, government institutions and cultural representation. Such racisms are deeply gendered, classed, and sexualized. For instance, the barring of Chinese women and families of male labourers into Canada in the early twentieth century left long lasting cultural and racial imagination of Asian women's victimization, promiscuity and unhygienic sexuality (Woon 2007). Subsequent Korean War, of which Canada was a participant, further entrenched fantasies of hyper feminine and hypersexualized Asian women at home and abroad (Kang 2020).

The deadly violence that took place in Atlanta on March 16, 2021, was not merely an American problem, but underlined global systemic gendered anti-Asian racism and anti-sex work moral politics shared across North America. In 2020, a Filipina massage parlour worker, Ashley Noell Arzaga, was murdered by a white teenager influenced by the incel movement in Toronto, Ontario (German 2020).[1] Such violence reveals the ways in which race, gender and white heteropatriarchal masculinity structure how Asian women, including trans, cis and gender nonconforming people, experience their own sexualities and agencies.

In the wake of 9/11 and the Western world's "war on terror," islamphobia has payed a critical role in Canada's foreign policy and militarization. The "war on terror" has eschewed waves of renewed gendered and sexualized tropes on Muslim and Arab women to garner support for imperialist invasion and war (Zine & Taylor 2014), instilling ideas of "imperiled Muslim woman" along with the "dangerous" Muslim man (Razack 2017: 65). In the past two decades, there has been an alarming rise in Islamophobic violence taking place both domestically and globally—including the tragic Quebec City Mosque attack on January 29, 2017, that claimed the lives of six individuals, injuring many others and leaving Muslim communities across the nation in fear. In 2019, Quebec upheld Bill-21, which effectively banned those working in the public sector from wearing religious symbols, such as a hijab. This signifies the continued engraining of Islamophobia and other religious discrimination after the tragedy, under the guise of secularism.

We put together this collection under the backdrop of these global, national, and local political and social burning crises, with intellectual and activist commitments to minorities' lived experiences and social change concerning Asian diasporas in Canada. For us, the pandemic challenged how we conceptualize and approach Asian Canada—who are Asian Canadians? What can categories of Asian Canadian do or achieve? What makes Asian Canadian studies important in decolonial, anti-racist and anti-capitalist struggles? What sorts of relationalities are possible? What are the possibilities of radicalizing Asian Canadian studies as a method and a field of inquiry? These questions illuminate throughout this book, and at times serve as guides for readers entering a conversation with the editors and the contributors. We do not claim to offer

1 The incel movement is a portmanteau of "involuntary celibate." It is an online subculture of people who define themselves as unable to find a romantic or sexual partner despite desiring one. Discussions in incel forums are often characterized by resentment and hatred, misogyny, misanthropy, self-pity and self-loathing, racism, a sense of entitlement to sex, and the endorsement of violence against sexually active people.

comprehensive answers to these concerns, rather, we want this book to be an opportunity to challenge, remake and ignite the fire within racialized peoples in settler Canada, particularly those who identify as "Asians". In this introduction, we share details about this book, the keywords we build on and how we put chapters in conversations with one another. We hope by reading this book, readers will have a sense of where Asian Canadian studies are at and question the categorical ways of thinking we inhabit in our discussions of race and ethnicity. Most crucially, we intend for readers to join us on a journey in co-theorizing and co-organizing a world without settler colonialisms, anti-Black racisms, white supremacy, racial capitalism, cis-heteropatriarchy and ableism.

1 What Is Burning, or What This Book Does for Asian Canadian Studies

We start our deliberation of the book's objectives by defining what is burning. This book includes academic and non-academic works that centre desire, intimacy, and affective relations rather than damage, injuries, and wounded subjects (Tuck & Yang 2014). Damage-centred research, as Tuck and Yang argue, extracts stories of pain in communities and takes the control of these narratives away from participants. Such extraction might lead to repair at best, but often results in further marginalization and disciplinary control of these communities. For Wendy Brown, politicized identity's investment in its pain might constrain the emancipatory potential such politicization sets out to do. As Brown makes clear, liberalism's conversion of political identity into political interests requires making a claim of 'lack' or 'exclusion' from a universalized political subject. Such claim risks turning identity-based group's critique of liberal capitalism and bourgeois politics into social identities manageable by regulatory power (Brown 1993: 395). Through funding to non-governmental organizations and Asian-led business, for example, the settler state demonstrates its capability to de-politicize rights claims into more regulatable ways of addressing pain and violence.

We echo these theorists' caution by directing readers' attention to three ways in which chapters in this book offer something more than damage-centered narratives. First, 'burning' as embodied experiences bring close the affective and bodily harm racism produces. As a metaphor, 'burning' highlights the imprints of trauma and systemic racism on various Asian settler and migrant groups. Several chapters in this book document how colonialism and racisms structure immigration and integration policy and shape people's livelihood and lived realities (Chapters 2, 3, 4, 5, 13 and 15).

These chapters recall a much longer histories of colonial labour migration, such as Indian/Chinese indentured labour (Li 1988; Yee 1993) and explore how such migration routes shape contemporary movement of people and diasporic formations. For example, waves of Chinese settlers arrived in the late eighteenth century as cheap and indentured labour in the gold mining and railway industries. Many Chinese labourers died while constructing the railway, as part of the settler colonial state's expansion. Those who survived encountered racist legislations. In 1875, Chinese labourers were banned from voting, working in mining, public services, law, and other professions in British Columbia. Shortly after the completion of the Canadian Pacific Railway in 1885, the Head Tax was enacted, preventing more Chinese migrants from entering Canada. The fear of Chinese labourers taking away white settler's jobs fuelled the Orientalist notions of "Yellow Peril". In 1923, the Chinese Immigration Act restricted all Chinese immigration.

In 1914, Canada's immigration further prevented the disembarking of the steamship Komagata Maru, and its majority Sikh, and other Hindu and Muslim passengers, leaving migrants detained onboard for two months with limited supplies outside of Vancouver (Mawani 2018). As Mawani (2018) writes, the ship's arrival to the Salish Sea, challenges and forces us to examine imperial projects beyond land, and to see how water and the free sea are turned into raced spaces embroiled by histories of colonial and racial dispossession.

In 1942, after the War Measures Act was enacted following Canada's declaration of war on Japan, 22,000 people of Japanese descent were removed from their homes and incarcerated; and following the war, forcibly displaced and dispersed throughout the country. Through surveillance, policing, incarceration, expulsion and dislocation, Japanese Internment highlights how racial orders and hierarchies were produced and reproduced materially and through social constructions (Oikawa 2012).

This book contends that historical injustices have not passed. The economic and political structures that have produced injustices remain in place to make new kinds of yellow perils (Billé 2018). The rage, anger and sorrow emerging from anti-Asian racist attacks cross settler Canada speak to the impossibility of historical closure and the progress towards a race-blind liberal capitalist utopia. The metaphor of burning enables new ways of conceptualizing our histories beyond comparativity, but rather through relationality.

Therefore, we use 'burning' as a metaphor to center the heat, dynamic and emerging works by activists, junior scholars, and community members. We draw from the forms of vitality in *Paris is Burning*, a documentary about Black and Latinx ballroom culture in the U.S. In it, we see the fire of living, gathering, and community-making as crucial resources of queer of color survival. Several chapters in this book make a case for relationships and solidarity (Chapters 6, 8, 10, 11 and Part 3). Similar collections that present a case for activism remain limited. For instance, *Outside and In-Between: Theorizing Asian Canadian Exclusion and the Challenges of Identity Formation* (2021), edited by Rose Ann Torres, Kailan Leung and Vania Soepriatna, challenges the very idea of 'Asian Canadian' by centering the experiences of temporal residents from Asian countries. Their experiences are often excluded from 'Asian Canada', which features naturalized citizens and those identify as second/third generation diasporas (Torres, Leung, & Soepriatna, 2021). Another anthology, *Asian Canadian Studies Reader* (2017), edited by Roland Sintos Coloma and Gordon Pon, features more prominent and established scholars within Asian Canadian Studies.

Building on their work, our edited volume showcases both emerging and established Asian Canadian voices, crossing academic and community spheres. While we are critical of the university as a neoliberal institution, there are still initiatives that challenge what it means to be Asian Canadian and that we should examine (Kim 2016; Day 2016). For example, in the introduction of *Asian Canadian Studies Reader*, the editors rightly point out the lack of institutional support for Asian Canadian studies, Indigenous and Black Canadian studies under the guise of Canadian multiculturalism (Pon, Coloma, Kwak and Huynh 2017: 13). Our intentions in this volume are not to lament the absence of support. Rather, we are suspicious of claims of recognition. In our separate and intertwined work in communities, we see that interventions are taking place with or without the institution. For example, a two-day program organized by Scholar Strike Canada in 2021—entitled "Anti-Asian Racism Undone"—foregrounded the critical voices from artists, academics, sex workers and labour unionists across Asian Canadian communities. Our book builds on the momentum and the message of that program, underscoring what takes place within Asian Canadian scholarships and the spaces we congregate. Such theorizing and projects from below are burning with desire to make new worlds and create the otherwise. Hence, *Asian Canada is Burning* resists the normalized spaces, temporalities, and bodies that are afforded theorizing and centers the notion that theorizing exists and takes place in everyday life and occurs beyond the academy, and thus, must be recognized.

Thirdly, this collection's strength lies in its commitment to feminist, queer, and disability scholarship within Asian Canadian studies, these perspectives are burning for new conceptualization, attention, and foregrounding (Chapter 6 and Part 2). In "Queer / Asian / Canadian," an edited issue on queer Asian Canadian studies in *TOPIA: Canadian Journal of Cultural Studies*, the editors argue that queer bodies disrupt the taken-for-granted belonging to settler heteropatriarchy, a structure of feelings only warranted to heteronormative folks (Kojima, Catungal and Diaz 2017). In agreement with their assessments, *Asian Canada is Burning* focuses on the multiple forms of power and systems that co-constitute Asian Canadian experiences, with particular attention to gender, sexuality, and disability written by junior women of colour, queer, trans and disability scholars. We think by incorporating new locations, positions, and lived experiences, we might also challenge Asian Canadian studies on its gaps, and normalizing impulses.

While mobilizing the metaphor of 'burning', we remain ambiguous of the racial-geographical signifier of 'Asian'. On one hand, 'Asia' as an idea emerged as a part of the colonial cartography of the world, divided subsequently into sub areas such as East, Southeast, South, Central and Western Asia. People from said geographies are treated as homogenous groups locatable by an index of skin colour, facial feature, culture, and language (Sakai 2019). In this sense, the racialization of 'Asia' suggests the continuation of the racial-colonial-capitalist project of which Canada is an integral part. On the other hand, 'Asia' itself is diverse and heterogenous, fraught with internal tensions between ethnic groups and nation-states. Therefore, we deploy Asian Canadian experiences not as a fixed referent by time and space, but as an ongoing engagement with the settler state and other racialized groups. In other words, we treat Asian Canadian as a process of encounter rather than a given 'identity' we are born into. 'Asian Canadian' might be, at best, a way of describing how people who either identify as Asians or come from Asian countries experience settler Canada's state power, regulation, and governmentality, within a global capitalist system of exploitation and oppression. Depending on one's immigration status, caste, age, gender, sexuality, ability, and class, those perceived as 'Asian' might have completely different sets of experiences, identifications and affective relationships to settler Canada and their 'places of origins'. Simultaneously, these differentiated social structures also mean that people identifying themselves as 'Asians' become complicit in the exploitation, marginalization and oppressions of other groups, as well as, simultaneously implicated in global racial capitalism, colonialism, anti-Indigenous racism, anti-Black racism, homo and transphobia, sexism and ableism. 'Asian Canadian experiences', therefore, are best understood as relational, contradictory and becoming. This collection is concerned with moments and places of tensions, confrontations, relations, and solidarity.

With this title, we imagine the burning down of oppressive categories, hierarchies, structures and systems, as possibilities to build anew. Practices of slash-and-burn through ecological knowledge keeping of Indigenous and traditional communities, ensured sustainable renewing of the earth. To burn means that we are at a pinnacle in which we can reimagine what is next for us, amidst these changing and urgent times. To burn means to create space that can sustain new growth and changes. As Arundhati Roy writes in "The Pandemic Is A Portal" (2020: 132), within crisis emerges other possibilities for other worlds, "a gateway between one world and the next." Roy powerfully reminds us that with the effects of the pandemic, "nothing could be worse than a return to normality," and offers us the ability to leave behind rubble and "walk through lightly, with little luggage, ready to imagine another world. And ready to fight for it" (2020: 132).

To conclude, by centring emerging scholars and activists' work, this book offers interdisciplinary approaches within and outside the institution and hopes to support Asian Canadian Studies as a community-based research creation. But ultimately, *Asian Canada is Burning* brings forth potentials to address the crucial need to move beyond disciplines, as both pedagogies and praxes. As pedagogies, this book shows how to learn and study Asian Canadian experiences as process in relation to other racialized groups, together structured by settler colonialism. As praxes, this book demonstrates how to build community, practice solidarity and honor different forms of knowledge production.

2 How to Read This Book

Part 1 of this book consists of chapters collectively exploring ethnicity, migration and belonging in a settler state. These essays build on anti-racist feminist scholarship, which has for long argued against liberal inclusion into white and Eurocentric settler Canada (Ng 1995). These scholars and activists wrote of their racialized experiences and articulated challenges towards the Canadian nation state, by making connections between global histories of colonialism and imperialism of which Canada is a part. In the 1980's, women of colour organizing, such as grassroots press Sister's Vision Press (1985–2001) in Toronto foregrounded Black and women of colour led theories and publishing. For instance, this includes Himanji Bannerji's important edited contribution *Returning the Gaze* (1993) and Sharon Lim-Hing's edited volume *The Very Inside: An Anthology of Writings by Asian and Pacific Island Lesbians and Bisexual Women* (1994). These collections of essays, often explicitly Marxist and socialist, argued that systems of oppressions should be analyzed interlinkingly.

Along with Black and other racialized women, their work formed the first generation of women of colour feminism in Canada.

This volume takes seriously anti-racist feminist scholars' revolutionary visions, and adopts the view that racism is not a set of attitudes, but the very practices of self-identifying of European/Western societies (Bannerji 1995: 46). The politics of differences and inclusion that ethnic studies tend to adopt, unfortunately do not go beyond personal experiences and attitudes, thus fail to address the systems of oppression and settler colonial capital exploitation that shapes experiences of Asian immigrants, settlers, and other racialized groups. Experiences of Asian migrants therefore are produced by a continuum of settler colonial capitalism, patriarchy, white supremacy and racial formations in Canada (Day I. 2016: 7). Such experiences, both in the everyday and on an eventual level, are mediated by the interplay between the subjective and the objective. What is specific to Asian immigrants is both unique and a typification of the general, that is, one specific experience of the interlocking systems of oppression in settler economies such as Canada.

The first three essays in Part 1 therefore examine how the personal is structurally linked to colonial and racial formations by investigating the contradictions of homemaking in two different contexts. Shelly Ikebuchi's piece explores how the production of white domesticity and race are intertwined in the early 20th century B.C. Rajni Mala Khelawan's chapter takes us through Fiji as an unexpected place of South Asian diaspora, which, constructs contradictory yet intimate moments of "multiple Hinduisms" that unsettle the Western commodification of Hindulism and the Indian state's interpretation of Hindulism. Similarly, Krystal Jagoo's short creative writing investigates the history of transnational labour, or "coolies," to the Caribbean; as well as the memories of anticolonial independent movement as homemaking in the 20th century.

The rest of essays in Part 1 explore the connections between diaspora and Indigeneity made possible by colonialism's violence. Hyejung Jessie Yum and Jose Miguel Esteban's chapter both engage with questions of diaspora and settler colonialism. Yum focuses on writings of members of the Korean diaspora who question settler coloniality within religious institutions. Esteban takes us through an intimate narrative about dance, bodily movement and unbelonging as a Filipinx.

Chapters in Part 2 of this anthology deploy feminist and queer lenses to unravel gendered and sexual differences that have and continue to remain deeply intertwined with the processes of racialization. As Enakshi Dua (2007) writes, the building of a white nation relied heavily on processes of gendered exclusion and inclusion. Queerness of early Asian migrants became defining markers of the limits of settler colonial nations (Manalansan 2006). Applying feminist and queer lenses helps us to understand, unsettle and disrupt settler colonial and imperial building projects here and elsewhere.

To this end, the essays in Part 2 are organized by two themes. First, what are the limits and potentials of queer Asian Canadian studies? Elisha Lim's contribution questions the oftentimes romanticized potential of identify in social media activism. Their comic opens this section with a story about how social media influence a queer of colour couple. Ian Liujia Tian takes up the concept "intimacy" and surveys recent literature on queer Asian Canadian studies, arguing for attention to labour and class. The second theme highlights how Asians, queers or not, re-imagine and build family, kinship, romantic relations and love cross boundaries. Samuel Yoon's piece stages a temporal encounter between Gay Asians of Toronto and New Ho Queen in Toronto, a serious of events focusing on queer Asian diaspora. The next two chapters turn to queer art and activism. David Ng and Jen Sungshine, of Love Intersections, take us from Toronto to Vancouver, offering a generative analysis of race, homophobia and cultural politics. Monica Batac and colleagues' chapter positions three seemingly shared yet distinct subject positions: the Filipina American (Julia), Filipina/x Canadian (Psalmae), and Filipina diasporic (Chloe) student, each finding their place within the Canadian nation state and forging new kinds of intimacy.

Praxis is an important component of this book, not just in the sense of art making demonstrated by scholars in Part 2. By praxis, we mean embodied actions. All actions are praxis and guided by some understandings of social reality. For this book, we mobilize both theory and praxis for social justice (Bauman 1999). Without praxis, theories exist only in the realm of ideas; and without theories, praxis are only reproducing the status quo instead of pursuing transformative change. Theorizing, for instance, is a praxis in so far as it derives from material relations and tells us how and what we can do to build an otherwise world. Praxis exceeds artistic expressions to include activism in communities, kitchen tables and town halls. Therefore, in the last section of this book, we ask: How can the Asian community be better allies for Indigenous and Black communities in struggles against police violence, incarceration, settler colonialism and right-wing fascist politics as Asian settlers? How can we as Asians critically address racism, Orientalism and othering as the 'foreigner-within' in many political organizing without losing our potency?

We gathered short pieces from scholars and activists that take seriously solidarity in their work, championing a framework that sees solidarity as process rather than a set of criteria to follow. We define solidarity as embodied engagement with groups of people for social justice; such involvement requires relinquishing privileges, so that those who are participating in the community space can unpack tensions, learn from dialogue, and reimagine a future just for women, the poor, racialized, Indigenous, Black, differently abled, queer and trans peoples (Camangian and Cariaga 2022; Jaramillo and Carreon 2014).

The first two chapters focus on organizing around issues of gender, sexuality and labour. Coly Chau and Elene Lam, of Butterfly: Asian and Migrant Sex Worker Support Network, explore the ways in which massage parlour and sex workers mobilize against municipal anti-trafficking initiatives towards justice, likening how Chinese laundries historically organized against discriminatory by-laws. Chapter 14 historicizes the history of anti-racist labour organizing in Canada. Anna Liu meticulously traces the lineages of Asian Canadian Labour Alliance (ACLA) and the crucial role ACLA played in the history of labour organizing in Canada. Janey Lew's chapter points us to crucial reflections on decoloniality, settler colonialism and Asian Canadian identity. By centering 'love' as the affective grounding, Lew suggests that Asian queer and feminist histories and theories should be the channel through which we build solidarity with Indigenous resurgence. Similarly, In Malissa Phung's chapter, we get a sense of what solidarity with Indigenous and Black scholars means in the field of Canadian Literature.

We are fortunate to have Boycott, Divestment and Sanction (BDS) Toronto contribute a chapter on Palestine. In this piece, the writer discusses the history of BDS, and the forms of internationalism required of Asian diaspora. As Asians living in settler Canada, we must hold the Canadian state accountable for its connections and complicity with the state of Israel. For those of us involved in abolitionist movements, it also asks us to consider prison abolition in a global perspective, especially as Gaza is understood as "the biggest open-air prison."

We conclude with some reflections on the making of this book. We note areas the book falls short, including in terms of environmental issues, geographical locations, cultural and linguistic diversity. Creating an anthology in the height of the pandemic and amid various local and global crises, meant that we were not able to highlight as many crucial viewpoints and perspectives, as we had set out to. We want to acknowledge the scholars, organizers and groups that had to withdraw contributions or were unable to have their work included in the anthology as they tended to other urgencies. We recognize these gaps as important points of departure for next volumes of work on Asian Canadian Studies, and in understanding these opportunities, we ultimately turn to futurities. We echo Indigenous futurism, Afro-futurism and Gulf futurism and propose Asian diasporic futurism as a strategy to counter techno-Orientalism and gendered anti-Asian racism (Lai 2014). Asian diasporic futurism, we argue, move us from the nation states to reimagine a constellations of techno-Asian diaspora commons across the global. While Asian labour has long been associated with technology as mechanized clogs in capitalist productive systems, our vision of futurism builds on such attribution of Asian communities as perverse users of technology—through modes of copying, stealing, and mimicking. Such are the futures afforded to those of us who are living at the underside of global capitalism, that as already cyborg-like beings, our future predicates on our subverting of Eurocentric, capitalist and racial enclosure of technology.

References

Bannerji, Himani (1993) *Returning the Gaze: Essays on Racism, Feminism and Politics.* Toronto: Sister Vision's Press.

Bannerji, Himani (1995) *Thing Through.* Toronto: Women's Press.

Bauman, Zyumunt (1999) *Culture as Praxis.* London: Sage.

Billé, Franck (2018) Introduction. In: Franck Billé and Sören Urbansky (eds.) *Yellow Perils: China Narratives in the Contemporary World.* Honolulu: University of Hawai'i Press, 1–34.

Brown, Wendy (1993) Wounded Attachment. *Political Theory* 21(3): 390–410.

Camangian, Patrick, and Stephanie Cariaga (2022) Social and Emotional Learning is Hegemonic Miseducation: Students Deserve Humanization Instead. *Race, Ethnicity and Education* 25(7): 901–921.

Cheung, Jessica (2020) Black People and other People of Colour Make up 83% of Reported COVID-19 Cases in Toronto. *CBC*, July 30. https://www.cbc.ca/news/canada/toronto/toronto-covid-19-data-1.5669091.

Day, Ikyo (2016) *Alien Capital: Asian Racialization and the Logic of Settler Colonial Capitalism.* Durham: Duke University Press.

Dua, Enakshi (2007) Exclusion through Inclusion: Female Asian migration in the making of Canada as a white settler nation. *Gender, Place, Culture* 14(4): 445–466.

German, Mildred (2020) Filipina in Toronto Killed by a 17-year Old Inspired by Terrorist 'Incel' Movement'. *Philiphine Canadian News,* May 28. https://philippinecanadiannews.com/canada/filipina-in-toronto-killed-by-a-17-year-old-inspired-by-terrorist-incel-movement/.

Jaramillo, Nathalia E., and Michelle Carreon (2014) Pedagogies of Resistance and Solidarity: Towards Revolutionary and Decolonial Praxis. *Interface* 6(1): 392–411.

Kang, Laura Hyun Yi (2020) *Traffic in Asian Women.* Durham: Duke University Press.

Kim, Christine (2016) *The Minor Intimacies of Race.* Chicago: University of Illinois Press.

Kojima, Dai, John Paul Catungal, and Robert Diaz (2017) Introduction: Feeling Queer, Feeling Asian, Feeling Canadian. *Topia 38* 69–80.

Lai, Larissa (2014) Epistemologies of Respect: A Poetics of Asian/Indigenous Relation. In: Smaro Kamboureli and Christl Verduyn (eds.) *Critcal Collaborations: Indigeneity, Diaspora, and Ecology in Canadian Literary Studies.* Waterloo: Wilfrid Laurier University Press, 99–126.

Li, Peter (1988) *The Chinese in Canada.* Toronto: Oxford University Press.

Lowe, Lisa (1996) *Immigrant Acts: On Asian American Cultural Politics.* Durham: Duke University Press.

Manalansan, Martin F. (2006) Queer Intersections: Sexuality and Gender in Migration Studies. *International Migration Review* 40(1): 224–249.

Mawani, Renisa (2018) *Across Oceans of Law: The Komagata Maru and Jurisdiction in the Time of Empire.* Durham: Duke University Press.

Ng, Roxana (1995) Multiculturalism as Ideology: A Textual Analysis. In: Dorothy Smith (ed.) *Knowledge, Experience, and Ruling: Studies in the Social Organization of Knowledge.* Toronto: University of Toronto Press, 35–48.

Oikawa, Mona (2012) *Cartographies of Violence: Japanese Canadian Women, Memory, and the Subjects of the Internment.* Toronto: University of Toronto Press.

Pon, Gordon, Roland Coloma, Laura Kwak, and Kenneth Huynh (2017) Asian Canadian Studies Now: Directions and Challenges. In: Gordon Pon and Roland Coloma (eds.) *Asian Canadian Studies Reader.* Toronto: University of Toronto Press, 3–28.

Razack, Sherene (2017) The Muslims Are Coming: The "Sharia Debate" in Canada. In: Roland Coloma and Gordon Pon (eds.) *Asian Canadian Studies Reader.* Toronto: University of Toronto Press, 64–85.

Roy, Arundhati (2020) *Azadi: Freedom. Fascism. Fiction.* Chicago: Haymarket Books.

Sakai, Naoki (2019) The Regime of Separation and the Performativity of Area. *positions: asia critique* 27(1): 241–279.

Torres, Rose A., Kailan Leung, and Vania Soepriatna (2021) *Outside and In-Between: Theorizing Asian Canadian Exclusion and the Challenges of Identity Formation.* Leiden, Netherlands: Brill.

Tuck, Eve, and K. Wayne Yang (2014) R-Words: Refusing Research. In: D. Paris and M.T. Winn(eds). *Humanizing Research: Decolonizing Qualitative Inquiry with youth and Communities.* Thousand Oakes, CA: Sage.

Woon, Yuen-Fong (2007) Between South China and British Columbia. *BC Studies* 156: 83–107.

Yee, Paul (1993) *Saltwater City*. Vancouver: Douglas & McIntype.

Zine, Jasmine, and Lisa K. Taylor (2014) The Contested Imaginaries of Reading Muslim Women and Muslim Women. In: Lisa K. Taylor and Jasmin Zine (eds). *Muslim Women, Transnational Feminism and the Ethics of Pedagogy: Contested Imaginaries in Post-9/11 Cultural Practice*. New York: Routledge.

PART 1

Situating Asia(ns) beyond Settler Canadian Nationalism

CHAPTER 2

Tearing Down Walls: Rethinking White Domesticity in the Context of Cultural Domicide

Shelly Ikebuchi

Citizenship and belonging are complex and polylithic, shaped by interlocking influences of many factors such as 'race', class, gender, sexuality, ability, immigration, community relations, culture, religion, and education, among others. Asian Canadian histories have highlighted the complexity of citizenship and belonging. Lisa Mar (2011) for instance, has examined how political and legal struggles around ethnicity and immigration shaped how Chinese in Canada 'brokered belonging' in a nation that was far from welcoming. Focusing on physical spaces, Kay Anderson's (1991) formative study on Vancouver's Chinatown highlighted the importance of space in shaping community and belonging. Japanese Canadian history of citizenship and belonging was also influenced by multiple factors including, but not limited to, immigration laws and Japanese Canadian internment during World War II.[1] The goal of this chapter is to introduce the domestic realm as a space of influence in the shaping of citizenship and belonging. By examining a religious institution, the Woman's Missionary Society (WMS), and their work with Japanese and Chinese women, this chapter interrogates how the spaces and practices of domesticity intersected with and utilized discourses and practices of citizenship and national belonging. Further, this chapter argues that the evangelistic endeavours of the WMS, while promising belonging, relied on ideas of white supremacy, which simultaneously painted Chinese (and later Japanese) Canadian women as potential citizens and as always already 'Other'. In their endeavours, the WMS relied on mimicry and metonymy. Mimicry took place through the requirement that Japanese and Chinese women (and their homes) be remade and refashioned in the image of white women and white domestic spaces. By equating the home with belonging (familial and national), metonymy justified their interventions. If white women were to be the standard against which Chinese and Japanese women were to be measured, then 'home' would become the place where they

1 For a deeper discussion of this history, see Adachi (1991), McAllister (1999), and Miki (2004).

might be made to belong. The effects of this were far-reaching, especially when one considers cultural loss.

This chapter takes two trajectories to mine the intersections of belonging and space. First, it examines how white women missionaries in British Columbia attempted to reshape Japanese and Chinese women in their own images and how this reshaping was extended to include the physical spaces they inhabited. Second, it examines the discourses necessary for these practices to take place, by considering domestic spaces as analogous to home and belonging. By equating the nation with 'home', the WMS were able to use the domestic realm as a proxy for inclusion and citizenship. Home spaces, thus, were made and remade in order to erase 'foreignness', and thus allow the residents to be included in the national (and religious) family. These two trajectories combined to produce whiteness as the currency of belonging, and 'Asian-ness' as a signal of 'stranger-ness'. This required that 'foreign' practices and ideologies in the home be dismantled. Thus, in the concluding section, the argument is made that these practices were a form of cultural domicide, which resulted in a loss of culture, community, and in some cases, family. To provide some context, a brief history of the Woman's Missionary Society and their work in communities along the coast of British Columbia is necessary.

Much of the WMS work among the Chinese and Japanese women in BC began in the Chinese Rescue Home (the Home). The Home was started in 1886 by Reverend John Edward Starr and John Gardiner. Initially, it was envisioned as a refuge for women who were (or who were assumed to be) Chinese prostitutes and slave girls. Early residents of the Home were often 'spirited away' from their own homes through pretence or subterfuge, in an attempt to free them from their lives of slavery and/or prostitution. When Starr and Gardiner decided that two men could not possibly maintain a rescue home for women, they reached out to the Woman's Missionary Society and pleaded with them to take over the running of the Home. The WMS agreed to do so in 1887. While their work in the Home began as rescue work, eventually their mandate broadened to include education, prompting the name change to the Oriental Home and School in 1909. Eventually, the evangelism of Chinese and Japanese women would also include interventions outside of the Home. As part of these evangelistic endeavours, the WMS sent 'Bible Women' to Vancouver and Victoria. Much of their work included visiting communities on Vancouver Island and along the southern coast of BC. Here, they focused their energy on women, visiting them in their homes or offering courses designed to bring Western ideals and practices into their homes. This, I argue resulted in a form of domicide.

In their book, *Domicide: The Global Destruction of Home*, Porteous and Smith (2001, p. 3) define domicide as the "deliberate destruction of home against the will of the home dweller." While much of their work focuses on the destruction of physical spaces, this paper adopts the conceptual framework of cultural domicide to examine how metonymical discourses of 'home' and practices of mimicry in home*making* resulted in the cultural 'whitewashing' of Chinese and Japanese homes. This making, unmaking, and remaking of homes occurred on multiple registers, including the shaping of physical spaces and the teaching of home-making skills.

1 Mimicry

While the motivation for most of their endeavours was evangelism, the WMS sought not only religious adherence from their charges, but domestic adherence as well. In the Chinese Rescue Home, the 'inmates', as they were often called, were moved into domestic spaces. It was in these domestic spaces that attempts at cultural erasure would begin. The spaces themselves were not inconsequential, as this would be the first form that mimicry would take in the systematic erasure of Chinese (and later Japanese) culture in the inmates' lives. The spaces of the Home were designed to mimic the domestic spaces that white women inhabited. Removing Chinese (and later Japanese) women from their own homes and placing them in such domestic spaces was not only about rescue but also about distancing them from what the white women saw as destructive or negative cultural practices. The first space used in this way was a house on Cormorant Avenue in Victoria. Later, in 1909, the WMS would build a new home which would take the form of an even grander and more impressive domestic space.[2] Both of these spaces were meant to replace, temporarily for some and permanently for others, the homes where the women (and later, children) had previously lived. Although the women's homes were not physically destroyed, the removal of women from their homes signalled a symbolic destruction. The importance of domesticity in transforming Japanese and Chinese women was evident in both the spaces that were chosen and in the names that would define the institution. When the name changed in 1909, from the Chinese Rescue Home to the Oriental Home and School, the only thing that remained the same was the word 'home'. The movement of Chinese and Japanese women from their own home spaces to these new domestic

2 As I argue elsewhere (2015), this new space was fashioned after the Georgian manor home and reflected investments in empire-building, evangelism, and domesticity.

spaces was only the first step. Coming home also required that new lessons in proper domesticity would need to be learned.

Lefebvre's (1991) triad of space as conceived, perceived, and lived, provides an entry point into understanding how the spaces of the Home were complicit in cultural domicide. The physical spaces of the Home were conceived in gendered and racialized ways and therefore were planned and ordered as spaces of white domesticity. Therefore, the training that took place within those walls often revolved around specific forms of home-making: if the spaces of the Home were meant to replicate white domestic spaces, so too were the tasks that women were to learn. Miss Bowes, one of the Home's early Matrons, explained that "in winter the girls spend their leisure filling orders for knitting, children's underclothing, etc. In summer they mend and help make articles for the Home."[3] The roles that white women played in their own homes were to be reproduced in the Home. The expectations of white womanhood were literally built into the spatial organization of the houses in the form of kitchens, parlours, and sewing rooms. The adage 'a woman's work is never done' was doubly so in the Chinese Rescue Home. The work that the women and girls were expected to do arose out of three imperatives. First, given that the Home was envisioned not as an institution or even a boarding house, but as a domestic space, the women and girls were expected to contribute as family members to its cleaning and maintenance. The mimicry of white domesticity, thus, was a requirement of familial relations and a marker of belonging, of being home. Second, work such as sewing and knitting were regarded as useful training for the women. Third, the work contributed to the project of mimicry, as the women were trained to produce western clothing which they were then required to wear. Dressing the women and children in western clothing was a decision that was meant to elevate them, act as a sign or signal of their transformation to those outside of the Home, and to distance them from their former lives and communities.[4]

White domesticity, seen as an appropriate focus of training for Asian women, was based on gendered, classed, and racial logics. Indeed, much of the training learned within the walls of the Home was also meant to train Japanese and Chinese women to take on serving positions in the homes of white women. Thus, the spaces of the Home were not simply conceived of as providing homes for the women who lived there, but also as producing a useful workforce to provide 'service' to white women in the community. Thus, mimicry helped to

3 Annual Report of the Woman's Missionary Society of the Methodist Church of Canada, 1895–1896. Toronto: The Ryerson Press, 24.

4 For a more detailed discussion, see Ikebuchi (Ikebuchi, 2015), especially Chapter 3.

establish racial hierarchies, defined the parameters of belonging, and offered economic opportunities. These imperatives also contributed to how the spaces were perceived by the women who lived and worked within them.

Razack (2002) explains that perceived space (the second of Lefebvre's triad) "emerges out of spatial practices, ... Through these everyday routines, the space comes to perform something in the *social order*, permitting certain actions and prohibiting others" (9, emphasis mine). Class and cultural expectations were built into the spatial organization of the houses. The physical space of the Home dictated how cultural home-making practices were to be carried out. It was in these spaces that the inmates were taught Western ways of 'home-making'. Even tasks such as building a fire needed to be unlearned and relearned. The matron explained that it "is a very practical piece of work even teaching them to make fires. One of my Japanese girls was two weeks learning that simple process, for Oriental-like, she persisted in putting in the coal first."[5] The work of unlearning was meant to dissociate the 'girl' from her 'Orientalness'. Thus, the physical spaces of the Home were the training ground upon which cultural 'whitening' was to take place. For white women, it was taken for granted that their cultural practices were superior and would therefore serve as the standard for running and maintaining the Home. In fact, the household 'chores' that the inmates performed were often framed as educational, and later, the formal curriculum in the school would include 'home-making' or domestic skills. These practices affected how Chinese and Japanese women lived within the Home and for some, came to shape the practices that they engaged in once they left. Domesticity shaped not only the practices within the Home, but the WMS also used it as a standard against which homes in Japanese and Chinese communities would be measured.

The homes in Chinatown were of utmost concern to the Woman's Missionary Society. Reporting on the success of their work, the WMS explained that while the evangelistic work "to a stranger may seem meagre, it is where one sees the greatest progress, because it is there that the greatest obstacles have been overcome." They continued, by explaining that "Chinatown has entirely changed. The many half tumbled down shacks, whose outside appearance was a true index to the squalor and filth within, have been burnt or taken down, and on their sites new brick stores, with comfortable dwelling rooms above, have been built."[6] That Chinatown was becoming ordered and structured in ways similar

5 Annual Report of the Woman's Missionary Society of the Methodist Church of Canada, 1899–1900. Toronto: The Ryerson Press, XCIII.

6 Annual Report of the Woman's Missionary Society of the Methodist Church of Canada, 1899–1900. Toronto: The Ryerson Press, XCIV.

to Western notions of home was what the WMS saw as evidence of success. However, the rebuilding of physical structures was not enough. Instead, the home had to be remade from the inside out. Key to this was the learning and reproducing of whiteness and white domesticity.

Assessing how closely Chinese and Japanese women could approximate whiteness and white domesticity became a focus of many of the WMS reports. One missionary report in 1919, for instance, boasted how Chinese women in the WMS auxiliaries mostly "speak English, wear Canadian dress and are more or less in touch with the church at the Chinese Mission."[7] The writer continued by comparing this group with more recent immigrants who she describes as "quite a different class of women – [who] still wear their native costume, understand no English and seldom leave their homes in the cheerless tenement blocks of 'New Chinatown'" (CXVI).[8] The description offered of this latter group of women emphasized their foreignness, and signalled their homes as outside of the nation, situated as they were in the 'cheerless tenements' of 'New Chinatown'. Both inside and outside of the Home, clothing and home spaces became targets of disciplinary actions designed to aid in the civilization and domestication of Chinese and Japanese women. Thus, domestic training was an ongoing practice both inside the Home and outside of it. While the mimicry of whiteness was a requirement of belonging, this required continual work, as "in order to be effective, mimicry must continually produce its slippage, its excess, its difference" (Bhabha, 1994, p. 122). For mimicry to take place, then, hierarchies of difference would be continually assessed, defined, and then managed in order to produce an approximation of sameness. Despite that mimicry dictated that white women were to be viewed as superior, mimicry was professed by the WMS to be a tool of inclusion and belonging.

2 Metonymy

Metonymy was a discursive tool used to encourage inclusionbut only after disciplinary techniques such as domestic training and evangelism had taken place. By equating home with nation, metonymy justified interventions into the homes of Japanese and Chinese women in exchange for the promise of belonging and cultural (if not legal) 'citizenship'. Being at 'home' in the nation came to mean being part of a larger family, which was conceived and modelled

7 Annual Report of the Woman's Missionary Society of the Methodist Church of Canada, 1919–1920. Toronto: The Ryerson Press, XCVI.

8 Ibid.

after the white, Christian family. Thus, to be at home required that Chinese and Japanese women be remade in white women's images and their homes refashioned in much the same way. This happened through disciplinary practices of 'domestication'. The assumption that Chinese and Japanese women were foreign, and therefore not ideal candidates for belonging and citizenship, meant that the only way to include them was to domesticate them, to remake and refashion both them and their homes. Thus, the requirements of belonging and citizenship were the destruction of 'foreign' practices, especially as they related to domestic spaces. In short, it required a form of cultural domicide.

The erasure of 'foreign' cultural practices and the embracing of white standards of domesticity were necessary for the promise of inclusion and belonging to be realized. Key to belonging was both religious adherence (Christianity) and national/cultural adherence. By equating home with nation, metonymy offered belonging and cultural citizenship. This was accomplished through equating cultural adherence to Western ideas of home with citizenship.[9] Central to linking home with belonging were discourses of family. References to the Home as a family were evident in the labelling of photos and throughout the reports of the WMS. The photos often referenced the Home 'family' and often family references were prominent in the WMS reports. Within the Home, matrons were often referenced as mother-figures, and as having 'motherly oversight' over the Home.[10] Japanese and Chinese women, on the other hand, were framed as (God's) children in some contexts, and as 'sisters' in others.[11] These familial references both challenged and maintained racial hierarchies that were prevalent at the time. By framing Chinese and Japanese women as children or as sisters, inclusion was offered. But, at the same time, white women were portrayed as authorities and parental figures through their symbolic roles as mothers and hierarchies of race were maintained through the infantilizing of Japanese and Chinese women. The family metaphor was completed by God as father. Therefore, being at 'home' in the nation, required both domestic and religious interventions.

Evangelism was necessary to bring Japanese and Chinese women into the family fold. In addition to teaching the superiority of white domesticity, offering domestic training through cooking and sewing classes also served the

---

9 As I have argued elsewhere, the "ideological processes that made Japanese and Chinese women targets of moral regulation and reform were part of the same processes that allowed for their inclusion into the 'family of God'." (Ikebuchi, 2015, p. 186).

10 Annual Report of the Woman's Missionary Society of the Methodist Church of Canada, 1896–1897. Toronto: The Ryerson Press, LXXIV.

11 For a more detailed discussion these familial relations see Ikebuchi (2015).

purpose of recruiting them into the Church. When other forms of outreach failed, one missionary explained that she "cut off about fifteen skirt patterns, and announced [that she] ... would give them to anyone who came to [the] next meeting" (XCVII).[12] While the response was not as rewarding as she had hoped, teaching domesticity would later become a common practice used by missionaries and 'Bible women'. One 'Bible woman' wrote that "Steveston is regularly visited and a cooking class has been opened for the women."[13] Later, referencing this class for Japanese women, the Bible Woman argued that these classes gave "promise of becoming a real factor in the home life of our women. We earnestly hope that a path to God may be opened up through this meeting."[14] In the following year, her report read "The cooking class reported as opened last May has fulfilled our expectations ... The practical influence of this class on the home life is one of its chief attractions. It is also a helpful means of training the women for membership in more directly spiritual meetings."[15] Thus, domestic training was seen as contributing to both spiritual training and to the potential membership or inclusion in future endeavours. This strong link between domesticity and citizenship also meant that the evaluation of domestic spaces was used to measure women's worthiness as Canadian cultural citizens.

'Canadian' culture was framed as superior, as a marker of civilization, and therefore, as a gateway to belonging. In this sense, 'home' became a metonymical marker of belonging and citizenship. Westernizing Japanese and Chinese women was viewed as a way of ridding them of 'heathen customs'. Often reports included descriptions of domestic spaces that missionaries visited in Japanese and Chinese communities. One missionary reported the following:

> In the homes one frequently sees the god shelf. In one home I visit there is a god shelf in the sitting-room and another in the adjoining bedroom. The good woman in a certain home feared that the frequent illness in their family might have been caused by the god shelf facing towards the north, which is regarded as an unlucky omen of sickness ... Here then was

12 Annual Report of the Woman's Missionary Society of the Methodist Church of Canada, 1902–1903. Toronto: The Ryerson Press, XCVII.

13 Annual Report of the Woman's Missionary Society of the Methodist Church of Canada, 1917–1918. Toronto: The Ryerson Press, CXIV.

14 Annual Report of the Woman's Missionary Society of the Methodist Church of Canada, 1917–1918. Toronto: The Ryerson Press, CXVI.

15 Annual Report of the Woman's Missionary Society of the Methodist Church of Canada, 1918–1919. Toronto: The Ryerson Press, CXII.

> our opportunity to point to better things, to seek for possible unhygienic causes and above all to give the light and cheer of that Truth which alone can fully illumine the darkness of the soul[16]

In this report, it is evident that cleanliness was equated with white domestic practices and non-Christian religious beliefs were a sign of inferiority and spiritual darkness. In another report, a missionary outlined how the home visits could stem the problem of heathenism. She wrote that "after [the Bible woman] had given the Bible lesson, [one] woman said she would not burn incense to her ancestors any longer."[17] Thus, the elimination of heathen practices or the removal of cultural artifacts from domestic spaces was viewed as a measure of spiritual maturity, and therefore, allowed for greater acceptance of the women in question.

As the work of the Home progressed, the Matrons of the Home and other missionaries in the area began to focus not just on 'Christianizing' but also 'Canadianizing', as these projects went hand in hand. One wrote:

> The longer we work among the Orientals in Canada, the more fully we realize that our work is twofold. First, to give our Orientals the knowledge of God as their Father and Jesus Christ as their Saviour. Second, to help them to become good citizens of Canada. … These strangers from across the sea need help when they come to this new land, and it is our duty and privilege to help them to become as the *home-born*.[18]

The possessive language of 'our Orientals' marked off Japanese and Chinese women as the objects of white women's ministrations. Further, the language of stranger[19] and of 'home-born' signalled that Japanese and Chinese women were viewed as outsiders and, therefore, it was only through missionary interventions could they become cultural citizens.

Canadianization took many forms, such as how one missionary described the outcome of a cooking class.

---

16 Annual Report of the Woman's Missionary Society of the Methodist Church of Canada, 1911–1912. Toronto: The Ryerson Press, LXXXVIII.

17 Annual Report of the Woman's Missionary Society of the Methodist Church of Canada, 1909–1910. Toronto: The Ryerson Press, LXXXI.

18 Annual Report of the Woman's Missionary Society of the Methodist Church of Canada, 1918–1919. Toronto: The Ryerson Press, CXI.

19 In other Chapter 5 of my book, I utilize Sara Ahmed's (2000) discussion of the stranger, to argue that discourses of strangeness and the stranger served to mark the Chinese as a "body out of place," as outside of proper family or domestic relations (Ikebuchi, 2015).

> At our June meeting the members of the cooking class prepared a *Canadian* dinner, to which we invited the church people. Thirty guests sat down to the pretty tables that looked very inviting with their white cloths and decorations of pink roses. A well cooked dinner, consisting of meat, vegetables, salad, strawberry short-cake, ice cream and coffee was served. All had a good time and after the dinner, many told me it was the first properly served Canadian dinner they had ever partaken of.[20]

The success of such transformations, according to one WMS report, was not only about saving souls, but also about making Canada "safer for all time because of the work that is being done."[21] Without intervention, these cultural 'strangers' were not only viewed as always already foreign, but also as a threat or danger to the nation. Ahmed (2000, p. 37) explains that "'the stranger' is produced as a figure precisely by being associated with a danger to the purified space of the community, the purified life of the good citizen, and the purified body of 'the child'". The danger associated with the 'stranger' here, is that they are a threat to the home, both in a national sense and in a familial one. The stranger can never be at home in the nation. However, through domestication, they could be made safer. If, through domestic mimicry, Japanese and Chinese women could approximate whiteness, or become, to use Bhabha's (1994, p. 127) turn of phrase, "almost the same, but not quite" white, then they could find a space of belonging, of being 'home'. Although the promise of inclusion was likely well-intended, the privileging of white imaginings of home reinforced ideas of white superiority. Bhabha (125–6) explains the paradox of mimicry: the mimic can only "repeat, rather than re-present" and thus the attempt to "emerge as authentic" is futile. Although Japanese and Chinese women could, repeat or reproduce white domesticity, they could not fully embody them. Domestication was always a partial project because while Chinese and Japanese women might learn English and 'English ways', they would never *be* English. Despite their domestication, Japanese and Chinese women could not be considered fully Canadian, as the promise of belonging was based on racial logics that precluded their full inclusion.

To be at home, in the metonymical sense, was to belong, yet belonging was based on whiteness, which could only be repeated.

---

20 Annual Report of the Woman's Missionary Society of the Methodist Church of Canada, 1920–1921. Toronto: The Ryerson Press, CXXIX, emphasis mine.

21 Annual Report of the Woman's Missionary Society of the Methodist Church of Canada, 1920–1921. Toronto: The Ryerson Press, CXXXI.

Although Japanese and Chinese women could not be deemed *fully* Canadian, the degree to which Canadianization was deemed successful was measured through the ability of the women to mimic white domesticity. One report read: "The Japanese W.M.S. ladies provided and served the refreshments; dainty sandwiches, cake, ices, candies, tea and coffee. There was an excellent programme of Canadian and Japanese music. About one hundred guests were present, and all agreed that they had seldom attended a more delightful missionary function."[22] While the music included both 'Canadian' and 'Japanese' selections, these performances of Canadian-ness and Japanese-ness were meant to signal the successful transformation of the always already foreign 'Other'. Further evidence of the successful project of Canadianization was the house itself. The report went on to indicate that most of the "Canadians were greatly surprised to find how thoroughly Canadianized many of our Japanese are. One lady, after going through Mrs. Ishizaki's rooms, said 'One couldn't tell this from a *real* Canadian home'."[23]

Despite that this report was meant to show the success of the WMS endeavours, the Japanese woman referenced here was not framed as 'Canadian', but instead as 'Canadianized'. Her home was not a 'real' Canadian home, but was, instead, offered up as a close facsimile of one. Like their homes, Japanese and Chinese women became the objects upon which the work of Canadianization was to be applied, rather than Canadian subjects. This meant the stripping away of previous cultural behaviours and then, the imposition of white cultural forms. So, while the WMS saw this mimicry as evidence of successful Canadianization, this portrayal also implies a loss of culture, as evidenced by the notable absence, music notwithstanding, of non-white cultural artifacts or foods in the home.

3 Cultural Domicide

While usually painted by the WMS as positive, their interventions undoubtedly resulted in cultural loss for many. Evidence of domestic 'improvements' in Chinese or Japanese communities was outlined in the yearly WMS reports. One Matron wrote that "Chinatown is not the disagreeable place it was twenty years ago, as the old buildings have been replaced by brick blocks, and the streets are paved and clean and just as surely the old customs are being

22 Annual Report of the Woman's Missionary Society of the Methodist Church of Canada, 1923–1924. Toronto: The Ryerson Press, CXXIII.

23 Ibid. emphasis mine.

replaced by new and we hope better ones."[24] Here, we see the evaluation of physical spaces taking on significance even in the realm of cultural practices. In other reports, matrons described the homes of former 'inmates' as evidence of the success of their mission. One wrote: "It is a delight to report that ... those who have married are in general carrying out the lessons they have been taught, and establishing Christian homes."[25] Another Home Matron reported that: "In Ladysmith, I spent a day with Ethel, one of our girls who was married last October. I was much pleased to find her happy and comfortable and *seeking to carry out in her own home what she was taught while in the Home* here."[26] The lessons the women learned in the Home, thus, shaped practices and behaviours even after the women left the Home.

Speaking of Japanese and Chinese women, the WMS noted in one of their reports: "We notice gain in social conditions. Increasingly both nationalities are scattering out into the suburbs of the city, living in nice well-furnished homes" (XC). Later, the report read: "We consider it an encouraging fact that many of our Chinese are moving out of Chinatown into nice roomy homes in *good parts* of the city ... These homes are furnished in Canadian style, and we have been more than pleased to see how beautifully clean and orderly the women keep their houses, and how proud and happy they are to be in a 'real home'. Here they will have true home life, something which I fear is little known in the crowded apartments of Chinatown."[27] This report shows that prior to the interventions of the WMS, the homes of Chinese and Japanese women were not to be seen as 'real homes' from which one could have a 'true home life'. While the 'crowded apartments' provided close contact and sociality, for white women missionaries, this type of domesticity fostered the wrong type of cultural exchange. For this reason, both Chinese and Japanese women were encouraged to move away from their communities and into 'good parts' of the city. For many of the women who complied, this would most certainly have meant a loss of community and links to culture. In fact, it was common to find reference in the WMS reports of Christianity as a dividing force within the communities, as they discussed how some women found it difficult to 'stand for Christ' because of reactions from their religious and cultural communities.

24 Annual Report of the Woman's Missionary Society of the Methodist Church of Canada, 1919–1920. Toronto: The Ryerson Press, CXIV.

25 Annual Report of the Woman's Missionary Society of the Methodist Church of Canada, 1917–18. Toronto: The Ryerson Press, VIII–IX.

26 Annual Report of the Woman's Missionary Society of the Methodist Church of Canada, 1909–1910. Toronto: The Ryerson Press, LXXVII.

27 Annual Report of the Woman's Missionary Society of the Methodist Church of Canada, 1912–13. Toronto: The Ryerson Press, CI, emphasis mine.

Choosing Christianity, thus, for some, meant severing ties (both emotionally and spatially) with their communities.

The removal of Japanese and Chinese women from their homes, as well as interventions into the domestic lives of other Japanese and Chinese women *in* their homes, resulted in changes to the community and culture. The spaces of the Chinese Rescue Home and later, the Oriental Home and School mimicked white domestic spaces and the education that the women received there was meant to train them in Western cultural habits and behaviours so that they would sever religious and cultural ties to their communities. Further, missionaries also went into homes to train women to transform their domestic practices. Despite that these strategies were meant to improve the lives of Japanese and Chinese women, it is important to also acknowledge the losses that resulted from such interventions. Tearing down what were seen as cultural barriers to inclusion required that new walls be built, and within these whitewashed walls only white domesticity could prevail.

References

Adachi, K. (1991) *The Enemy that Never Was: A History of Japanese Canadians.* Toronto: McClelland & Stewart Inc.

Ahmed, S. (2000) *Strange Encounters: Embodied Others in Post-Coloniality.* New York: Routledge.

Anderson, K. (1991) *Vancouver's Chinatown: Racial Discourse in Canada, 1875–1980.* Montreal: McGill-Queens University Press.

Bhabha, H. (1994) *The Location of Culture.* London: Routledge: Routledge.

Ikebuchi, S. (2015) *From Slave Girl to Salvation: Gender, Race, and Victoria's Chinese Rescue Home, 1886–1923.* Vancouver: University of British Columbia Press.

Lefebvre, H. (1991) *The Production of Space.* Oxford: Blackwell Publishers.

Mar, L. (2011) *Brokering Belonging: Chinese in Canada's Exclusion Era, 1885–1945.* Toronto: University of Toronto Press.

McAllister, K. E. (1999) Narrating Japanese Canadians In and Out of the Canadian Nation: A Critique of Realist Forms of Representation. *Canadian Journal of Communication* 24(1), 79–103.

Miki, R. (2004) *Redress: Inside the Japanese Canadian Call for Justice.* Vancouver: Raincoast Books.

Porteous, J. D. and Sandra Smith (2001) *Domicide: The Global Destruction of Home.* Montreal: McGill-Queen's University Press.

Razack, S. (2002) When Place Becomes Race. In: S. Razack (ed.) *Race, Space, and the Law.* Toronto: Between the Lines, 1–20.

CHAPTER 3

Unpacking the Festival of Diwali in Canada: Where have Rama, Sita, and Lakshman Gone?

Rajni Mala Khelawan

"Why do we celebrate Diwali, Mummy?" Once again I was five years old, clinging to my mother's sari.

"Questions, questions!" she would sigh, but I always knew she loved to give the answers. "With his faithful brother Lakshman on his right-hand side, the divine king Rama left his jeweled crown on his dying father's pillow," she would begin. "He strapped on his bow and arrow and took out for the woods to rescue his beloved wife, Sita. Even though, Sita was a common girl, a common girl whose chastity was in question even in those days." My mother would soak the white cotton wicks in ghee and light them with a matchstick, one by one.

"What does chastity mean, Mummy?"

"Never mind what it means, Kalyana." She would blink her round eyes to brush my question aside. "Do you want to hear the story or not?"

I would nod my head, eager and alert.

"Ravana kept Sita imprisoned in a small hut, in a wooded area. Oh, Ravana thought he could one day convince her to forget about her husband, Rama, and become his kept wife. For fourteen years, God Rama fought lions and tigers, cheetahs and cougars, wolves and hounds, bears and gorillas too. Oh yes, every animal, Kalyana, and more, for he even fought four-limbed and three-eyed monsters, hideous beasts of demonic nature. Yet he defeated them. One by one, the beasts would fall to the ground, panting and weak, then take their last breaths and turn to dust. In the end, after fourteen long years of exile, the victorious divine King Rama killed the demon Ravana and rescued his beloved wife Sita, and brought her home. That is why we light the pathways, the verandas, and the gardens. It is to help him find his way back home." (237–238)

Excerpt taken from Khelawan's (2016) novel *Kalyana*

∴

1 Introduction

The religious rituals and the oral tradition of storytelling are what I miss the most. When I immigrated to Canada from the Fiji Islands on October 10, 1988, which coincidentally falls on the country's Independence Day from the British rule, I did not know that it would be the last time I would hear the stories of the mighty deeds of God Rama and his half-brother Lakshman, or experience the vulnerability and strength of our beloved Goddess Sita. It would be the last time I would engage in the communal lighting of the *diyas*. Even though the Indo-Canadians form the third largest non-European immigrant group in Canada, as noted in the *Canada Immigration Newsletter* (2014), Diwali is not celebrated with the same enthusiasm or vigor here as it is in Fiji. The stories of Rama, Sita, and Lakshman that I grew up with, the Gods and Goddesses of the Great Epic *Ramayana*, the heroes and heroines of Diwali, are nowhere to be found in Canada.

Stuart Anderson (2020) and Kareem El-Assal (2020), both report that there is a recent uptick of immigration of Indians from India to Canada under the Trump administration, given that his policies discourages racialized immigration to the U.S.. However, contrary to as one would expect, their rituals and oral traditions have not followed them here. In fact, these rituals and traditions are generally absent from their public celebrations and private communal gatherings involving Diwali that, it no longer resembles the sacred festival of the Hindu people of Canada, connecting them to the larger diaspora, but it becomes something different altogether; perhaps even a Western non-religious festival. Is this erasing of the religious and cultural ritual practises of minority culture in the Canadian context justified?

In this essay, I will attempt to illustrate two points: First, the importance of rituals in connecting individuals to a larger collective in this case, the Hindu diaspora. Second, I will apply Satya P. Mohanty's realist theory of cultural and social identity to show how erasing stories of Rama, Lakshman, and Sita from Diwali celebrations shifts and dismantles 'personal cultural identities', and subsequently affects the 'collective cultural identities' of Hindus transnationally. I also think it is important to note here that my discussion of the religion of Hinduism in this chapter is through the diaspora location of Fiji, and does not address Hindu nationalism or Hindutva movements that have come to characterize the Modi government. I believe that is beyond the scope of this chapter and would require a separate thorough discussion elsewhere. Nonetheless, while examining these points through the lens of Indo Fijian communities (the majority of whom were brought as indentured labour by the British empire), I will explore why maintaining these cultural identities and ritual practises (in other words, rejecting colonial ideals) are important in development of self in relation to a wider culture or diaspora. In this space, I will attempt to unpack the Festival of Diwali.

2 Ritual and Diwali

In this section, I will discuss Diwali and its significance, the specific religious rituals associated with its celebration; and the role these rituals play in strengthening an individual's bond to the greater diasporic community. I will use personal experiences to illustrate what a typical Diwali celebration looks like in Canada today, and drawing from Bell's research on the importance of rituals in individual lives, I will restate why it is important to reignite an engagement in Diwali's ritualistic traditions in Canada.

Diwali is a religious festival that celebrates the triumph of good over evil. It encourages communal and familial bonding through storytelling and shared ritual practise. For Hindus, transnationally, Diwali symbolizes an end to suffering and a celebration of life's joys. It usually falls in the months of October and November, and is celebrated twenty days after the emergence of the new moon. According to Om Lata Bahadur's (2006) essay, this date is taken from the Hindu calendar. She states that, it is difficult to pin point exactly when Diwali is going to occur using the Western system; however, when it does arrive, it lasts for five days.

From my recollection of my late mother's stories, Diwali marked the day God Rama, Lakshman, and Sita, returned to the city of Ayodhya, Kosala, after fourteen years in exile.. Kaikeyi, Rama's step mother, desired her own son, Bharat, to become the king and rule over the city of Ayodhya. Thus, her last wish to her dying husband, Dasharatha, the King ofKosala, was to banish his oldest son, Rama, to the forest for fourteen years, and make her son, Bharat the king instead. The conflicted King, with great distress, asked Rama to do as his queen wished. Rama, to uphold the request of his dying father, prepared for exile. Lakshman and Sita, not bearing to see him take the journey alone, followed him. In the forest, Rama, Sita, and Lakshman encounter many adventures and hardships. During this time, Sita meets Ravana, the Lord of the demons, who kidnaps her. Rama and Lakshman, with the help of Hanuman (the flying monkey God) and his troop of monkeys, find Sita, rescue her, and defeat Ravana by setting fire to his kingdom and killing him. In this way, the noble God Rama becomes victorious over the evil demon, Ravana. The two brothers and Sita journey back to Kosala. The people of Ayodhya, upon hearing the news of

Rama's return, light up the verandas and pathways with *diyas* and lamps to help them find their way back; upon their arrival, theythrow a feast to celebrate the coming of their king, and the victory of good over evil. They engage in gift giving, make noise, and light firecrackers to mark this festive occasion. Diwali is meant to be a continuing celebration of this kind; it is meant to honour the return of God Rama, in our spiritual lives.

In Fiji, the preparations of Diwali took place days before Diwali arrived. From what I remember, my mother would meticulously instruct everyone to clean the house: she would ask the brass to be shined; the walls to be wiped down; the drapes to be washed; and the floors to be scrubbed. No speck of dust or grime would have been acceptable anywhere in the house on Diwali day. To complete the preparations, our front doorsteps would be decorated with *rangoli* – an art form where dry chalk or powdered colored rice is used to fill in the elaborate design patterns on the cement floors. My mother would then make candies and desert, for the purpose of giving them to relatives and friends. The women of the household would receive new saris and clothes; the children would be given money and driven to town to purchase firecrackers that light up the skies on Diwali night. This kind of gift giving and preparations are common in Diwali celebrations. Bahadur (2006) documents that in some parts of India, a *Madhubani* (a type of painting) depicting God Rama, Sita, Lakshman, and other major deities, are created by the best artist of the family. The wall becomes the canvas. She states that all the members of the family then come together and fill in the colours. This binds the bonds between the family members. Bahadur (2006) notes that this is a dying tradition;as this kind of togetherness is now rarely found in modern India.

On the final day of Diwali, ritualistic preparations for the *puja* or prayers take place. Several *diyas* (i.e., small clay bowls) are filled with *ghee*, and a small cotton wick is placed in the center of them. These are lit after the *puja* rituals are performed during the evening hours.

Bahadur (2006) elaborates on the rituals performed during Diwali *puja*. The prayer starts at dusk. Bahadur (2006) states that first, the *mandir*, or the place of worship that holds many pictures and statues of the variousdeities, including those of Rama, Sita, and Lakshman, are decorated with candles and *diyas*. In Fiji, a variety of flowers are picked from the gardens, and placed all around the *mandir*. Bahadur (2006) further states that a tray is assembled with sweets, fruits, and *kumkum*, a red paste made from mixing turmeric powder and lime. A small silver dish is filled with puffed rice mixture. *Puja* begins when a *tika* or a mark is placed on the foreheads of all the gods and goddesses sitting in the altar, and then on all the devotees assembled in front of them. In Fiji, softened sandalwood paste is also substituted in place of *kumkum*. The deitiesare bathed in pure water, *roli*, *aipun*, and rice mixture (Bahadur 2006). Bahadur (2006) notes that everyone holds a bit of rice in their hands, as stories of Lakshmi, the Goddess of Prosperity, are told. It is believed that, on Diwali night, she enters a well lit house and blesses the family living there with an abundance of wealth. After the storytelling cycle completes, everyone showers the gods and goddesses with puffed rice, after which, the females of the house distribute the *prasad* or the fruits and sweets previously offered to the divine, amongst everyone. In Fiji, families also perform the *havan* or a sacrificial fire ritual, in which they gather around a contained fire and drop offerings of puffed rice mixture into it when the Head of the Household completes the chanting of the mantras by saying'*Svaha*'. The first diya is lit after the *puja* closes. Then the celebration, eating, socializing, and lighting of the candles and firecrackers begin. This merriment continues long into the night. This is what I remember about how I used to celebrate Diwali.

In her book, *Ritual: Perspectives and Dimensions*, Catherine Bell (1997) argues that, rituals functions to strengthen bonds attaching the individual to the society that an individual is a member of (25). She cites a study that Julian Huxley did on ritualized patterns of behaviour among animals, in which he concluded that rituals, like in animal kingdoms, act to provide human communities with bonding; he also claimedthat, it was unfortunate that this was discouraged in modern communities.

Bell (1997) cites another study on ritualistic traditions by Victor Turner in which he expands on Emile Durkheim's views that rituals are means by which individuals are brought together as a collective group; he states that ritual plays an important role in maintaining the unity of a group, and also acts as a mechanism for recreating this unity. In other words, he states that "rituals did not simply restore social equilibrium; they were in fact, a part of ongoing process by which the community was continually redefining and renewing itself" (39).

Furthermore, Bell (1997) states that theorists such as Erik Erikson and Jean Piaget have argued that ritual activity does not just enhance community bonding, but is also linked to particular dynamics in the brain wherein the ritualistic acts are correlated to a release of harmful emotions and thoughts (i.e., catharsis) in individuals. Moreover, the emotional responses that are evoked in the practise of engaging in rituals have the effect of people identifying their innermost selves to a larger reality (Bell 1997). In other words, ritual traditions such as those found in Diwali celebrations,which I have outlined here, are important devices in maintaining individual identity and mental equilibrium, and on a grander scale, continuing the unity of the wider diasporic community. Now that I have provided a brief explanation for the importance of engaging in ritualistic traditions that separate Diwali from another Western non-religious festival, I wanted to expand on what Diwali celebrations currently looks like in Canadian Hindu communities.

Recently, I attended a Diwali festivity in Canada. I attended it with my five-year-old son, thinking that he will be educated about the spiritual significance of this gathering,or he would get a chance to light a *diya*, or at the very least, hear the stories of Rama, Lakshman, and Sita's great escape from the forest where Ravana dwelled. At some level, I was yearning to hear these stories myself, sharing the experience with like-minded group of people, whom I thought I shared a religious and cultural tradition with. I did not go to the gathering, expecting a *puja* ceremony, as that would be classified as a 'religious', thus a 'private' and a 'personal' affair, and in a secular society, I knew this wouldbe highly discouraged; or best kept to temples.

This was my actual experience of attending a Diwali event in Canada: there were about one hundred or so people of Indo heritage heritage that attended this annual event. There was ample vegetarian food present, considering it was a potluck, so everyone brought something. The Master of Ceremonies started the evening with various humorous results Google forfeits in a mad search for some foreign word – none of these words he searched in any way, shape or form, was related to Diwali. The evening proceeded with the people eating the foods, the children playing various games in another room, while the adults sat in a circle singing Bollywood songs. At no point in the celebration were the names Rama, Lakshman, Sita, or God Hanuman mentioned. After the night concluded, my son asked me, "So, Mom – Is this, what Diwali is all about?"

Prior to the birth of my son, I had bought tickets to another Diwali Festival. The tickets were priced at $50 for each adult, and again, the core stories of Diwali were never mentioned. However, many amateur dancers went up on stage, and performed Bollywood dances to many film songs. The true spirit of Diwali was nowhere to be found in any of these annual social events planned around celebratingthis religious holiday. This event was also attended by hundreds of people, almost all of them of Indian origin. It was saddening to witness.

As Bell's research has shown, rituals and ancient tradition of storytelling forms the basis of human bonding. It works to bring a set of individuals with shared values together, binding them to a common set of identity. This, in turn, maintains their inner sense of mental equilibrium. Rituals, therefore, are necessary for the functioning of the individual and the society as a whole. Thus,this lack of acknowledgement of what the religious festival of Diwali is or the failure to honour even a simple ritual such as lighting of the *diya*, has a great potential to impact an individual's sense of self and their connection to the wider diasporic community, which in turn can disrupt the continuation and unity of that community. To sum up, it affects their 'personal' and 'collective' cultural identities.

3 Social and Cultural Identities

In this section, I will first, expand on the definition of culture, and then I will turn to Satya P. Mohanty's realist theory of cultural identity for a discussion on social and cultural identities in the context of a diaspora Hindu-ness in Fiji that decenters the South Asian continent. Jack David Eller (2009) defines culture as "ways of thinking, feeling, and behaving, and the social and material products of those ways, which are shared among a group of people not on the basis of innate or physical traits but rather on the basis of common experience and mutual learning" (p. 26). Succinctly, he claims culture is learned, shared, symbolic, integrated, and adaptive. He notes that in an integrated societal structure, religion can be seen as being part of a larger cultural system that consists of other domains such as economics, politics, and kinship.

First, Eller (2009) claims culture is learned, shared, and symbolic: he states that culture is not innate, but acquired through enculturation. Eller (2009) asserts that, because culture is learned, it is shared between people and passed down from generation to generation, often times through symbolism; and in instances where children grow up separated from all cultural learning (such as in cases of a severely abused or neglected child or a feral one who grows up isolated in the woods), he claims that they do not reach their full potential. According to Eller (2009), these children mature to behave no differently than an animal interested in satisfying its basic need such as hunger; such a child, he writes, is incapable of showing or receiving love, which is nothing short of a tragedy.

Second, Eller (2009) posits that culture is adaptive: he notes that even though culture is learned and shared, it is not stable and unchanging. He states that justas all living creatures adapt to their environments with their bodies, humans adapt with their behaviour. Ulf Hannerz (1996) similarly argues that culture is ever changing.

Third, Eller (2009) notes that culture moves beyond geographical and social boundaries. A common cultural practise or religion has the power to link a group of people across national geographical boundaries. However, Eller (2009) also cautions that this can have severe consequences for minority groups of people living in a society in which the dominant group discourages and minimizes the value of minority people's culture and religion, thus leading to either acculturation or deculturation.

Satya P. Mohanty (2000) proposes his Realist Theory of Cultural Identity on this very notion that culture is fluid, and changing due to a cultural group's experience in a larger societal system. He argues that essentialist theory of identity do not take this fact into account, thus are inaccurate in their conclusions about cultural identity of minority people.

Mohanty (2000) argues that essentialist theories are falsely based on the assumption that identities common to members of a social (or cultural) group is based on a common shared experience, therefore is stable and unchanging. In other words, to the Essentialists, the historical changes or the internal differences that exist between members who are part of a group do not matter. Hindus then everywhere would behave, act, and think the same way as they belong to a society of people that practise the religion of Hinduism transnationally. This is not true as I have demonstrated how Hindus gathering to celebrate Diwali in the Western culture behave and act much different than Hindus celebrating the same Festival in Fiji per se. For this reason, it is important to understand these diasporic communities transnationally.

Postmodernist Theorists, on the other hand, as Mohanty (2000) states, insist that identities are fabricated and constructed, and not deduced from experience, and basing identity on personal experiences is problematic as experiences, in their view, is not a source of objective knowledge. Therefore, postmodernist theories discount peoples' individual and collective experiences. The experiences that come from exclusion of one's religion in the community that one lives in, according to postmodernist theorists, would have no effect at all in shifting one's cultural identity. They rationalize that personal experiences cannot be substantiated or taken seriously. Mohanty (2000) states that it is limiting for postmodernists to think that a person's personal experience does not form the basis of the creation of a person's cultural identity, as much as it is problematic for essentialists to think that all people that belong to a similar group have the same experiences and identify with one single unchanging identity. Mohanty (2000) asserts that a person's experience matters a great deal in the formation of his or her cultural identity.

"Personal experience" as Mohanty (2000) argues, is socially and theoretically constructed, and it is precisely in this manner that it yields knowledge. Moreover, Mohanty (2000) states that the cognitive component of experience is what grounds objective knowledge. To illustrate this point, Mohanty (2000) draws upon the work done by Naomi Scheman. Mohanty (2000) states that Scheman held a consciousness raising group for women where she rearranged the narratives of an individual's relationship with the world, exposing the socially constructed narratives, mediated by the values and visions that are political in nature. This led to a "political redescription" of a woman and her world, thus leading her to discern features of the social and cultural arrangements of her world that defined her sense of self, the choices she was taught to have, and finally, the range of personal capacities she is expected to exploit and exercise. The women's confusion and ambiguity turned into anger. In other words, the way she made sense of an experience, in the end created a whole new experience for her (35).

This study done by Scheman did not just establish that personal experiences are a source of objective knowledge, but also provided evidence against Essentialist Theories of Identity. It showed that due to the constructed nature of experience, there is no guarantee that an individual's personal experience will lead that individual to some common values or beliefs that will link the said individual to every other member of the individual's cultural group (Mohanty 2000). Furthermore, our personal feelings are dependent on social narratives, paradigms and ideologies (Mohanty 2000).

Mohanty (2000) goes on to state that any attempts made to explain identity in terms of objective knowledge by discounting subjective experiences of individuals living in a set social structure only aids to promote and maintain the ideologies of powerful, dominant and established groups. Mohanty (2000) quotes Sandra Harding who asserts that "objective knowledge is dependent on theoretical knowledge that activism creates, because without them, our efforts to interpret and understand the dominant ideologies and institutions are limited to those created and sanctioned by these very ideologies and institutions" (40).

Paula Moya (2000) supports Mohanty's arguments by stating that identities are both constructed and discovered from experience. She states that identities and experiences that underlie material for construction of identity are mediated by theoretical understanding of the world and one's place in it, and oppressive experiences that arises from the individuals social locations is an interpretive framework – a way of understanding their world and their experiences in it; acknowledging this fact is the first step towards creating a progressive change that is familiar with the notion that past and present structures of inequality are correlated with creation of new identities. In other words, Moya (2000) states that knowledge is not produced simply by understanding social relations, but by understanding experiences in terms of social relations.

Social and cultural identity then can only be understood in terms of objective social location. Whether we inherit an identity (i.e., whether we identify ourselves in terms of our sex – male or female), or actively choose one on the basis of our political or religious views, our identities are ways of making sense of our experiences (Mohanty 2000). Our identities are theoretical constructions that enable us to read the world in specific ways. Therefore, experiences are valuable and taken seriously, as through them we learn to define and reshape our values and our commitments, and in the end, our sense of "self" (Mohanty 2000). To conclude, as Moya (2000) states, cultural identities are enabling, enlightening, and enriching structures of attachment and feeling that is crucial to development of a sense of "self" in relation to a group – who we understand ourselves to be, will have consequences for how we experience and understand our world.

Thus, in the case of a person practising Diwali living in a context where they find themselves as minoritized, such as in Fiji or in Canada, having to constantly hide or dismiss their cultural and religious identification will affect their sense of 'self'. In Fiji, Diwali is a cultural and religious ritual that enhances the Indo-Fijin community whose presence on the island was the product of British colonialism. In Canada, the erasure of certain traditions and rituals send messages to the diaspora that their ceremonial and religious rituals are not "secular" enough in a Western secularism framework. This may lead diaspora members to transmit this shame on to their children and any opportunities to teach their children about their cultural heritage will be lost in their ambiguous feelings about "proper" ways of celebration in a multicultural framework. These "hidden" regulations and frameworks, under the guise of secularism, relegate the use of public space to only certain kinds of celebration (e.g., commercialized parties), but not to others. People of minoritarian culture may internalize these new ideologies about space, ritual, and race as being "normal and modern" and dismiss their own cultural practises as being "inferior and of ancient world."

4 Conclusion

The notion of the individual and collective identity being rooted in culture is not a new one. In the words of the German Historian and Philosopher Johann Hender (1744 – 1803), "every nation of humanity had its own unique spirit or soul expressed in their language and culture" (316). Thus, protecting, maintaining and encouraging oral tradition and ritual practises of minority cultures become crucial and necessary in our modern secular Western countries. For Hindus living in Canada, one way to do this is by celebrating Diwali with stories of Rama, Sita, and Lakshman's heroic adventures. It is by remembering or retrieving age old cultural traditions and rituals left behind in a distant location. In the words of Hannerz (1996), "sometimes it is perhaps not so much 'reinventing' that is needed, but to begin with, at least some mere 'remembering' or 'retrieving' in so far as previous generations have left certain unfinished yet worthwhile business behind" (7).

It is also important to remember that by retaining your own culture, and being proud of it, does not necessarily entail a rejection of other values. In other words, a Hindu person can celebrate Diwali proudly and still embrace Christmas and throw a traditional turkey dinner. What will be missing is the shame one feels for one's own cultural heritage. To conclude, giving a detailed description of what the Festival of Diwali is, and how I learned to celebrate it in Fiji, the rituals and stories associated with it, in some ways, is my small attempt to reclaim my cultural identity.

References

Anderson, Stuart. (2020) "Indians Immigrating to Canada at an Astonishing Rate." *Forbes*, February 3.

Bahadur, Om Lata (2006) "Divali: The Festival of Lights." In: John Stratton Hawley and Vasudha Narayanan (eds.) *The Life of Hinduism*. Berkeley: University of California Press.

Bell, Catherine (1997) *Ritual: Perspectives and Dimensions*. Oxford: Oxford University Press.

CIC News. 2014. "The Story of Indian Immigration." *Canadian Immigration Newsletter* April 16.

El-Assal, Kareem. (2020) "A Quarter of Canada's Immigrants Arrived from India in 2019." *Canadian Immigration Newsletter*, February 11.

Eller, Jack David (2009) *Cultural Anthropology: Global Forces, Local Lives*. New York: Routledge.

Hannerz, Ulf (1996) *Transnational Connections: Culture, People, Places*. London: Routledge.

Khelawan, Rajni Mala (2016) *Kalyana*. Toronto: Second Story Press.

Mohanty, Satya P. (2000) "The Epistemic Status of Cultural Identity: On Beloved and Postcolonial Condition." In: Paula M. L. Moya and Michael R. Hames-Garcia (eds.) *Reclaiming Identity: Realist Theory and the Predicament of Postmodernism.* Berkeley: University of California Press, 29–66.

Moya, Paula M. L. (2000) "Postmodernism, Realism, and the Politics of Identity: Cherrie Moraga and Chicana Feminism." In: Paula M. L. Moya and Michael R. Hames-Garcia (eds.) *Reclaiming Identity: Realist Theory and the Predicament of Postmodernism.* Berkeley: University of California Press, 67–101.

CHAPTER 4

Seeking Pappy's Approval

Krystal Kavita Jagoo

I worried that Pappy might never understand why I feel the need to dismantle white supremacy with every breath I take. I mean, my grandfather passed away before I turned 10, when we still lived in Trinidad, with its mostly Black and brown population, so I doubted this would have dominated his consciousness like mine. There, he taught me the value of hard work to achieve success, and the need for humility and generosity should that come, as he put himself through school to become the first Trinidadian navigator for the national oil company. I remember him giving back to his village freely and never flaunting his accomplishments. While he had not ever claimed that he pulled himself up by his bootstraps, that was how I had come to think of his story over the years, embodying model minority status in my mind.

As I became increasingly aware of the deeply flawed reality of Canada through my career as a social worker, intent on anti-oppressive practice, I understood the hypocrisy of my field's absence of work explicitly dismantling white supremacy. Especially as a racialized woman, I have a responsibility to disrupt this problematic status quo by challenging colleagues to confront their complicity. As my consciousness developed, I wondered if my grandfather would be proud of me for standing up for these issues in my career, even as it threatens it. When that psychologist in North Bay would email me every single time that he could not locate a book of his, I initially assumed that everyone in our workplace got those annoying messages. Eventually, I realized that they came only to me, and in a meeting, he laughed as he told me that I would not believe that Bev had that book about which he recently emailed me! I clarified that I would have no difficulty believing that as I have never had any of his missing books and compared his assumption that the only racialized member of the team stole his books to the driving while Black phenomenon, for a reference he might grasp! Instead of the accountability I had hoped for, with what I now recognize to be an anti-Black statement, he said that he sometimes searched my office in my absence as he never believed me.

I comforted myself that it would get better when I escaped the north as I applied for jobs in the GTA with a fervor that exceeded their white supremacy! After clearing my student debt, I decided that the toll on my emotional wellbeing was worth a ten grand pay cut annually to avoid getting called a terrorist in Walmart! I accepted a job offer at a medical practice an hour outside of Toronto after 52 long months there, and naively dreamed of greener GTA pastures. Within a year, the facade became apparent as although this organization had co-opted the talk of anti-oppressive practice, their walk was violently white supremacist! As Trump came into power across the border, I was being terrorized by another white man at my job that was far different from the GTA of my dreams! Initially, I focused on the value of my work with patients, but eventually took a medical leave when migraines and sleep issues debilitated me.

Thanks to this white supremacist workplace harassment, I had much more time to reflect about my grandfather and how he would feel about my explicitly anti-racist social work practice, while worrying if I would ever reclaim my hijacked career. Over many long months, I realized that it was I who had put Pappy in that model minority box after his death, as I desperately tried to hold onto the memory of a man who had taken on the status of a legend in my world. Before my grandfather completed the training, our national oil company had only brought white men from England to work as navigators, but he became the first Trinidadian to be employed for Trintoc in that capacity. While Pappy may never have used the words white supremacy once, upon further reflection, it became obvious that we had a shared understanding. Over time, I recognized that my grandfather could never have aspired to occupy that position only before held by British men had he not fundamentally opposed the notion of white supremacy!

Over 2017, I had worked in a paid capacity for under 45 days before being told by an old British woman with only a high school diploma that I did not meet her standards for continuing past probation. Unfortunately, even with a Master's degree in Social Work, and a decade of employment in my field, including clinical, teaching, and writing experience, it turns out I was born with war paint for my very skin. Searching for solace and sustenance, I read over four hundred books from marginalized authors that year, desperately looking for hope. What I found was that racialized folx more brilliant than me had managed to get published, but often died in abject poverty. I also wondered then whether my grandfather could have ever imagined the challenges I would face when he raised me back home with the audacity to have integrity and speak truth to power! Did he anticipate that I would settle on this stolen land full of post-racial myths fuelled by white mediocrity gaslighting, derailing, and silencing me daily?

Given the finality of death, I will never unequivocally know if Pappy would have supported my work to dismantle white supremacy even as it threatens my employability. Obviously, that little girl whose grandfather made her believe that her brilliance could change the world wants to hold onto that conviction. What I do know though is that I never hesitated to oppose him in childhood when we disagreed, so the emotional safety he provided me then paved the way for my anti-oppressive practice. Maybe Pappy thought I would face less barriers in adulthood because he pictured that I would spend it amongst folx who looked like us back home so it never occurred to him to teach me to be less opinionated to survive white supremacy in Canada.

On my best days, I like to believe that he expected me to end up in this context and believed in my profound ability to disrupt white supremacy! If Pappy showered me with unconditional love even when he ground his teeth, and sighed in frustration with me in childhood, I know he raised me to make decisions that I can stand behind, in his absence. It is his blood that courses through my veins, the man, for whom, our national oil company changed its hiring practices! Should that not be enough to convince me that this foreign land too can evolve in response to my determination? Did Pappy not teach me how to make waves when he took me out in his boat as a little girl? Did I not begin my time here skipping three grades in high school? I hope to remember these answers when next white mediocrity questions my competency in this sorry excuse for what passes for equity in my field. Thankfully, like my grandfather, I too know the value of my contributions even when whiteness undermines my work.

CHAPTER 5

Vulnerable Resisters: Decolonizing Voices of Asian Migrants in a Settler Colonial and Religious Context

Hyejung Jessie Yum

1 Introduction

In late May 2021, Indigenous communities and Canadian society mourned when the remains of 215 children were found buried on the site of the former Kamloops Indian Residential School in British Columbia. The school was one of the residential schools operated by the Catholic Church from 1890 to 1969, and operated by the government later as a day school until it was closed in 1978.[1] Since the 1980s, churches in Canada began to recognize their colonial legacy practiced in the name of mission and civilization. Anglican, Roman Catholic, the United Church of Canada, Mennonite, and other churches and missionaries operated residential schools, supported by the Canadian government. In 2015, the Truth and Reconciliation Commission (TRC) of Canada published Calls to Action to redress the legacy of settler colonialism against Indigenous people. In the report, Church Apologies and Reconciliation section (Calls to Action #58–61) calls for church leaders and institutions to collaborate with Indigenous leaders and survivors to educate their clergies and people about historical and ongoing wrongdoings of colonial legacy. It also asks to respect Indigenous spiritualties, thereby preventing spiritual violence.[2] Paulette Regan, director of research for the TRC of Canada, claims that non-Indigenous settlers need to go through their own decolonizing process to move towards transformative possibilities of restorative relationships.[3]

Since the initiation of TRC, the decolonizing approach to the relations between Indigenous people and white settlers has noticeably increased in a Canadian Christian discourse. In addition to such efforts on redressing white

1 https://www.cbc.ca/news/canada/british-columbia/tk-eml%C3%BAps-te-secw%C3%A9pemc-215-children-former-kamloops-indian-residential-school-1.6043778.

2 Truth and Reconciliation Commission of Canada, *Calls to Action* (Truth and Reconciliation Commission of Canada, 2015).

3 Regan, 2010: 168, 192.

settlers' colonial practices, it is also necessary to recognize that the colonial relations in a multicultural Canada are more complicated than the Indigenous-white settler relations. To address the complexity, this chapter highlights the importance of Asian migrants' decolonizing voices beyond the binary relations in religious discourse. I sketch Asian Canadian stories briefly to show how Asian immigrants have been involved in the construction of Canadian society. Furthermore, I address Asian immigrants' ambivalent relationship to settler colonialism, which demonstrates the complexity of colonial relations in a multicultural context. Lastly, I present Asian immigrants as vulnerable resisters by engaging the works of Asian religious scholars who have sought decolonizing solidarity with Indigenous people in the Canadian context.

2 Asian Immigrants in Contradictory Demands of Canada

Asian immigration in Canada began with and continues to be conditioned by the demand of labour for capitalist expansion. At the same time, however, Asian immigrants were a stumbling block to the desire to form a white national identity in the process of nation building. Such contradiction led Canada to implement discriminatory policies towards non-white immigrants, including Asian immigrants, so that Canada could construct and maintain a white identity.[4]

Chinese immigrants' experience is a notable example of discriminatory history in the contradiction. In *A Space for Race*, Kathy Hogarth and Wendy L. Fletcher demonstrate how legitimate racism disturbed belonging of non-white groups such as Chinese immigrants in Canada. Chinese immigration began with the gold rush in British Columbia in 1858 before Canada was formed as a nation. The immigrants mainly worked to build infrastructure, such as roads for the gold rush. When the industry declined in the 1860s, the remaining Chinese became the target of hostility in the local community as they were regarded as those taking away jobs from Caucasians.[5] Yet Chinese immigration was once again encouraged when cheap and tractable labours were needed for the construction of the Canadian national railroad in 1881. From 1881 to 1884, 15,000 Chinese came to Canada. Under the harsh working conditions, more than six hundred workers died at work. At that time, while the local communities opposed burying the Chinese in the area, First Nations communities

4 Dhamoon, 2010: 76.

5 Hogarth and Fletcher, 2018: 58.

opened up their own burial grounds for the Chinese workers to be buried as a gesture of hospitality.[6] When the completion of the railroad reduced demand for labour in 1885, Canada began a policy to restrict Chinese immigration by imposing a "head tax" of $50, which was equivalent to two years' wages for the workers.[7] This was a discriminatory policy that did not apply to European immigrants. Most of the workers at the time were male, and if Chinese women came, there were concerns about the increase of the non-white population. Such discriminatory policies and views towards Asian immigrants continued afterwards. *Echoes Magazine*, published by *the Imperial Order of Daughters of the Empire* (IODE) in 1914, vividly describes the views that "oriental" migrants were a threat to the Canadian identity as a white man's country.

> The Chinese and Japanese immigration is a peril to white civilization. Many undesirable nationalities may settle in colonies and present a very difficult problem for assimilation, but the oriental races absolutely will not assimilate. If the number of yellow men and women increase, the inevitable will follow—a struggle as to whether or not the Pacific coast of our fair Dominion shall remain a possible white man's home—now the white laboring man has been superseded in the saw mills, the fishing industry, etc. by the oriental, who works for less wage, and the whole equilibrium of the industrial life of the West has been affected by depressing wages.
>
> *Echoes* Magazine, October 1914, 21[8]

In a response to this text, Marjorie Johnstone argues that *Echoes* disseminated imperial ideas by depicting Asian immigrants as being unassimilable to white society, in contrast to Southern and Eastern European immigrants who were also problematic but assimilable through reeducation.[9] As the historic case of Chinese immigrants shows, Asian immigrants were sacrificed and treated as foreign workers and even a peril to the state despite their contributions to constructing the significant part of the national infrastructure.

The exploitation continues to this day, for example, the temporary foreign worker program has been developed in such a way that it provides the flexible and low-cost labour needed by Canadian society but have rarely cared

6 Hogarth and Fletcher, 2018: 58.

7 Kim-Cragg, 2018: 110.

8 *Echoes Magazine*, October 1914, 21, quoted in Marjorie Johnstone, "Settler Feminism, Race Making, and Early Social Work in Canada," Affilia 33, no. 3 (August 2018): 331–45.

9 Johnstone, 327.

for their societal belongings and security. For several decades, many Asian women, including Filipino women, migrated to Canada through the Live-in Caregiver Program (LCP). They were vulnerable to insecurity and limited freedom because the LCP requires workers to live in their employer's home and a worker had limited freedom to choose her dwelling place and had minimal privacy. Also, because the LCP employer had the authority to determine the migrant workers' legitimacy to stay in Canada, workers were extremely vulnerable to excessive and inappropriate work and even sexual abuse.[10] In her book *Asian Immigrants in Two Canadas*, South Asian Canadian scholar Habiba Zaman argues that the law's stipulation concerning the designated employer and place to live "creates both systemic and legislated disempowerment designed to remove political, economic, labour, and social rights" from the workers, and "ultimately, to create a highly flexible, cheap labour force" in the market.[11] With significant criticism on its racialized and gendered aspects, the LCP, which allowed the workers to apply for permanent residency after two-year experience, was closed in 2014 and replaced with the caregiver program (CP), abolishing the requirement of live-in conditions yet imposing new requirements of language and license to apply for permanent residency in a limited quota.[12] It is still controversial whether the new policy improves "security" or deepens "precariousness."[13]

Through its discriminatory policies towards Asian migrants, Canada resolved the contradiction between the capitalist demands and the desire for a white dominant society. The white normative Canada has been constituted partly in the context where Asian immigrants were counted as force of labour yet cared for rarely as societal members.

3 Complex Relation of Asian Immigrants to Settler Colonialism

Asian immigrants have been discriminated by the white norm constructed through the racializing process of the nation building. Nevertheless, it is true that they also have benefitted from the European colonial settlement

10 Zaman, 2012: 64, 66.

11 Zaman, 2012: 41.

12 Refugees And Citizenship Canada Immigration, "Government of Canada," Canada.ca, August 29, 2023, accessed September 19, 2024, https://www.canada.ca/en/immigration-refugees-citizenship/services/work-canada/hire-permanent-foreign/caregiver-program/hire-caregiver.html.

13 Banerjee, Kelly, and Tungohan 2017: 7–8.

on Indigenous land. The place of Asian migrants in settler Canada, then, shows something more complex than that a dichotomous approach between Indigenous people and white settlers.

We might find such complexity in a religious context where churches have engaged with decolonization begun by their apologies for Indian Residential Schools. In a response to an Indigenous leader's request for churches' roles in colonization, the first official apology of church was made by United Church of Canada in 1986. The indigenous leader acknowledged the apology yet refused to accept it, leaving a significant message that settler colonialism is not just the past event, but ongoing reality that requires working further.[14] In 1993, former Primate of Anglican church also officially apologized to Indigenous Anglicans for the churches' errors that ran the residential schools and expressed the need to redefine Indigenous people in their mind.[15] Later, other churches such as Presbyterian and Mennonite churches responded to the pain from the legacy of the residential schools which they were involved in.[16] Although there has been controversy over the refusal of Catholic Pope Francis to acknowledge survivors of abusive residential schools, the Canadian Conference of Catholic Bishops explained that fifty "autonomous" Roman Catholic organizations, which engaged in residential schools, made an individual and collective apologies and compensated for the errors according to decentralized structure of Catholic church.[17] Begun by these apologies, churches and their institutions have increasingly engaged in research and educate their own colonial legacies and seek ways to build right relations with Indigenous peoples.[18] These

---

14 "The Apologies," The United Church of Canada, accessed September 19, 2024, https://united-church.ca/social-action/justice-initiatives/reconciliation-and-indigenous-justice/apologies. "The United Church of Canada: Working in Solidarity toward Reconciliation," World Council of Churches, accessed September 19, 2024, https://www.oikoumene.org/resources/documents/the-united-church-of-canada-working-in-solidarity-toward-reconciliation.

15 Woods, 2016: 4.

16 "Church Apologizes to Kenora Residential School Survivors," *Canadian Broadcasting Corporation* (CBC) (Toronto: CQ-Roll Call, Inc, Canadian Broadcasting Corporation, 2013). "Residential Schools Resolution: Mennonite Church Canada Christian Witness Council," accessed September 19, 2024, https://www.commonword.ca/ResourceView/82/22161. "MC Canada Shares the Pain of Indian Residential School Legacy," *Canadian Mennonite Magazine*, August 26, 2010, https://canadianmennonite.org/articles/mc-canada-shares-pain-indian-residential-school-legacy.

17 "Bishops Try to Clarify Pope Francis' Decision Not to Apologize for Residential Schools," accessed September 19, 2024, https://www.theglobeandmail.com/canada/article-bishops-try-to-clarify-pope-francis-decision-not-to-apologize-for/.

18 Anglican Mennonites.

religious involvements have been centred on the reflection of white Christian settlers' colonial practices such as civilizing mission and abuses towards the Indigenous people. Recognizing and redressing colonial violence carried out by white settlers is an important starting point for decolonization. Yet Indigenous-settler relations are more complex than the binary relation, especially when the Asian immigrants' ambivalent relationship to colonialism is considered. As I discussed above, Indigenous and other non-European immigrants have been produced as 'others' in different degrees through the racializing process embedded in settler colonial practices and discriminatory policies.[19] In this sense, Asian immigrants were victimized and minoritized by the colonial project. Nevertheless, Asian immigrants are not pure victims of the colonial legacy.

In "Decolonization Is Not a Metaphor," Eve Tuck and K. Wayne Yang claim that despite racialized minorities criticism of racism, such criticisms without acknowledging settler colonialism can be, at best, an effort to obtain their cultural and legal entitlement as brown settlers in a settler nation.[20] Despite the discriminatory treatment, Asian immigrants have also contributed to and benefited from the colonial construction of Canadian society on Indigenous land. The dual relationship of Asian immigrants as both victims and beneficiaries of settler colonial legacy reveals the multifaceted dimension of Indigenous-settler relations. For instance, in "Salmon and Carp, Bannock and Rice," Chinese Canadian religious scholar Greer Anne Wenh-In Ng addresses the complicity of Asian and Asian Canadian Christians belonging to and benefited from the churches built upon the colonial legacy in residential schools where Indigenous culture and spirituality were attempted to be erased.[21] Given that Indigenous people continue to be suffering and marginalized on their land as the consequence of the cultural and spiritual genocide, Asian Canadians and migrants in churches are also called for acknowledging and being responsible for their own complicity in the settler colonial legacy. In this sense, Ng recognizes the complex relation between Asian and Indigenous women, arguing that Asian Canadian women are potential allies with Indigenous women as visible minorities in Canada; however, Asian and Asian Canadian women can also be viewed as those who have benefitted from white settlers' society and consequently participated in oppression towards Indigenous people.[22] Not

19 Dhamoon, 2010: 74.

20 Tuck and Yang, 2012: 18.Tuck and Yang's claim has been reconsidered by Tapiji Garba and Sara-Maria Sorentino. The assumption that all racialized people are settlers ignores Black people's forced migrant experience through slavery. Garba and Sorentino, 2020.

21 Ng, 2007: 207.

22 Ng, 2007: 204.

only Ng, other Asian religious scholars also pay attention to the necessity of recognizing the complex identities of Asian and Asian Canadians to engage in a settler colonial and multicultural reality.

4 Asian Migrants as Vulnerable Resisters

Asian religious scholars in Canada have made decolonizing voices in a settler colonial and multicultural context. While addressing precarious and vulnerable status of Asian immigrants in Canada, they also demonstrate how such vulnerability can be transformed into a driving force to challenge colonial reality. By engaging in some works of Asian Canadian religious scholars, particularly Christian feminist theologians, this section proposes Asian migrants as vulnerable resisters seeking decolonial solidarity with Indigenous people in Canada.

4.1 *Religious Education towards Intercultural Community*

Greer Anne Wenh-In Ng is a religious scholar who notes the relationship between Asian Canadian and Indigenous people early on. On June 22, 2006, Canadian government officially apologized to Chinese Canadian community for its discriminatory history by imposing head taxes on Chinese immigrants. She recalls that it was the day after National Aboriginal Day, on which a celebration of Aboriginal culture and spirituality was broadcast in Canada. At the moment when colonial and discriminatory legacy of Canada intersected, she raised a question of how much non-European Canadians, including Asian descendants, engaged in their delicate relationship with First Nations people.[23] Although being aware that Canadians with Asian heritage were not directly involved in unjust treaties and residential schools and oppressed by the discriminatory history, Ng calls Asian immigrants for the necessity to acknowledge their own complicity in colonization as one of the beneficiaries from the continuing system in usurped land. As a way to resist structural racism in solidarity with Indigenous people, Ng suggests educational religious practices such as educating "communal histories of exclusion and oppression" and anti-racism, developing liturgies to lament the histories and to recognize stories of the minoritized, and initiating a deeper intercultural works outside the religious places.[24] Beyond dominant binary Indigenous-settler relations

I mentioned this in the footnote in "Unsettling the Radical Witness of Peace." See, Yum, 2020: 107.

23 Ng, 2007: 198.

24 Ng, 2007: 208.

between white and Indigenous peoples, Ng initiated to shift the view on Asian Canadians as the oppressed to those who involves in more complex relationship to settler colonialism both as settlers and racialized minorities and to call for the necessity for an intercultural approach to the colonial history of Canada.

4.2 *Radical Hospitality for Mutual Transformation*

Yun Jung Kim, Korean Canadian postcolonial feminist scholar and minister of United Church of Canada, demonstrates Asian immigrants, especially women, as vulnerable bodies in Canada, yet also transformative subjects in decolonial solidarity with Indigenous women.[25] In South Asian and Chinese immigrant history of Canada, Asian women were intentionally excluded and controlled to prevent Asian male migrants from permanent residence, who provided cheap labour yet were unwanted bodies for a white nation. This is evidently shown in Kim's quotation of an editorial note on South Asian immigration in *Vancouver Sun* in 1913:

> The point of view of the Hindu [in wanting Canada to admit wives and families] is readily understood and appreciated. But there is the point of view of the white settler in this country who wants to keep the country a white country with white standards of living and morality ... The white population will never be able to absorb them ... We must not permit the men of that race to come in large numbers, and we must not permit their women to come in at all. Such a policy of exclusion is simply a measure of self-defence.
>
> HELEN RALSTON, 2001[26]

Such intersectional body politics of gender, race, and class have constructed "Asian" bodies as undesirable permanent aliens in Canada where whiteness has been normalized.[27] In spite of their vulnerable and marginalized position as racialized and gendered bodies in Canada, Kim shows how Asian migrant women can be transformative agents through participating in decolonial solidarity with Indigenous women. As a concrete example, she takes the United Church of Canada's *Sounding the Bamboo Conference,* a biennial conference "for ethnic minority women" to support "intercultural, interracial,

---

25 Yun, 2021.

26 Ralston, 2001: 264, quoted in Kim, 26.

27 Kim, 26.

and intergenerational dialogue" from 1993 until 2010.[28] At the conference in Winnipeg in 2010, women of colour attendants, including herself, were awakened by Indigenous woman leader's call, "You must think of being immigrants or citizens with us. We are the people who welcomed you here in this land." Kim notes that the calls for women of colours led them to acknowledge that their narratives necessarily entangle with settler colonialism.[29] In line with Ng, Kim also acknowledges Asian immigrants as settlers who are socially and politically benefiting from colonial "civilization" at the cost of Indigenous displacement and victimization.[30] Furthermore, she points out the danger of essentializing and homogenizing Asian migrant women as the oppressed in that such overcomplication of Asian women's identity could result in them being forcibly located as marginalized outsiders. Instead, she understands their identities as multiple and hybrid, which makes them possible to negotiate various and intermixing narratives in their complex relations in Canada.[31] Embracing vulnerability and hybrid agenthood in the identities makes a creative space for Asian migrant women to work for "a border-crossing solidarity" and "co-liberation" with other minoritized women, particularly Indigenous women, in the settler colonial context.[32] By inviting them to practice radical hospitality and solidarity with people across difference in their context, Kim proposes a creative role of Asian migrant women as those who are vulnerable yet transformative subjects with restorative and liberative power in the mutual relationships.[33]

4.3 *Migrants as Vulnerable yet Resistant in Interdependent Life*

Another Korean Canadian postcolonial feminist scholar HyeRan Kim-Cragg pays attention to migrants' vulnerability as resistance in the contexts of colonial history and contemporary border imperialism in Canada. Concurring with Jewish Canadian historian Irving Abella, Kim-Cragg critiques the national myth of Canada as a welcoming nation for immigrants.[34] She points out that Canada was historically not hospitable for "non-white and non-Christian people," quoting Abella's note, "the Canadian record is one of which we ought not

28 Kim, 141.
29 Kim, 141–142.
30 Kim, 148.
31 Kim, 136–137.
32 Kim, 136–137.
33 Kim, 203.
34 HyeRan Kim-Cragg, *Interdependence: A Postcolonial Feminist Practical Theology* (Eugene, OR: Wipf and Stock Publishers, 2018), 109.

be proud. Our treatment of our native people as well as our abysmal history in admitting blacks, Chinese, Japanese, Indians and during 1930s and 1940s Jews, should lay to rest [this] myth."[35] Critiquing the myth of Canada as homogeneous and stable entity and the illusion of independence and control, Kim-Cragg argues that a migrant's vulnerability discloses the "instability of nation state" and thus becomes a way of resistance to border imperialism.[36] For example, visible religious presence of migrants in public sphere discloses Western society's "embarrassment or hostility toward religion" other than Christianity.[37] This case shows that migrants are not only vulnerable but also resistant, revealing the instability of the neocolonial power. Following Judith Butler's challenge to dichotomist view of vulnerability and resistance, Kim-Cragg claims that resistance always bears vulnerability, which links to "an exposure to another's power to act."[38] Modern belief views personhood as independent beings, yet our lives are interdependent.[39] Considering that vulnerability and resistance are inseparable living conditions, migrants are not always powerless yet resistant. In addition, concurring with Ng and Kim, Kim-Cragg also problematizes the tendency of totalizing and stereotyping migrants as a homogenous group in social and religious discourses. Although it is true that many migrants experience difficulties to adjust new society, they are also varied in their economic status, the degree of education, and many other social conditions.[40] In order to have right relationship, it is important to see the migrants "connectively" more than those in need in the paradigm of them versus us. For her, "[a]s long as migrants, especially non-Christians, are regarded as victims or villains, or model minority, we run the risk of patronizing, penalizing, and praising them, unable to see their vulnerability, agency, decency, and most of all, humanity that is tangled with our own vulnerability, agency, and decency."[41] Rejecting the ideal of independence and control from a masculine perspective, she invites us to acknowledge human vulnerability and agency to live together respectively among heterogenous people in interdependent lives.[42]

35 HyeRan Kim-Cragg, "A Postcolonial Portrait of Migrants as Vulnerable and Resistant," *Practical Matters* 11: 172–175.

36 HyeRan Kim-Cragg, "A Postcolonial Portrait of Migrants as Vulnerable and Resistant," *Practical Matters* 11: 172–175.

37 Kim-Cragg, "A Postcolonial Portrait of Migrants as Vulnerable and Resistant," 174.

38 Estelle Ferrarese, "Vulnerability and Critical Theory," *Critical Theory*, Issue 1.2 (Leiden; Brill, 2016), 81.

39 Kim-Cragg, "A Postcolonial Portrait of Migrants as Vulnerable and Resistant," 174.

40 Kim-Cragg, "A Postcolonial Portrait of Migrants as Vulnerable and Resistant," 171.

41 Kim-Cragg, 174.

42 Kim-Cragg, 176–177.

Beyond the dominant binary relation of Indigenous-white settler, the voices of Asians and Asian Canadians, such as Ng, Kim, and Kim-Cragg, have contributed to renewing Canadian religious discourse through a decolonizing and intercultural interactions. Instead of identifying Asian immigrants as a homogenously oppressed group, they situate Asian immigrants relationally in the setter colonial and multicultural context of Canada and, thus, recognize the complexity in multilayered relationships among Indigenous, racialized and white peoples.

5 Conclusion

Asian migrants have contributed to, marginalized by, and been complicit in the colonial construction of Canadian society. In the contradictory needs between the demand for cheap labour and the desire for Eurocentric national identity in Canadian history, they have been racialized and marginalized as unwanted and permanent foreigners. Nevertheless, they have migrated, settled, and benefited as settlers on stolen Indigenous land. With the keen awareness of such multilayered and ambivalent relations to settler colonialism in Canada, Asian religious scholars in Canada have strived for creating decolonizing voices in their contexts beyond the dichotomist Indigenous-white relations in the dominant religious discourse. Embracing complex identities of Asian migrants as vulnerable but resistant transformative agents, they call for lamenting together for marginalized Canadian history, solidarity with Indigenous peoples, racial hospitality for mutual transformation, and building intercultural community. Situating Asian migrants in multiple locations allows to create a nuanced agency as vulnerable resisters to participate in renewing Canadian society as a just and mutual space for people across differences.

References

Banerjee, Rupa, Philip Kelly, and Ethel Tungohan (2017) *Assessing the Changes to Canada's Live-In Caregiver Program: Improving Security Or Deepening Precariousness?* Toronto: Pathways to Prosperity.

Canadian Broadcasting Corporation (2013) *Church Apologizes to Kenora Residential School Survivors.* Toronto: CQ-Roll Call, Inc, Canadian Broadcasting Corporation.

Dhamoon, Rita (2010) *Identity/Difference Politics: How Difference Is Produced, and Why It Matters.* Vancouver: UBC Press.

Ferrarese, Estelle. (2016) Vulnerability and Critical Theory. *Critical Theory* 1.2: 1–88.

Garba, Tapji, and Sara-Maria, Sorentino (2020) Slavery Is a Metaphor: A Critical Commentary on Eve Tuck and K. Wayne Yang's 'De-colonization Is Not a Metaphor,' *Antipode* 52(3): 764–782.

Greer Anne Wenh-In Ng. (2007) Salmon and Carp, Bannock and Rice: Solidarity between Asian Canadian Women and Aboriginal Women. In: Rita Nakashima Brock (eds). *Off the Menu: Asian and Asian North American Women's Religion and Theology*. Louisville: West-minster John Knox.

Hogarth, Kathy and Wendy L. Fletcher (2018) *Space for Race: Decoding Racism, Multiculturalism, and Post-Colonialism in the Quest for Belonging in Canada and Beyond.* New York, NY: Oxford University Press.

Johnstone, Marjorie (2018) Settler Feminism, Race Making, and Early Social Work in Canada. *Affilia* 33(3): 331–45.

Kim, Yun Jung (2021) Toward Postcolonial Practice and Theology of Radical Hospitality in Canadian Diasporic Contexts: Transformative Relocation in Asian Migrant Women's Perspective, PhD Dissertation, St. Michael's College, Toronto, 2021.

Kim-Cragg, HyeRan (2018) A Postcolonial Portrait of Migrants as Vulnerable and Resistant. *Practical Matters* 11: 167–180.

Kim-Cragg, HyeRan (2018) *Interdependence: A Postcolonial Feminist Practical Theology.* Eugene, OR: Wipf and Stock Publishers.

Ralston, Helen (2001) State Control of Women's Immigration: The Passage to Canada of South AsianWomen. In: Sharon Anne Cook, Lorna R. Mclean, and Kate O'Rourke (eds.) *Framing Our Past: Canadian Women's History in the Twentieth Century.* Montreal: McGill-Queen's University Press, 263–266.

Regan, Paulette (2010) *Unsettling the Settler Within: Indian Residential Schools, Truth Telling, and Reconciliation in Canada.* Vancouver: UBC Press.

Truth and Reconciliation Commission of Canada (2015). *Calls to Action.* Truth and Reconciliation Commission of Canada.

Tuck and K. Wayne Yang (2012) Decolonization Is Not a Metaphor. *Decolonization: Indigeneity, Education & Society* 1(1).

Woods, Eric Taylor (2016) *A Cultural Sociology of Anglican Mission and the Indian Residential Schools in Canada: The Long Road to Apology.* New York: Palgrave Macmillan US.

Yum, Hyejung Jessie (2020) Unsettling the Radical Witness of Peace. *Anabaptist Witness* 7(2): 93–113.

Zaman, Habiba (2012) *Asian Immigrants in "Two Canadas":Racialization, Marginalization, and Deregulated Work.* Black Point: Fernwood Publishing.

Websites

"The Apologies," The United Church of Canada, accessed September 19, 2024. https://united-church.ca/social-action/justice-initiatives/reconciliation-and-indigenous-justice/apologies.

"Bishops Try to Clarify Pope Francis' Decision Not to Apologize for Residential Schools," accessed September 19, 2024, https://www.theglobeandmail.com/canada/article-bishops-try-to-clarify-pope-francis-decision-not-to-apologize-for/.

Dickson, Courtney, and Bridgette Watson. "Remains of 215 Children Found Buried at Former B.C. Residential School, First Nation Says | CBC News." *CBC*, September 19, 2024 https://www.cbc.ca/news/canada/british-columbia/tk-eml%C3%BAps-te-secw%C3%A9pemc-215-children-former-kamloops-indian-residential-school-1.6043778.

Immigration, Refugees And Citizenship Canada. "Government of Canada." Canada.ca. August 29, 2023 Accessed September 19, 2024. https://www.canada.ca/en/immigration-refugees-citizenship/services/work-canada/hire-permanent-foreign/caregiver-program/hire-caregiver.html.

"MC Canada Shares the Pain of Indian Residential School Legacy," *Canadian Mennonite Magazine*, August 26, 2010. September 19, 2024. https://canadianmennonite.org/articles/mc-canada-shares-pain-indian-residential-school-legacy.

"Residential Schools Resolution: Mennonite Church Canada Christian Witness Council," accessed September 19, 2024 https://www.commonword.ca/ResourceView/82/22161.

"The United Church of Canada: Working in Solidarity toward Reconciliation," World Council of Churches, accessed September 19, 2024 https://www.oikoumene.org/resources/documents/the-united-church-of-canada-working-in-solidarity-toward-reconciliation.

CHAPTER 6

Unboxing Our Narrative of Space and Place: An Unsettling Dance of (Un)Belonging

Jose Miguel Esteban

> What moves us, what makes us feel, is also that which holds us in place, or gives us a dwelling place.
>
> AHMED 2014: 11

∵

Left foot. Right foot.

Left foot. My weight shifts back and forth.

Right foot. I cannot stand still in this place.

This is a room I rarely return to, yet so much of me and so much of who I am lies here. Boxes containing objects, objects containing memories fill up this room. Their stories rest in this space, but their meanings can never belong to any one place.

I close my eyes.

I shift. My body's weight pushes my left foot further against the hardwood floor. My weight shifts right. My foot pushes deeper beyond the floor. I feel my toes sink beyond the surface that previously pushed against them. As my weight transcends the surface on which I stand, I feel my feet being engulfed by warm and smooth granules of sand. I hear the crash of distant waves and smell the salty breeze. It caresses my skin, cooling it after a long day of being kissed by the tropical sun.

I open my eyes.

I find myself still in this room of boxes. I look down half expecting to see my feet buried into the sand of my memories. They are still pushing against the floor. They long to sink into this space. As I try to push further beyond gravity's force, I notice an object peeking out of a box.

Stuck in the crevice of a torn corner, it desires to stay hidden while calling out to be found. I excavate it from its home, handling it as carefully as when I first received it from the hands of my *lola*, my grandmother. We were on a vacation in the islands of Palawan in the Philippines when my grandmother handed me this fish, made from the weaving of a single palm leaf. Once green and smooth, it is now brown and brittle. Holding it in my hands I feel one of its edges poke my palm. I remember the feeling of fish nibbling at my legs during a fish feeding session. All of this took place at the resort where I was going to receive the "true" island experience. There were opportunities to go island hopping on "authentic" *bangka* boats. We were served "traditional island cuisine." The employees of the resort even took part each night in a performance of cultural dances from around the Philippines. This was supposed to give me a taste of my culture and my heritage. This was supposed to connect me to the place from where I have come. Yet what kind of connection was being made for me? How could I feel connected to that place, to that space of my memory? Standing in this room, I feel no connection to this place either.

I am Filipino[1]-Canadian. I am Canadian-Filipino. I am a Filipino in Canada. I am a Canadian in the Philippines. In neither place do I fully find belonging. As a citizen of Canada, I am a settler on this land. As a citizen of the Philippines, I have lost a connection to the land of my birth. Where do I belong? Where *should* I belong? I search within these boxes. I search within myself for the story of how I got here.

My family immigrated to Canada to realize the dream of new possibilities, to embrace the ideals of multiculturalism and to thrive in its promise. We were drawn to a nation that would "promote the full and equitable participation of individuals and communities of all origins in the continuing evolution and shaping of all aspects of Canadian society," as described for us in section 3(1)(c) of the Canadian Multiculturalism Act (Canada 1988). My family arrived full of hope. We were ready to establish new roots, to find a new place to belong. And still, I question this belonging. I feel a presence moving me to unsettle my taken-for-granted place in this space of belonging.

---

1 Debate surrounds the use of the term *Filipino* and its implications for gender identity. In particular, activists and scholars living in the Philippines argue that the formulation of gender-neutral forms of *Filipino* by those in the diaspora (e.g. Filipinx, Filipin*, Filipin@) erases its gender neutrality within the Tagalog language, centreing an American/Western perspective to language and identity (Toledo 2020). In this chapter I use *Filipino* not to fall on a particular side of the debate, nor to disengage with this important conversation. Rather, I use *Filipino* as a critical and creative return to the ways in which I have come to know, and have been made to know, my own identity.

1 Disability's Uncertain Belonging to Space

A new partner is moving me through this dance. The figure of disability inhabits the spaces of my, now *our*, dance. This is a movement I have felt before.

I blink.

I find myself standing in front of the doors marking the entrance to a school. This is where I will complete my final practicum placement. This is where I will put everything I have learnt to practice. This is where I will prove that I am ready to become an elementary school teacher. I am early. I am not yet ready to step inside. As I look at my watch and wait for the hands to hit the prescribed time for my arrival, my weight shifts back and forth.

Left foot. I am ready.

Right foot. I am nervous.

I face that all too familiar feeling of encountering a new place.

I do not know what to expect. This placement is unlike any of my previous practicums. This school is unlike any school I have ever stepped foot in. It is described as catering to a certain "type" of student. My weight continues to shift from left to right, from certainty to uncertainty:

Left. I've done this dance before.

Right. I should be confident in my skills.

This is a new dance.

How will I navigate my relationships with these "certain" students? My weight shifts back and forth as I list out the different markers identifying the students that I am expected to encounter. Forward onto my toes, I wait to meet these students with "developmental differences." Backward onto my heels, I anticipate supporting these students with their "special needs." Forward, I will have to face the task of addressing their "learning exceptionalities." Backward, I look forward to celebrating their "different abilities." Leaping from one label to the next, my dance partner surprises me as it moves through these words. The figure of disability reveals its presence by gesturing to its absence. I realize that its presence has been excluded from the space of my memory, of my remembering. These words seek to describe my future students. They also seek to define my partner. Yet the appearance of disability does not rest in any of these words. It is not permitted to take part in its own identification. It resists capture in the desire for its definition.

The time has almost come for me to start this placement. I will soon have to find a place within this school. I will soon have to navigate the spaces through which I will relate to my future students. I re-encounter this memory and once again enter into the school. I find myself moving with an appearance of disability as we dance through our *re*-entrance into this moment.

In my desire to find belonging in this new community, to find certainty in my place and within this space of uncertain relations, I bring with me a potential map. In my backpack lies a book, *Design and Deliver: Planning and Teaching Using Universal Design for Learning* by Loui Lord Nelson (2014). This book has been described to me as a method, *the* method, of transforming my teaching practice into one that is more inclusive. I take the book out of my bag. I open it, landing on page twenty-nine where the appearance of disability invites me to dance with a cartoon of its depiction.

This black and white cartoon is set on a snowy day and takes place in front of what appears to be the front doors of a school. Leading to those doors are two paths. Both are covered in snow. One snow-covered way to access the doors is a set of stairs. The other one is a ramp. Standing in front of both options are a group of what I perceive to be students wanting to enter the school. All except one are huddled in a group in front of the stairs. This group is depicted as a mass of backs of heads with toques on, although one member of the group seems to be "too cool" for the winter protection, donning a baseball cap instead. The one student separated from the group is depicted as more than a back of a head. Half of their face is visible in profile. This student is sitting in a wheelchair in front of the ramp. This wheelchair-using student calls out, through a speech bubble. They speak to whom I interpret to be an adult working for the school. This adult is holding a shovel and standing on the stairs. The student's speech bubble says, "COULD YOU PLEASE SHOVEL THE RAMP?" The shovel-holding adult's speech bubble replies, "ALL THESE OTHER KIDS ARE WAITING TO USE THE STAIRS. WHEN I GET THROUGH SHOVELING THEM OFF. THEN I WILL CLEAR THE RAMP FOR YOU." Below this is another speech bubble in which the wheelchair-using student replies, "BUT IF YOU SHOVEL THE RAMP, WE CAN ALL GET IN!" Underneath this cartoon is a caption that exclaims, "CLEARING A PATH FOR PEOPLE WITH SPECIAL NEEDS CLEARS THE PATH FOR EVERYONE!" (Nelson 2014: 29).

I look at the image of the student sitting in their wheelchair. I recognize this image as an embodiment of disability. I look at the cartoon as a whole. I recognize it as a call for the inclusion of that student, the inclusion of disability. I look up from the book and at the school in front of me. I see a ramp. Perhaps this school has responded to this call for inclusion. I wonder if the wheelchair-using student from the cartoon would feel a sense of belonging here. Yet as I recognize this act of inclusion, I pause and wait for the figure of disability to reveal its movement through the inclusionary promise of universal design for learning (UDL). Through this cartoon's attempt to access an inclusionary mindset within a social model of rethinking disability, disability appears to me through its exclusion, through its absence.

"BUT IF YOU SHOVEL THE RAMP, WE CAN ALL GET IN!" These final words from the wheelchair-using student draw my attention to the adult's choice to shovel the stairs first as an indication of the necessary intervention of a UDL mindset. UDL invites me to consider how, "a rich learning environment (i.e., the location where learning is taking place) is designed around the needs of all students, not just those with an identified need (e.g., students with disabilities, students who are English language learners students who are gifted)" (Nelson 2014: 2–3). Accessibility measures, through the erasure of barriers, are suggested to me as the key to everyone's success. The ramp becomes a space of access, a place in which the wheelchair-using student can belong. And still a question persists: *How* does disability appear in such "universal" success? I wonder whether it even does.

The cartoon pleads with me to provide access to the disabled student and thus to *every* student I teach. It draws my attention away from the stairs and towards the ramp. The ramp now becomes a site for this dance of inclusion, the space where disability can find belonging. Although such a move is important and necessary in the cause for disability justice, I am moved to consider whether accessibility's erasure of barriers also causes an erasure of disability.

I return to the stairs. As the wheelchair-using student faces this barrier to access, we encounter the social model of disability choreographing my partner's dance. If such a model were to locate disability "squarely within society" and thus its built environment (Oliver 2009: 21), then it is the stairs that embody disability. Disability no longer belongs within the space of the student's identity nor in their wheelchair, but rather in the stairs that prevent the wheelchair-using student from accessing the doors and their education. Through the student's inclusion into the now "universal" society, their disability becomes buried beneath the snow along with the stairs. If disability is solely constituted through the barriers that disabled people face, then their inclusion into "universal" spaces requires that their disability be erased, or rather removed. Their disability must remain absent within spaces of access and their embodied differences to be understood as no difference at all. Where then can disability belong? How can it ever belong as anything other than a barrier? How can the embodied differences of disability become valued as ways of moving through the world?

I drop the book as I allow the cartoon to fall back into my memories. I allow that moment of me waiting in front of those doors to unravel itself into my remembering and my forgetting of this appearance of disability's (un)belonging in my dance. I return to the room of boxes, the room of my memories. I find the fish falling from my hands. As it slowly falls onto the floor, it too begins to unravel itself. It reveals the original palm leaf from which it was made.

2 Unsettling Relationships to Place

I reach down to pick up the palm leaf but instead find my hands grasping another potential map. This time the map takes the shape of a program for the performance I am about to witness. Sitting in this theatre, I once again feel my weight shift from side to side. This time my movement is rooted not in nerves or anxiety, but in excitement.

It is February 5, 2016. I am about to witness *Going Home Star*, a production created by the Royal Winnipeg Ballet (RWB) in response to the Truth and Reconciliation Commission of Canada's (2015) calls to action. My excitement comes from its framing through Martha Schabas' (2016) review in *The Globe and Mail*. She describes it as "the first major artistic project to come out of Canada's Truth and Reconciliation Commission," seeking to bear witness to the atrocities of the Indian residential school system. As a citizen of Canada, I am expected to learn about this part of this nation's history. As an immigrant studying to become a citizen, or rather helping my parents to study for their citizenship test, I was expected to memorize that "in 2008, Ottawa formally apologized to the former students" of these residential schools (Citizenship and Immigration Canada 2012: 10). As a Canadian dance artist, I am expected to respond to the call for "non-Indigenous artists to undertake collaborative projects and produce works that contribute to the reconciliation process" (Truth and Reconciliation Commission of Canada 2015: 9). In attending this ballet performance, I am supposed to learn how I can respond to this call in my future work. As the performance begins, my weight continues to shift. My excitement transforms into that all too familiar feeling of uncertainty. This time this uncertainty is saturated with a sense of disappointment as I watch the final curtain fall. The audience begins to leave this space. I stand up to join them. Something seems wrong to me. I cannot quite grasp what seems to be missing. I search for my partner to fill this hole and to reveal what is causing this uncertainty.

My past movement with the appearance of disability invites me to unsettle my relationship and belonging to this space of reconciliation. My partner asks me to wait with my shifting weight as I return to the room of my memories. I pick up the palm leaf from the floor and slowly try to recreate each fold, attempting to form it back into its original fish shape. With each fold I reconstruct my narrative of belonging. I reshape my remembering of the places I call home. I recreate my forgetting of the spaces that I occupy. First fold, I am wearing my *barong*[2] to school for our annual multicultural day. Second fold, my

---

2 A barong is a traditional long-sleeved shirt worn on formal occasions in the Philippines. It is traditionally woven from a silk made of pineapple fibres and embroidered with intricate designs.

mom is coming into my classroom to teach my peers the Tagalog alphabet. Third fold, my mom is coming into my classroom to demand an answer from my teacher as to why I had been placed into the lowest levelled reading group. Fourth fold, I am using as many "academic" words as I can to convince the private high school admissions officer that English, the only language I am fluent in, is my native language. I want to belong to the multicultural narrative that expects me to be proud of my Filipino culture and heritage. I want to belong to the multicultural narrative that expects the embodiment of such pride within Canadian citizenship. Folding this palm leaf, however, I find myself unable to form the fish. I keep missing a fold and can never quite return my remembrance into its original memory. I question if I can still remember its original shape. How can I be certain in this leaf ever having an *original* shape? Just as the figure of disability moves through belonging and not belonging within "inclusive" places and "accessible" spaces, I begin to feel my constant movement into and away from "inclusion" through Canadian citizenship and "access" to the universal prosperity of Canadian multiculturalism. My dance with disability's appearance moves me to unsettle the very ground on which I stand and to unsettle my belonging to this land.

How do I belong within the Canadian state, this multicultural nation? Sunera Thobani (2007) suggests the ways in which the state expects me to belong:

> The state organizes the rights that nationals come to acquire by treating these as rooted in their own intrinsic worthiness and not in the colonial violence, political, racial and ethnic dominations, or in the classed and gendered exploitations and resistances that characterize nation formations. The qualities that are said to be shared by nationals bring them directly into the orbit of the state.
>
> 11

I am expected to see my belonging and my success as intrinsic and reflective of my individual actions and choices of how to engage in society. The multicultural framework allows me to wear my barong to school and invites my mom to teach my friends about our Filipino language; our cultural differences are incorporated into the multicultural mosaic. However, as Himani Bannerji (2000) suggests, through the conception of multiculturalism "all is not as harmonious as it should be" (50). I'm required to ensure that these multicultural embodiments are all done within the state's permissible ways of moving. I can only succeed and be included if I prove that I can converse in English and further be able to converse at a level that transcends and overcomes my "native" language of Tagalog, a language I can barely even understand. My mom is invited, encouraged and expected to push me to learn English over Tagalog so that I may find belonging, all while teaching my friends the Tagalog alphabet.

Frantz Fanon (2004) reminds me that the colonizer and colonized "confront each other, but not in the service of a higher unity [...] There is no conciliation possible, one of them is superfluous" (4). This reminder gestures to the ways in which my dance is not necessary within the dance of multiculturalism. The figure of disability simultaneously gestures to its own movement, cast away from spaces of inclusion and recognized as the excess waste of society (Bauman 2004). Our dance is not needed in the dominant narrative; this narrative of universality claims to desire our inclusion while simultaneously threatening our exclusion. Or maybe we are needed and even desired to be included but must ask ourselves, as disability studies scholar Tanya Titchkosky (2011) suggests, if we are in *"what are we 'in for'"* (27)? My belonging into the multicultural narrative can only be achieved if I subscribe to the state's choreographies of belonging and move through the prescribed interpretations of my dance. I can only belong if any aspect of my being that contradicts the expectations of those choreographies, any aspect that becomes a barrier to my inclusion within multiculturalism becomes buried away under the snow, along with the stairs and the cartoon student's disability.

I return to my shifting weight as I begin to exit the performance of *Going Home Star*. How does my belonging into the expectations of Canadian citizenship frame how I encounter truth and reconciliation? As I wait with what I have witnessed and re-enter the space of this performance, the missing fold in this recreation of the Indian residential school narrative reveals itself to me. I am reminded of Schabas' (2016) review and recall a statement made by Tina Keeper, a Cree film producer, actor, and political activist who became a member of the RWB board of directors, taking on the role of associate producer for this work: "We knew from the beginning that we didn't want to do a fusion. We wanted to make a ballet." I am moved to applaud the inclusion of Indigenous artists who led the creative processes of storytelling (through the writing of author Joseph Boyden, who's own heritage will come to questioned and who will be referred to as a "pretendian"—see Barrera 2016; Lewis 2023), scenic design (through the multi-media art of KC Adams), and musical composition (through collaborations with Inuit throat-singer Tanya Tagaq and the Northern Cree Singers). I am moved to my feet as I become inspired by Joseph Boyden's determination for this ballet to "[become] an opportunity to cross boundaries, to reclaim what is often considered a colonial art form" (Knapp 2015). I am moved to join in a standing ovation to celebrate the desires for relationship building as Mark Godden reflects on his experience of choreographing this ballet as more than just a process of creating a dance work:

> Tina [Keeper] wanted more from this ballet—an awareness from everyone involved about the culture and who they are. So we had sweat lodges and people from the Aboriginal community came to speak with us. They even blessed the beginning of the project with a smudging ceremony.
>
> GELLER 2016

And yet as I rise from my seat to leave the theatre, the figure of disability reminds me to attend to the absences found within the inclusion of those present. As I move with this reminder, the presence of the Indigenous dance artist is made absent. Indigenous choreographers or dancers were not invited to take part in the creation and performance of the work. The presence of Indigenous dance practices and the embodied ways of knowing that flow from such traditions has been excluded. This memory, my remembering, gestures to the question of who is invited to dance within spaces of truth and who is expected to choreograph our movement within places of reconciliation.

I hear Tom Clark, Ravi de Costa and Sarah Maddison (2016) asking me, "How do we escape the colonial desire to shape indigeneity in its own image?" (3). My movement with the appearance of disability gestures to a similar question, how do we escape normalcy's desire to shape disability in its own image? I am moved to ask a similar question for myself within my dance. How do I escape the dominant choreographic narratives that desire to shape me through my interpretations of an expected movement? I recognize that I too have desires based on the constraints of these narratives that choreograph my being. I desire to belong in the spaces created for me. I work to reside in these places that are expected of me, and yet my belonging is uncertain. These spaces may have been created *for* me but they have not been created *with* me. My belonging must then rely on the expectations of those who have created the places in which I desire to move. And still, as I move, am I not also creating and shaping these spaces and the expectations they hold?

I feel Dean Itsuji Saranillio (2013) suggesting with whom I should desire to belong, with whom I might begin to reimagine how I should shape the contours of my relationship with the space of my belonging:

> Settler states have no interests in non-Natives identifying with Native movements, as it opens their purview to processes of settler accumulation

> by Native dispossession, thus serving to oppose a system set by White supremacy that while *differently*, ultimately comes at the expense of *all of us*.
>
> 291

He moves me to wonder whether the multicultural narrative, and its place for me within the Canadian mosaic, was ever intended for my belonging. I unravel this "belonging" and begin to recognize it as the colonial tool that severs me from the formation of any relationship with those who belong to this land. Without creating a relationship to the original caretakers and knowledge keepers of this land, I can never come to know the spaces in which I reside. I can never come to understand how I can belong in relation to this place. And yet, I question whether I can truly belong to this land. I am not and will never be indigenous to this place. I realize that I am not and will never be indigenous in any space. I question my desire to belong anywhere.

3 Unravelling Our Shifting Weight

I allow my attempts at recreating the fish to unravel. I allow the folds to be released as the brown, brittle and bent palm leaf dangles from my fingertips. I desire to release this leaf into its original shape. Yet it will never return to its untouched state. It will never return to the vibrant green hue it once inhabited. It has been plucked from its tree and manipulated by the hands of the resort employee. It has been bought by my grandmother and delicately passed down to me. It has travelled by plane across oceans and been weathered by time. It has been placed into the box in front of me and in this room surrounding me. It has been unravelled, folded and refolded. But it will never return to where it came from. It will never rest in one place as it belongs to nowhere and everywhere.

I am the palm leaf. I no longer belong to the land of my birth. I can no longer return to my original indigeneity. I cannot even claim a relationship to indigeneity. My knowledge of the land has been plucked from me and manipulated for colonial expansion. I have sold my belonging, my responsibility to the land and a connection to my ancestors, for the American dream through the Canadian dream,[3] for the capitalist promise of prosperity. I have abandoned

3 Much of Philippine culture has been influenced by American culture and media leading to a desire, shared by many, for the American dream of capitalist success. For those, like my family, who could not access the American dream directly, the Canadian dream has become an alternative to strive towards.

a home in search for this dream, and I have been weathered by the expectations of these new places I am forced to inhabit, the spaces I have chosen to desire. I have placed my original belonging into boxes, allowing myself to escape from my memories. I build a narrative of what it means to be a citizen of the Philippines, of what it means to be a Filipino citizen of Canada. And in this choreography of my belonging, I forget that I do not belong anywhere.

My partner returns to our dance as it moves with my shifting weight. The presence of disability within my story unsettles my taken for granted movement through the Filipino roots and the mad/queer routes that have brought me to the present place I inhabit, the diasporic spaces of my past memories and of my future dreams. The appearance of a figure of disability within my narrative invites me to move differently. Disability as a difference, the difference of disability (Michalko 2002), invites me to return to my story and invites me to move through *our* story, a story of unravelling desires and needs for (un) belonging. As the palm leaf unravels, as I unravel, my weight placement has remained unsettled.

Left.

Right.

Forward.

Backward.

The difference of disability moves through each subtle transfer of my centre of gravity. The difference of disability moves me to push further into this weight transfer. We push the limits of my balance as we exaggerate this gesture. My arms begin to swing as my head rocks back and forth. My spine begins to release itself as each vertebra begins to ride the waves emanating from my weight shifting from left foot to right foot, from toes to heels. I lose control of my body as I stumble back and forth. I succumb to the turbulence of my movement. The room is spinning, and the difference of disability invites me to inhabit this whirlwind. We are moving. We inhabit somewhere, nowhere and everywhere. I am disoriented. I witness passing images, passing objects, passing places. While I dance within the narratives of these spaces, I remain restless, never resting in any single narrative. In this constant movement, I find myself resting in this restlessness, and for a brief moment, I wonder if I have been touched by a sense of belonging.

References

Ahmed, Sara (2014) *The Cultural Politics of Emotion* (2nd ed.). Edinburgh: Edinburgh University Press.

Bannerji, Himani (2000) *The Dark Side of the Nation: Essays on Multiculturalism, Nationalism and Gender*. Toronto: Canadian Scholars' Press Inc.

Barrera, Jorge (2016) Author Joseph Boyden's Shape-Shifting Indigenous Identity. *APTN News*, December 23. <https://www.aptnnews.ca/national-news/author-joseph-boydens-shape-shifting-indigenous-identity/>.

Bauman, Zygmunt (2004) *Wasted Lives: Modernity and its Outcasts*. Cambridge: Polity.

Canada (1988) Canadian Multiculturalism Act. <laws-lois.justice.gc.ca/eng/acts/c-18.7/page-1.html>.

Citizenship and Immigration Canada (2012) Discover Canada: The Rights and Responsibilities of Citizenship. <publications.gc.ca/collections/collection_2012/cic/Ci1-11-2012-eng.pdf>.

Clark, Tom, de Costa, Ravi, and Maddison, Sarah (2016) Non-Indigenous People and the Limits of Settler Colonial Reconciliation. In: Sarah Maddison, Tom Clark and Ravi de Costa (eds.) *The Limits of Settler Colonial Reconciliation: Non-indigenous People and the Responsibility to Engage*. Singapore: Springer.

Fanon, Fanon (2004) *The Wretched of the Earth*. Translated by Richard Philcox. New York: Grove Press.

Geller, Leah (2016) Godden of Going Home Star on Telling Residential School Stories Through Dance. *Apt613*, January 26. <apt613.ca/choreographer-mark-godden-of-going-home-star-on-telling-residential-school-stories-through-dance/>.

Knapp, Millie (2015) Going Home Star: Reconciliation by Ballet. *American Indian Magazine* 16, 3. <americanindianmagazine.org/story/going-home-star-reconciliation-ballet>.

Lewis, Haley (2023) What Are 'Pretendians' and How Are They Causing 'Severe Harm' to Indigenous Communities? *Global News*, March 9. <https://globalnews.ca/news/9450313/pretendians-canada-indigenous-ancestry/>.

Michalko, Rod (2002) *The Difference that Disability Makes*. Philadelphia: Temple University Press.

Nelson, Loui Lord (2014) *Design and Deliver: Planning and Teaching Using Universal Design for Learning*. Baltimore, London and Sydney: Paul H. Brookes Publish Co.

Oliver, Michael (2009) The Social Model in Context. In: Tanya Titchkosky and Rod Michalko (eds.) *Rethinking Normalcy: A Disability Studies Reader*. Toronto: Canadian Scholars' Press Inc.

Saranillio, Dean Itsuji (2013) Why Asian Settler Colonialism Matters: A Thought Piece on Critiques, Debates, and Indigenous Difference. *Settler Colonial Studies* 3: 3–4.

Schabas, Martha (2016) Winnipeg Ballet Going Home Star puts Truth and Reconciliation in Motion. *Globe and Mail*, January 29. <theglobeandmail.com/arts/theatre-and-performance/winnipeg-ballets-going-home-star-puts-truth-and-reconciliation-in-motion/article28458551/>.

Thobani, Sunera (2007) *Exalted Subjects: Studies in the Making of Race and Nation in Canada*. Toronto, Buffalo and London: University of Toronto Press.

Titchkosky, Tanya (2011) *The Question of Access: Disability, Space, Meaning*. Toronto, Buffalo and London: University of Toronto Press.

Toledo, John (2020) [Opinion] Filipino or Filipinx? September 15. <rappler.com/voices/ispeak/opinion-filipino-or-filipinx>.

Truth and Reconciliation Commission of Canada (2015) Truth and Reconciliation Commission of Canada: Calls to Action. <publications.gc.ca/collections/collection_2015/trc/IR4-8-2015-eng.pdf>.

PART 2

Gender, Sexuality and Other Intimacies

CHAPTER 7

The Bee

Elisha Lim

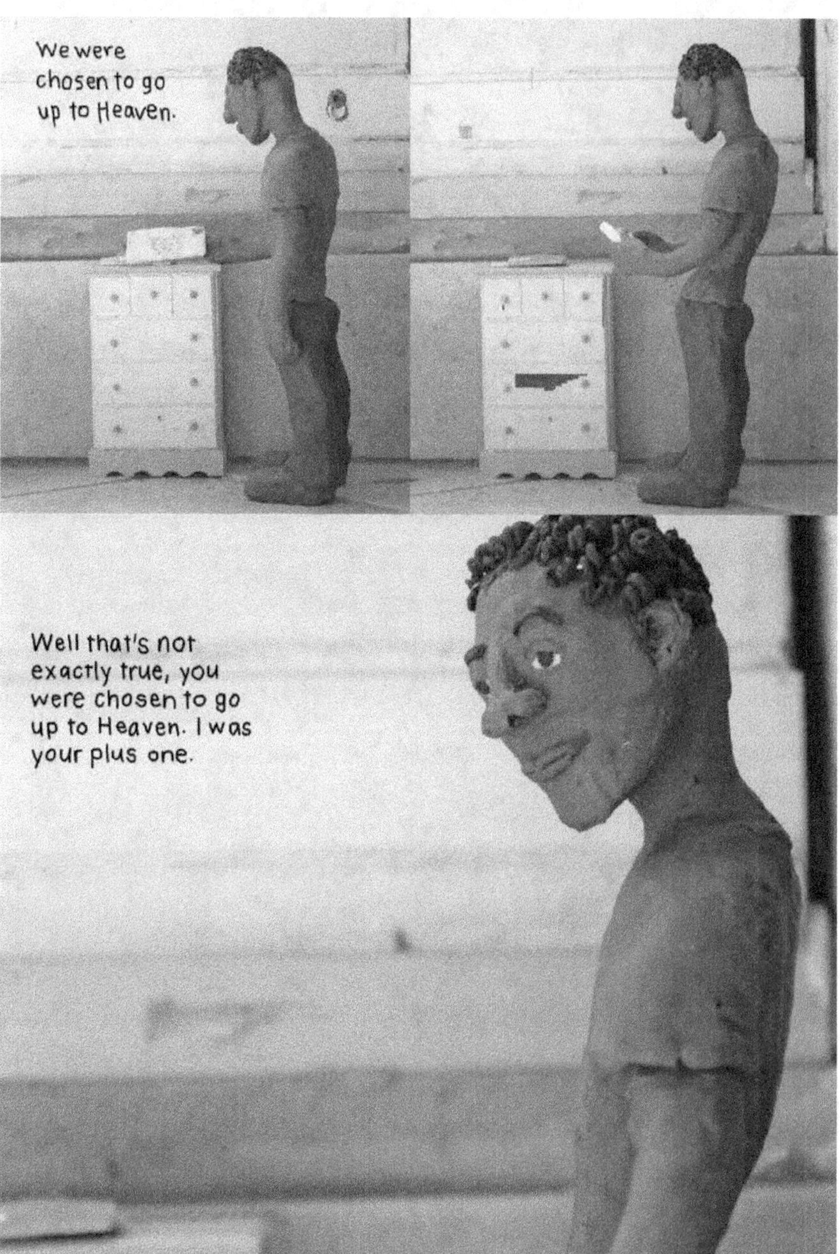

Once we eventually
ascended, Heaven
turned out to be a
farm.

But the first night I woke suddenly in the darkness.

A benevolent hum loomed outside our bedroom doorway.

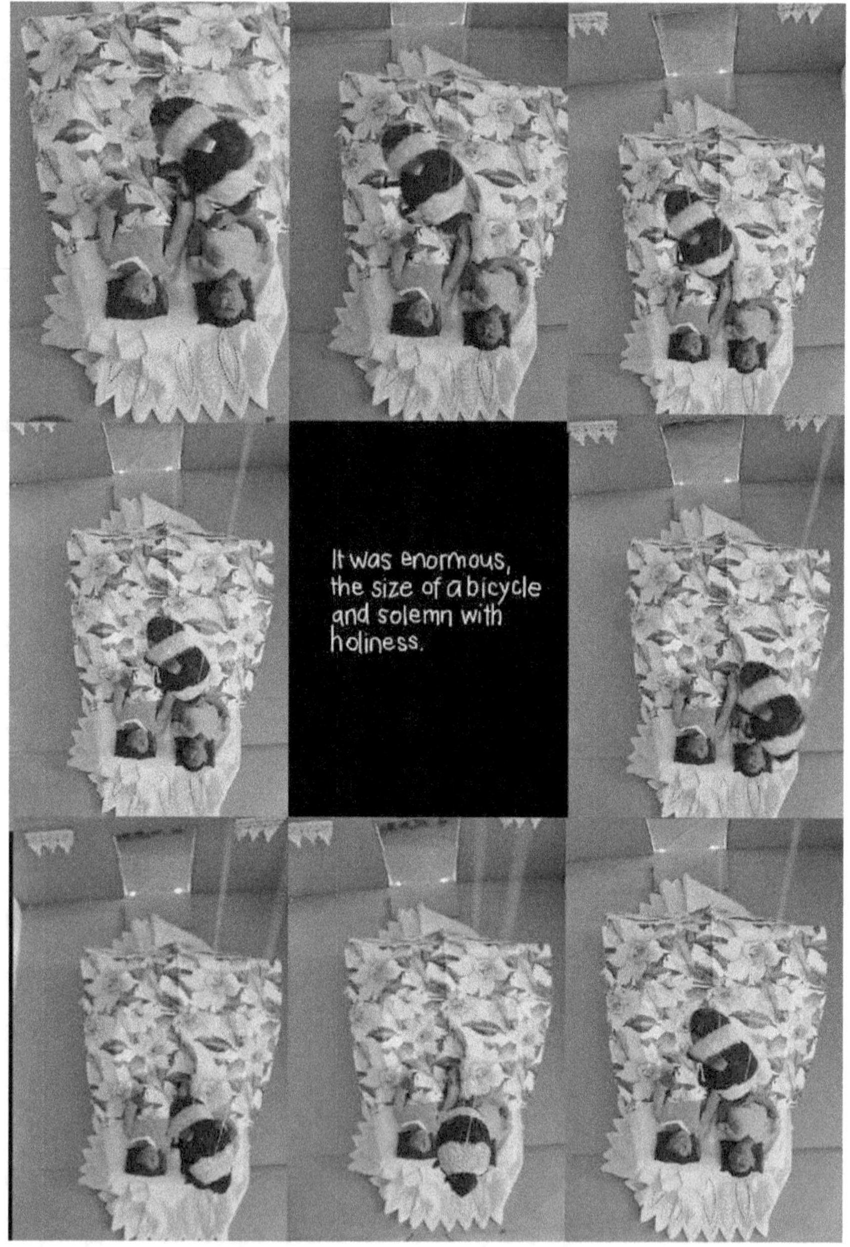
It was enormous,
the size of a bicycle
and solemn with
holiness.

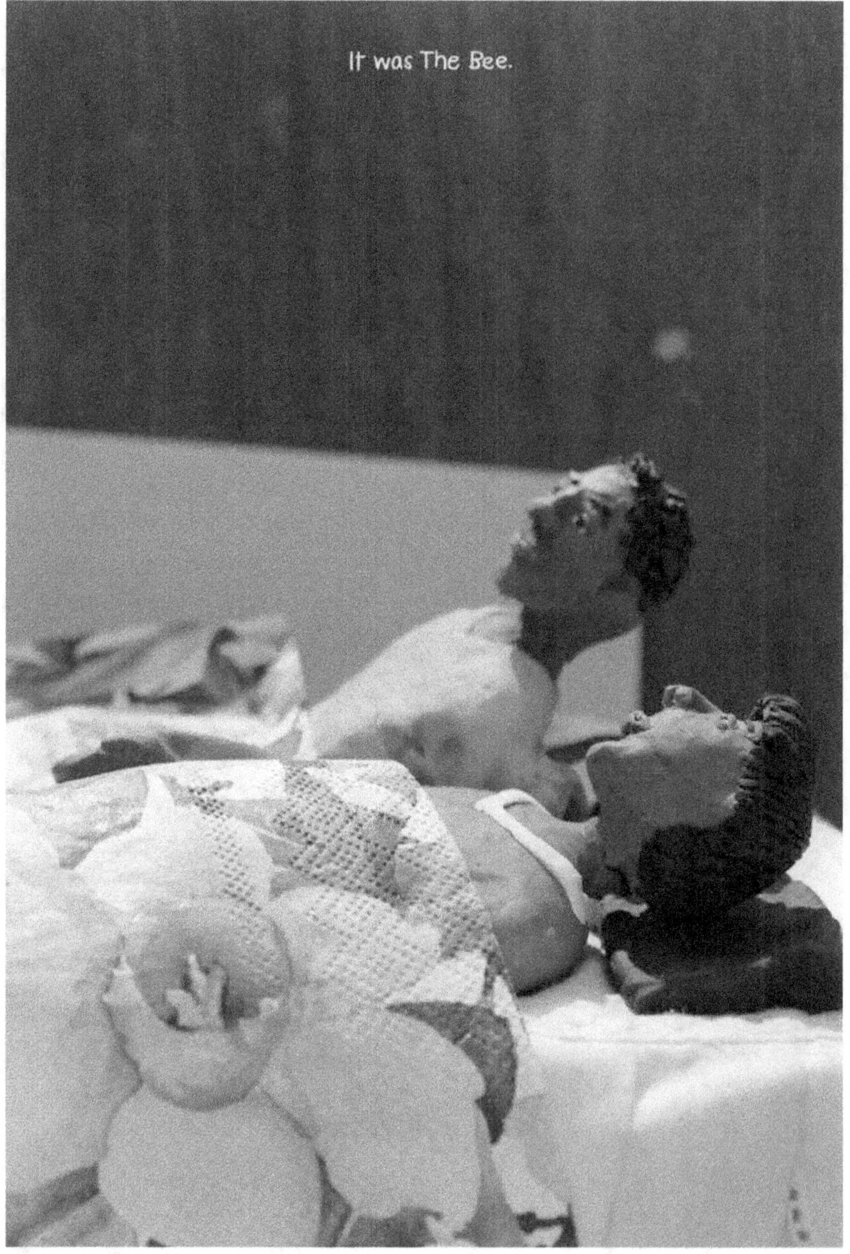
It was The Bee.

A childhood of Bee stories had theoretically prepared us for this moment, but I was still stunned. To be honest, I'd stopped believing.
Now, faint with gratitude, my eyes brimmed with tears.

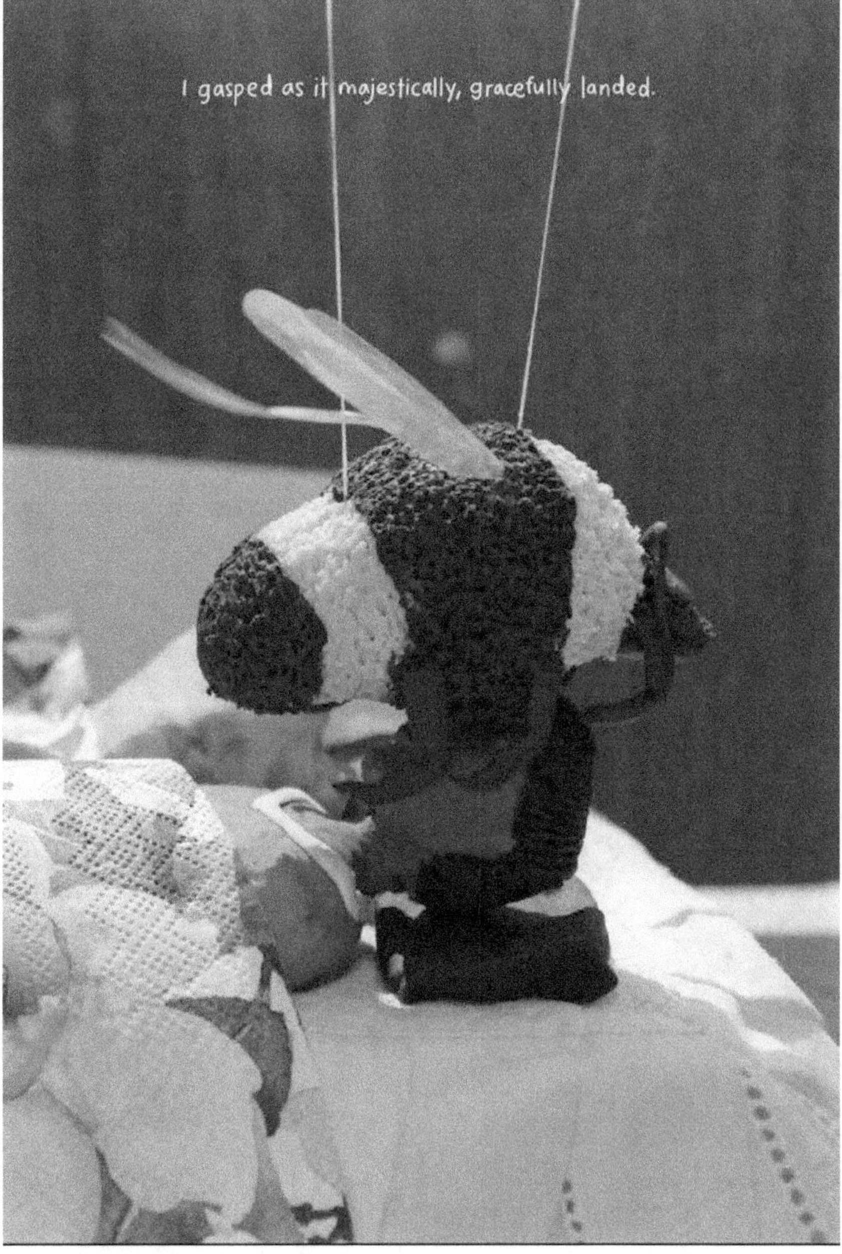
I gasped as it majestically, gracefully landed.

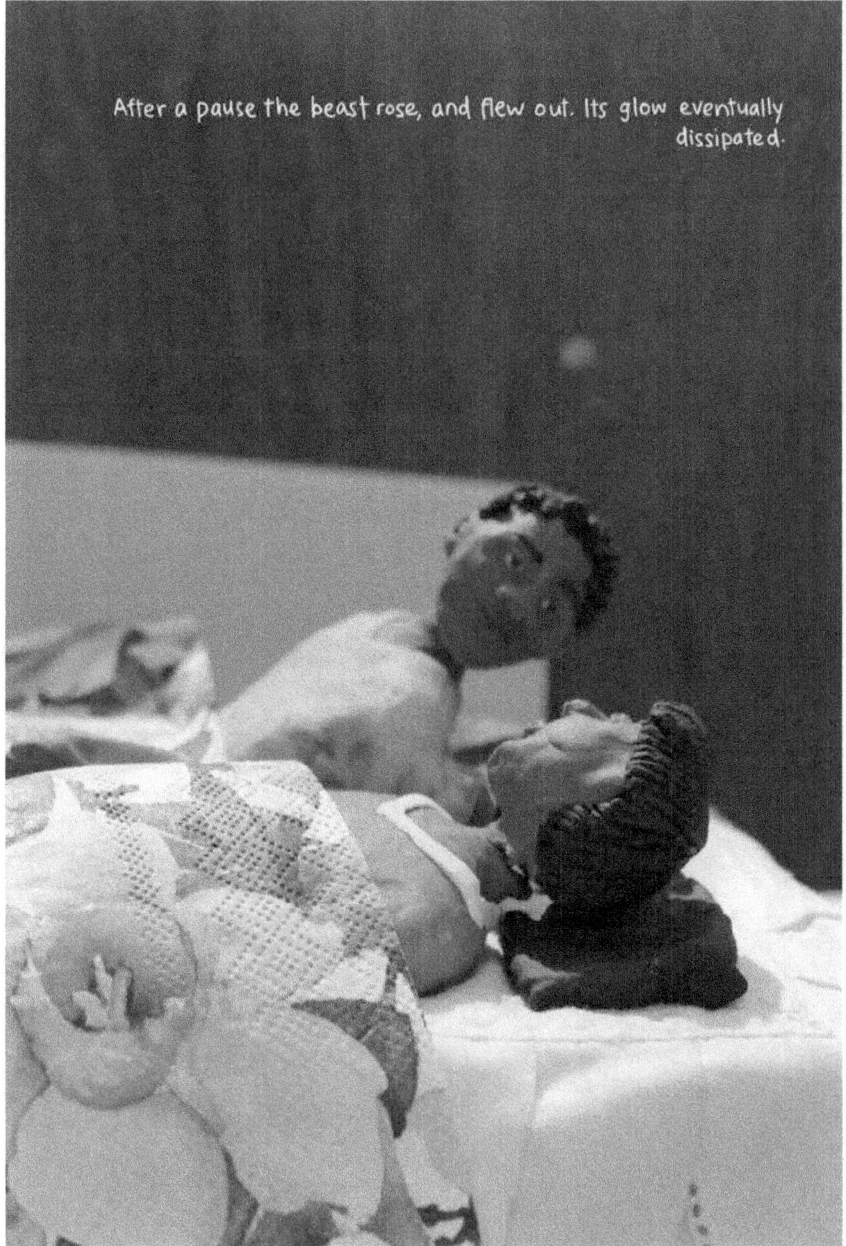
After a pause the beast rose, and flew out. Its glow eventually dissipated.

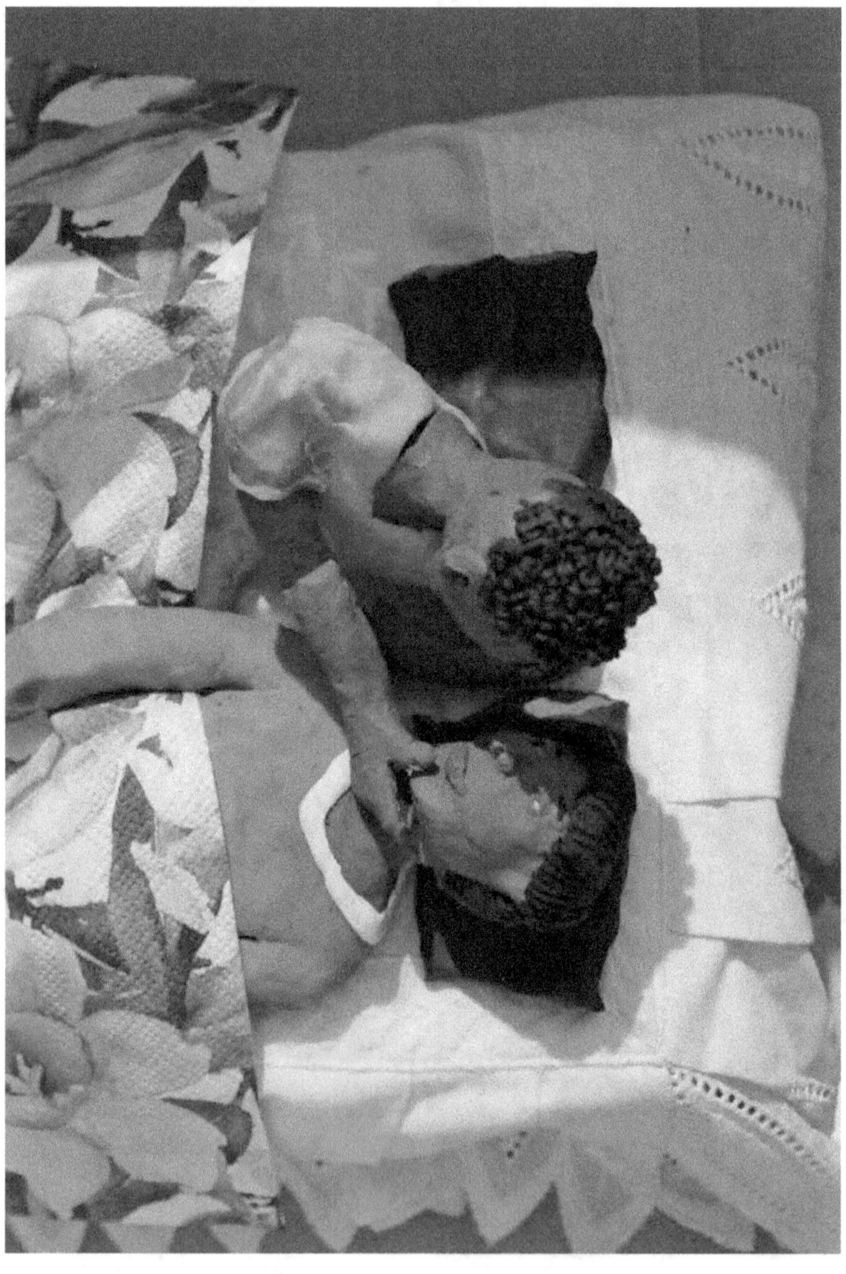

Anti-Asian violence has mounted in North America during the pandemic after Donald Trump's dog whistling campaign labeled covid-19 as the "China virus" and "Kung flu." In Canada, the Chinese Canadian National Council's Toronto survey reported a spike in anti-Chinese racism since March, up to 1,000 cases in 2020. But after the mass-shooting of 6 Asian sex workers in Georgia on March 17th 2021, some Asian activists treated the tragedy as a flash point to demand the same attention that Black communities garnered in their protests against extrajudicial police killings. Parroting the tactics of Black Lives Matter, the social media hashtag #asianlivesmatter emerged, as well as demands for greater funding and resources to be directed towards Asians communities. Northeastern University, for example, circulated a petition signed by 1250 Northeastern students, faculty and staff demanding more Asian support – although according to Data USA, Northeastern already boasts more Asian students than any other minority. Elsewhere, Asian influencers like Harvard Professor Laura Huang, angrily tweeted that BLM supporters need to stand up equally for Asians. "Those of you who were so vocal w BLM, where are you on the 1900% increase in Asian-directed hate crimes?" (@LauraHuangLA).

I'm a social media scholar, and I write about how algorithms make identity politics into commensurable market tokens and brand assets. Anti-Black racism is not new to Asian communities, but on social media, Asian grief has rapidly pivoted to attacking, appropriating and undermining successful Black social media activity. Online ranking metrics pit issues against each other as competing products. This is not a glitch in the system, it's the design. Corporate social media platforms are commercial spaces that aim to transform all of life into fungible units of commerce. Recent identity politics battles on social media compare their success in virality contests that I call "identity economics" (Lim 2020).

Social media activism reduces nuanced social problems into single-issue marketing campaigns, and the false equivalence between Asian and Black experience is just one of its casualties. The Georgia shootings did not only target Asians, but sex-workers – a specificity that demands solidarity around class access and undocumented status. Meanwhile, the scapegoats of the pandemic are not only Chinese. In Switzerland, covid-19 has been a pretext to target Jewish communities; Malaysian authorities blame asylum-seeking Rohingya; in India, Muslims are violently attacked for allegedly causing the disease; in many countries vulnerable front-line migrant workers face new levels of hostility, policing, mandatory checks and ostracization. In China itself, Black people are believed to spread the pandemic. According to articles in *The Guardian* and *The Washington Post*, they have been evicted by landlords, refused service in hospitals, and many have been forced to sleep in the streets. McDonalds in Guangzhou banned Black diners. The pandemic has launched a rise in xenophobia around the world, and the backlash that Asian-Canadian's face isn't about us. It is about racism deployed worldwide to preserve political popularity and state and capital interests – a reality that calls for urgent internationalist solidarity.

In this sense, social media metrics and their market-ready ranking systems effectively conduct neoliberal goals to divide and conquer collective social organizing. Distracting ranking metrics are part of a business strategy that hails back to the 1970s, when, frightened of the interracial, popular support of Black Power and American Indian movements, pro-business activists in the US started to attack countercultural movements, union organizing and publicly funded community strongholds like universities and community centres (Duggan 2003). In Canada, the Trudeau administration skillfully rearticulated growing working class solidarity movements as an "ethnic tension" to be placated with multicultural fairs, religious celebrations, target funding and diversity grants (Bannerji 2000). Canadian anti racist theorist Himani Bannerji notes how radical anti-racist movements were eroded and replaced by apolitical minority actors who were happy to embrace multiculturalism as a form of upwards mobility. "Hardheaded businessmen, who had never thought of culture in their lives before, now, upon entering Canada, began using this notion and spoke to the powers that be in terms of culture and welfare of their community" (48).

Social media algorithms amplify this business model of diversity optics. Users who seek the social justice of representation and visibility optimize their behaviour according to algorithmic relevance and align themselves with competitive traditional market norms (Marwick 2013; Chun 2016; Bucher 2018; Tufekci 2018). Activists looking to promote social causes align with the algorithmic rules of product marketing and promotion, unconsciously adopting market logic into all of their online sociality of posts, tags, shares and utterances. Social media promises to connect and amplify voices, while at the same time, grooming users into a receptive commercial and political landscape that commodifies traditionally non-commercial things.

A Medium blog post critiquing Asian resentment of BLM writes, "The inevitable problem with [Professor Laura] Huang's framing is that it portrays a sense of entitlement to the fruits of others' activism" (Sang 2021). This is the entitlement of identity economics: social media reifies identity into a historic colonial legacy of liberal individual property. This entitlement is the subject of my graphic novel, which features eight nightmares I had about my growing brand anxiety. My reputation, my Asian activism, my interracial allyship, my power couple identity – all became assets that I defended at great expense to my self respect and personal safety.

Activism is not a metric or a popularity contest, but an interdependent set of relations that demand equitable resource redistribution. Bannerji writes,"a substitution through the language of diversity and colour distracts us from what actually happens to us in our raced and gendered class existence and culturalizes our politics." Anti-racism is a class war and we need each other, to fight.

References

Bannerji, H. (2000) *The Dark Side of the Nation: Essays on Multiculturalism, Nationalism and Gender*. Canadian Scholars' Press.

Bucher, T. (2018) *If … Then Algorithmic Power and Politics*. Oxford: Oxford University Press.

Chun, W. H. K. (2016) *Updating to Remain the Same: Habitual New Media*. Cambridge: MIT Press.

Duggan, L. (2003) *The Twilight of Equality?* New York: Beacon Press.

Lim, E. (2020) The Protestant Ethic and the Spirit of Facebook: Updating Identity Economics. *Social Media + Society* 6(2).

Marwick, A. E. (2013) *Status Update: Celebrity, Publicity, and Branding in the Social Media Age*. New Haven: Yale University Press.

Sang, E. (2021) Asians Must Stop Comparing Our Issues to Black Lives Matter. *Medium*. Feb 16. https://gen.medium.com/asians-must-stop-comparing-our-issues-to-black-lives-matter-2879b105 1d2a.

Tufekci, Zeynep. "How social media took us from Tahrir Square to Donald Trump." *MIT Technology Review* 14 (2018): 18.

CHAPTER 8

Labour, Intimacy and Diaspora: Queer Asian Studies in Canada

Ian Liujia Tian

In the introduction of *Queer/Asian/Canadian* feature section, Kojima, Catungal and Diaz (2017) reiterate the importance of sustained critique against the settler state as part and parcel to queer Asian Canadian studies. They suggest that queerness is not just LGBTQ+ identities but also an opposition to notions of normalcy, especially those of the nation-states. Continuing their antinormative position, I discuss queer Asian studies in Canada in the past ten years, which can be roughly grouped into two topics: migration and diasporic formations. I then propose directions for other kinds of queer work to come by analyzing a recent documentary *Migrant Dreams,* directed by Min Sook-Lee.

1 Queer Asian Studies in Canada

Queer Asian Studies is rooted in community formation and activism. In 1980, Richard Fung, Gerald Chan, Nitto Marquez and Tony Souza founded Gay Asian Toronto (GAT), one of the first of such organizations in North America. The birth of GAT was not a coincidence, rather, it was the result of transnational organizing. Prior to GAT, the first National Third World Gay Congress was held in Washington DC in October 1979, sponsored by the National Coalition of Black Gays in the US. One of the outcomes was the formation of an Asian Caucus, which became an important network for collaboration and political support in the context of third world decolonial movement.

The transnational feature of GAT suggests the deep political connections earlier activists forged, and the anti-imperial, anti-colonial and anti-racist orientations shaping the beginning years of gay Asian movement in Canada. It is therefore not a stretch to say that the histories of queer Asians in Canada intertwine with other global struggles.

In the 1980, during the AIDS crisis, gay Asian communities again demonstrated marvelous organizing in a time when state biopolitics decided who would live or die (Li A. 2019). The AIDS organizing prompted several HIV prevention NGOs across Canada, many of them still operating today. Since then, the world has shifted to neoliberal governance where individuals and heterosexual nuclear families are taking responsibilities for services previously provided by the Canadian state. Queer and trans of colour critique, an insurgent academic discourse, has responded to these changes, delineating how race, gender and sexuality are co-constitutive of each other (Ferguson 2004; Chen 2019). It is under such socio-economic and intellectual context that most recent scholars are dissenting against the settler Canadian state from at least two angles.

The first group of scholarships focuses on migration. Many queer people of Asian descent, broadly defined, are new immigrants, refugees, or temporal residents. Immigration agencies, the police, employers are crucial institutions of power that shape their experiences beyond LGBTQ+ identities. For example, Poon, Li, Wong and Wong's (2017) recent research argues that the experiences of new queer immigrants from China challenge Canada's homonationalist narrative. In a similar vein, Murray's (2014) interviews with queer refugee claimants reveal how terms and ideas about gender and sexuality emerging out of North American place refugees in vulnerable positions. While Murry's research does not center queer Asians, the experiences shared by his interlocutors will speak to queer Asian refugees and immigrants.

In this sense, Asian queer migration is intimately connected to a long history of Asian exclusion in Canada's settler policies. From the Hayashi-Lemieux Gentlemen's Agreement (1908) to the Chinese Exclusion Act (1923), Asian men were constructed as gendered, racial and sexual threats to the reproduction of white Canada (Anderson 1991). Their perceived sexual deviancy was exemplified by laws that restrict white women's employment in Chinese restaurants in cities such as Vancouver and Saskatoon in the first half of the twentieth century (Backhouse 1996).

While the settler state has scraped these laws and policies, new forms of immigration control was put in place. In 1967, a new point system was implemented, and various programs were established to fill Canada's shortage. Waves of skilled workers, temporary migrants and students from various Asian countries come to settle, work or study. Some of them are sexual minorities in hope of being in a place without discriminations. However, the barriers, racism and discriminations do not go away, rather, new kinds of legal restrictions linger. For instance, White's (2014) archival work discusses documents and files queer refugees and migrants must prepare for their cases to be heard by the Canadian Border Service Agency (CBSA). White theorizes the trauma and intimacy people need to authenticate as 'technologies of affect', revealing how the state bureaucracies are not neutral but held belief of who is queer and what constitutes repression (White 2014).

The second body of work orbits around the idea of 'queer diaspora'. One way to understand queer diaspora is to consider how non-normative gender and sexuality disrupts nation-states' coherence based on heteropatriarchal families. The existence of racialized queer people poses a challenge to Canadian nationalism and various diaspora nationalisms (e.g., Chinese nationalism within Chinese communities in Canada). Another way to approach the concept is to examine how migration shapes sexual and gender identities as bodies move, stay, and linger (Patton & Sánchez-Eppler 2000).

Recent scholarship has offered diverse experiences of queer diaspora based on places of origins. For example, Dai Kojima (2014) provides in-depth stories of Japanese gay migrants in Vancouver, while Robert Diaz (2016) discusses the of intricacies of Filipinos drag performances during World Pride within the context of transnational culture. Some research also brings other identarian categories to bear on queer lives. Helen Leung (2017) considers the racial and homonationalist politics unfolding regarding the 2014 sexual education curriculum in Vancouver. Fritz Pino (2018) explores older Filipino gay men's alternative vison for intimacy and community. Other innovative and interdisciplinary approaches have tried to queer the otherwise normative cultural production and concepts, such as Tiger mom (Lee A. 2017) the Korean missionary in Canada (Lee R., 2017) and music produced by Filipinx diaspora artists (Mecija 2020).

Both groups of scholarships are not separated from each other. Their topics converge and diverge at times. My categorization here works more as an introduction to my two suggestions: a more explicit engagement with labour and class within Canadian queer Asian studies and a more expansive understanding of who queer 'subjects' are. First, as Martin F. Manalansan reminds us, queers migrate not simply as sexed subjects but as racialized, classed and gendered ones from uneven regions (Manalansan 1995). Queer people's migratory routes are crafted within inequal relations between nation-states, such relations are the product of colonialism and the global regime of accumulation. While queers move, some of them move as temporary workers and others move as economic migrants. Thus, we will benefic greatly from more sustained exploration into how social-economic and political relations on the global scale shape queer Asians's experiences and identities.

Second, we might also think of the queer, following other scholars, as more than sexual and gender minorities. Seitz (2017) has considered refugees in waiting rooms as queer figures. My own work also looks at detention centers in Canada, suggesting the queer nature of how value is extracted in places of confinement (Tian 2020). What such an expansive view of the queer might enable is futhering queer Asian Canadian project to engage with Indigenous, Black and critical migration scholarships.

Overall, the field of queer Asian studies in Canada is growing as more scholars are making visible not just settler state violence but also the community formations that sustain queer lives. My mapping is therefore not to be taken as a static review but as a starting point to engage with new, exciting, and interdisciplinary work to come. In the next section, I demonstrate one of such methods by analyzing a documentary about temporary migrant workers and suggesting them as queer characters both literally and metaphorically. In doing so, we might see how 'normal' procedures of immigration paperwork and documentation are actual regimes of power that produce distributed vulnerabilities. Thus, there is nothing 'normal' about a program that exploits migrant workers, there is nothing 'normal' about the amount of paperwork workers must fill and submit to work or stay, and there is nothing 'normal' about the global capitalist regime that moves through patriarchy.

2 Labour of Intimacy, Intimacy of Labour

Min Sook Lee's recent documentary *Migrant Dreams* (2016) focalizes around a group of Indonesian migrant workers (mostly women) working at greenhouses in Ontario, Canada; the film unpacks the working of capital, citizenship machinery, race, and gender through the workers' legal battle with their brokers and employer who brought them to Canada under the Temporary Foreign Workers Program (TFWP). Through this program, Canadian employers can hire overseas workers to fill vacancies that have not been taken by Canadian citizens and permanent residences. In recent years, agriculture, caretaking, and resource extractions are increasingly dependent on racialized migrants.

The TFWP has been criticized as modern-day indentured labour because workers and their legal status are tied to their employers (Strauss and McGrath 2017; Callon 2016). There is a growing tendency for employers to use the TFWP to meet long-term labour demand, subjecting racialized migrants to harsh and heavy manual labour (Cundal and Seaman 2012). Studies that focus on migrant workers, especially the feminization of trans-continental/transnational migration, have been arguing that a global racialized and gendered pool of labour moves through the regulation and captivity of the receiving states (Susan and McNally 2015; Zaman 2006; Maurizio 2014). Their mobilities, however, are structured around inequalities in the sending states as well.

For example, these Indonesian women's journey started with a broker who would 'help' them to Canada, promising them with decent salaries and remittances (at least twenty-five hundred per month). Having difficulties finding jobs in Indonesia, they had to seek work elsewhere to support their families. The male broker withheld actual information about the TFWP (workers are tied to one employer, and if the work is not 'high-skill' it is very difficult to obtain PR); charging them flights that were supposed to be paid by their employers. After coming to Canada, the broker took advantages of their unfamiliarity with Canada, providing terrible housing where more than five people live in one house.

Their experiences are telling examples of global inequality and flexible accumulation in neoliberal economy. The hyper mobile migrant bodies are simultaneously captivated by their employers, the broker and the settler agricultural economy that depends on their labour (Walia, 2021). In my reading, however, I will pursue another line of inquiry that tries to suggest workers as queer subjects produced by such inequalities. In doing so, I show how queer Asian study might intervene into normative structures that organize settler Canadian social and economic life.

Consider Nanik, one of the workers who came to support her children back home. Her family patterns disrupt what we consider as normative nuclear family living in one household. Her transnational mothering tells us who can spend intimate time with one's children and whose love for their kids takes a queer form, through video calls. In thinking about mothering, we might see how women become mobile assets whose bodies are offered up for their children and their sending states, often disguised by gendered notions of women's virtue (Sedef 2006; Tadiar 2012).

Their queerness also manifests through the racist and anti-immigrant rhetoric directed against them. Not unlike the anti-Chinese sentiment in the earlier 1900s, white settlers view temporary migrant workers as dangerous, foreign, and perverse. Thus, it is perhaps not a conceptual leap to say that temporary migrant workers are queer figures of white settler futurity, a future that ironically depends on the deplored racialized labour for its existence. Employers bring temporary migrant workers not to reproduce but to produce, not to settle but to pass through, and not to become part of the settler nation but to exist outside of it. As queer figures, temporary migrant workers reveal that the normative settler economy depends on their labour to continue, the same bodies that only to diminish once exhausted. What we consider as a normal trip to the grocery stores is not normal in any sense, each tomato is a transit point of migrant dreams that are too queer for white settlers to manage.

In one scene in the documentary, they are told by their employers that their work permits have expired two weeks ago, and they don't have status anymore. Thinking through queerness, we can see how the normative citizenship and immigration machineries, documents, papers and files produce non-normal people as 'illegal' migrants. What the settler state considers to be standard procedures are sites of power that name some as legal and others as illegal, producing valued and devalued beings (Cacho 2012).

If queerness suggests power from below, in the documentary, we also see resistance on the part of the workers. To begin, Asian women are deemed to be timid, docile thus easy to control. Cutting hours of rebellious workers, surveilling workers' apartments and threatening of deportations are tactics used to destabilize and manipulate female workers. Yet, they were able to reach out to migrant advocacies groups, labour lawyers and activists even though they still have trouble communicating in English.

Importantly, we also see how a queer couple, Rahmi and Dwipa, confronts and struggles against regimes of power. In a conversation after their wedding, they were both excited but frightened by the impact of their marriage on their jobs. The broker told Rahmi's family about their union as retaliation, which had an unexpected impact on her mother. Despite setbacks on their legal status, on their dreams and queer futures, they remain hopeful.

At the end of *Migrant Dreams*, Dwipa reflects upon his life in Canada: 'where I work it's just like in Indonesia'. This statement is significant in several registers. It suggests how labour exploitation is both global and national and how settler Canada as a safe place for LGBTQ+ people discounts working class, migrant, and racialized queer bodies. Such disavowal of queers like Dwipa exposes the violence of patriarchy, nation-states and settler economy.

At first glance, *Migrant Dreams* is a documentary about temporary migrant workers, yet as I have tried to suggest, we might read the life stories in the film from a queer Asian lens. Not only because they are Asians, but also because they tell us about how intimacy compels people to work (e.g., Nanik) and how labour produces intimate relations (e.g., Rahmi and Dwipa). A queer Asian study up for the task of thinking with migration and labour is capable of answering more urgent questions around life, time and survival in our present.

3 Conclusion

This chapter serves as an entry point to a growing field of queer Asian Canadian study. My mapping of recent literature is limited by the scope, time, and language. For example, I did not include literature from two decades ago, and I am not able to provide studies written in French. Having said these, the argument is clear: a more robust engagement with class, labour and migration is crucial for our collective queering of settler Canada.

I have used the film *Migrant Dreams* to show how such a queer view might work. In attending to migrant lives, I also hope to challenge settler colonialism's structural impact on Indigenous peoples on this land. In centering the settler state, I highlight how immigration agencies and employers are sites of power that discipline and valorize some bodies not others. Feminized, queer, and racialized subjects tend to become the targets of dispossession and exploitation; yet they also demonstrate intimacy, care, and hope.

This is the implicit point I want to reiterate: how queer and trans issues are productive points for labour and class analysis of our contemporary world. Questions of desire, intimacy and sexuality are deeply policed and disciplined by the need for labour and consumption. From the queer vantage point, we might see how the normal arrangement of intimacy is a fantasy reserved for some not others. This ideal reveals how global inequality structures and distributes unevenly intimate events, family formation and reproduction (Murphy 2017).

In the era of rising right-wing nationalism, the narrative of an imagined 'queer other' who threatens the national border renders Black, Indigenous, brown, and other racialized people targets of hatred and devaluation. During my involvement with migrant justice organizations, I personally have seen white nationalists repeatedly showed up at anti-racist rallies and even live-streamed their display of hatred. At these moments, I am thinking about what kind of queer Asian studies can do to unsettle nationalism, citizenship machinery and the liberal political structures. I argue for a queer Asian study that does not assume the homogeneity of identity; but more importantly, one that transgresses borders of class, race, gender, disability, space, nation-state systems, and heteropatriarchy (Mohanty C. 2003).

References

Anderson, Kay (1991) *Vancouver's Chinatown: Racial Discourse in Canada, 1875–1980.* Montreal-Kingston: McGill-Queen's University Press.

Backhouse, Constance (1996) The White Woman's Labor Laws: Anti-Chinese Racism in Early Twentieth-Century Canada. *Law and History Review* 14(2): 315–368.

Cacho, Lisa M. (2012) *Social Death: Racialized Rightlessness and the Criminalization of the Unprotected.* New York: NYU Press.

Callon, Emma (2016) Unbalanced Scales of Global Capitalism: Analyzing Temporary Foreign Worker Programs in Canada. *Canadian Graduate Journal of Sociology and Criminology* 5(1): 32–43.

Chen, Jian Neo (2019) *Trans Exploits: Trans of Color Cultures and Technologies in Movement.* Durham: Duke University Press.

Cundal, Kerry, and Brian Seaman (2012) Canada's Temporary Foreign Worker Programme: A Discussion of Human Rights Issues. *Migrant Letters* 9(3): 201–214.

Diaz, Robert (2016) Queer Unsettlements: Diasporic Filipinos in Canada's World Pride. *Journal of Asian American Studies* 19(3): 327–350.

Ferguson, Roderick A. (2004) *Aberrations in Black.* Minneapolis: University of Minnesota Press.

Kojima, Dai (2014) Migrant Intimacies: Mobilities-in-Difference and Basue Tactics in Queer Asian Diasporas. *Anthropologica* 56(1): 33–44.

Kojima, Dai, John Paul Catungal, and Robert Diaz (2017) Introduction: Feeling Queer, Feeling Asian, Feeling Canadian. *Topia* 38: 69–80.

Lee, A.W. (2017) ManChyna's Queer Tiger Mom. *Topia* 38:135–144.

Lee, R. (2017) Using Indigenous Feminist Land Ethics to Queer the Korean Missionary Position in Canada. *Topia* 38: 108–113.

Leung, Helen Hok-Sze (2017) Our city of Colours: Queer/Asian Publics in Transpacific Vancouver. *Inter-Asia Cultural Studies* 18(4): 482–497.

Li, Alan (2019) Power in Community: Queer Asian Activism from the 1980s to the 2000s. In: Jin Haritaworn, Ghaida Moussa and Syrus Marcus Ware (eds.) *Marvellous Grounds: Queer of Colour Formations in Toronto*. Toronto: BTL, 47–60.

Manalansan, Martin F. (1995) In the Shadows of Stonewall: Examining Gay Transnational Politics and the Diasporic Dilemma. *GLQ* 2(4):425–438.

Maurizio, Atzeni (2014) *Workers and Labour in Globalized Capitalism.* Basingstoke: Palgrave Macmillan.

Mecija, Casey (2020) Skin as Ecstatic Surface: Listening to Queer Diaspora in the work of Patrick Cruz. *Journal of Canadian Studies* 58 (2–3): 508–525.

Mohanty, Chandra (2003) *Femenism without Borders.* Durham: Duke University Press.

Murphy, Michelle (2017) *The Economization of Life.* Durham: Duke University Press.

Murray, David A.B. (2014) Real Queer: 'Authentuc' LGBT Refugee Claimants and Homonationalism in the Canadian Refugee System. *Anthropologica* 56(1): 21–56.

Patton, Cindy, and Benigno Sánchez-Eppler (2000) *Queer Diaspora.* Durham: Duke University Press.

Pino, Fritz Luther (2018) Older Filipino Gay Men in Canada: Bridging Queer Theory and Gerontology in Filipinx Canadian Studies. In: Robert, Diaz, Marissa, Largo, and Fritz, Pino (eds.) *Diasporic Intimacies: Queer Filipinos and Canadian Imaginaries.* Evanston, Illinois: Northwestern University Press, 163–82.

Poon, M. K., Alan T. Li, Josephine P. Wong, and Cory Wong (2017) Queer-friendly Nation? The Experience of Chinese gay Immigrants in Canada. *China Journal of Social Work* 10(1): 23–38.

Sedef, Arat-Koç (2006) Whose Social Reproduction? Transnational Motherhood and Challenges to Feminist Political Economy. In: Kate Bezanson and Meg Luxton (eds.) *Social Reproduction: Feminist Political Economy Challenges Neo-Liberalism.* Montreal-Kingston: McGill-Queen's University Press, 75–92.

Seitz, David (2017) Limbo life in Canada's Waiting Room: Asylum-seeker as Queer Subject. *Environment and Planning D: Society and Space* 35(3): 438–456.

Strauss, Kendra, and Siobhán McGrath (2017) Temporary Migration, Precarious Employment and Unfree Labour Relations. *Geoforum* 78: 199–208.

Susan, Ferguson, and David McNally. 2015. Precarious Migrants: Gender, Race and the Social Reproduction of a Global Working Class. *Socialist Register* 51: 1–23.

Tadiar, Neferti X.M. (2012) Life-Times of Disposability within Global Neoliberalism. *Social Text* 31(2):19–48.

Tian, Ian Liujia (2020) On Rescuable and Expendable Life: Bioavailability, Surplus Time, and Queer Politics of Reproduction. *Journal of Canadian Studies* 54 (2–3): 483–507.

Walia, Harsha (2021) *Border and Rule: Global Migration, Capitalism, and the Rise of Racist Nationalism.* Chicago: Haymarket Books.

White, Melissa A. (2014) Archives of Intimacy and Trauma: Queer Migration Documents as Technologies of Affect. *Radical History Review* 120: 75–93.

Zaman, Habiba (2006) *Breaking the Iron Wall.* Toronto: Lexington Books.

CHAPTER 9

The Past in the Present: An Encounter between Gay Asians of Toronto and New Ho Queen

Samuel Yoon

On the front cover of Gay Asians of Toronto's (GAT) first newsletter entitled "CelebrAsian", is a black and white photograph of a group of gender diverse Asians standing on a stage. The year is 1983 and we see a combination of smiles and clapping that suggests the completion of an event. The faces are undiscernible to me; I do not recognize any of these individuals even with my growing knowledge of this organization and its members. Even when I have the ability to say anything about this moment in time, it is through a second-hand retelling of memories by past leaders and members. I only know of the details of this photograph from Alan Li's (2018) essay "Power in Community: Queer Asian Activism from the 1980s to the 2000s". The front cover of the newsletter clearly states, "Gay Asians" and hails me, a process of interpellation. By recognizing myself on the basis of this identity category I have some claim to this object and the histories it belongs to but, when turning to the photograph and its unintelligible contents, I realize my status as non-belonging. Encountering this recent past is an experience of disorientation that is inflected with feelings of loss but also moments of recognition, always partial and never quite satisfying.

Amongst this sense of unfamiliarity, I see a resemblance to moments of celebration and communal joy in the parties thrown by New Ho Queen (NHQ), a Toronto queer Asian collective that formed in 2018. While these collectives are separated by almost thirty years, there is no denying the intimacy between these two sites since they both existed as spaces of queer Asian communal gatherings in Toronto. This essay is a comparative discussion that reflects on the temporal divide of past and present queer Asian formations with an emphasis on the possibilities and limits in claiming and forming a community based on the identity of queer and Asian. In this process, I resist detailing a linear timeline that espouses a narrative of progress and development, rather it imagines and reveals the fraught intimacies that NHQ and GAT share. This reading practice will reveal the ways the past lingers into the present but also the way the present breaks from the past in notable ways. In order to reflect on GAT, I turn to a queer Asian archive through Richard Fung's documentary work and GAT's newsletter entitled "CelebrAsian". In the case of HQ, I reflect on my own participation in the space and its queer Asian diasporic aesthetic and performances. My reading practice is not only a way to make the past visible to ensure younger queer Asians (like me) as the beneficiaries of recuperative histories so they can know themselves better or claim a visibility in queer history, but instead, I emphasize a different stake in these relationalities. I am interested in the maps to an otherwise and other ways that can reimagine and reinvigorate queer Asian formations in Toronto.

The questions I pose in having the past and present encounter one another is informed by Richard Fung's documentary work. Fung's' "Orientations" (1986), has been a foundational work in the queer Asian Canadian archive and documented the lives of Lesbian and Gay Asians, interviewing fourteen individuals as they detail their diverse life experiences of racism, community building, and coming out. In a follow up film, "Re:Orientations" (2016) returns to the lives of seven of the original participants. As Richard Fung says, "Three decades later, I am curious to see how we have changed, how the world has changed". I am also curious in regard to these changes, but rather I focus on what it means to encounter the past in the present in these queer Asian communities. While the arrival of community signals possibilities it also necessitates reflecting on the politics of forming and maintaining a community based on identity. I begin with an extended quote from feminist geographer, Judy Han as featured in Fung's "Re:Orientations":

> To meet with other queer Asian Americans, to meet with other queer Asian activists ... felt like we were trying to radicalize some sort of community building. Today, with so many of us involved in a variety of social justice movements, ... having asserted our queer subjectivity in a number of different ways, without necessarily convening under the umbrella of queer Asian, it seems like we need to imagine a different kind of gathering. ... I'm not sure what that is exactly, but I don't think that kind of identitarian—that kind of identity-based politics—is all there is. There's got to be more.

This provocation for a 'more' or an 'otherwise' is always in the process of taking place in different social movements although, there continues to be a sense that a non-identity politics is marked by a question of the unknown. Identity is persistent in many contemporary political projects even for those that may hold a critique of identity politics and its shortcomings. I do not suggest that GAT or NHQ enact a successful 'otherwise', but rather I am interested in tracing the ways 'queer' and 'Asian' was and continues to be contested in these formations in order to consider what it means to gather as queer Asians in this particular social and political moment.

My reading practice of these two queer Asian collectives attempts to surrender paranoia that is only critical of shortcomings and rather I engage in the reparative that is open to surprises, both good and bad (Sedgwick 2003: 136). In reading across these two sites, I ask, who shores up in this identity category and how do they arrive? I tend to the problematics of visibility, representation, and exclusion that circulate within this identity category although still account for the significance of this kind of identity politics.

1 Queer Asian and the Politics of Identity

The means to which I learned about GAT is through mediated forms that rely on the selection of particular individuals to speak about their experiences of being gay Asians and their participation in this organization. The traces of GAT are not simply the archive but the living archive, that is, the very leaders of this organization that continue to speak of the past and their involvement with GAT. Richard Fung and Alan Li are notable examples of those that have been most visible. In result, they have been positioned with the role of being representatives of Toronto's gay Asian community from the 80s. As a Fourth generation Trinidadian Chinese, Fung explains how he feels this tenuous claim to being "Asian". The specificity of Fung's identity illuminates the fraught ways that Asians may not inherently have any cultural or political affinities with another even if they do share experiences of being racialized as Asian in Canada. Fung (1995: 124) refers to this as the 'burden of representation' and draws attention to how identity can obscure particularities and produce the expectation that subjects that align in some way with queer and Asian have to speak some truth in regard to this 'experience'. Feminist historian, Joan Scott (1991), writes how providing visibility to minority experiences may actually naturalize difference as it takes experience as uncontestable evidence. Scott (1991: 777) suggests that instead we should explore "how difference is established, how it operates, how and in what ways it constitutes subjects who see and act in the world". None the less, speaking about one's experience from a particular identity category and the knowledge it produces can be a meaningful political act that resists the ways the majoritarian sphere has simply excluded or spoken on behalf of queer Asians. On the other hand, as detailed in Linda Alcoff's (1991) seminal essay "The Problem of Speaking for Others", there are a number of concerns about the ways that speaking for oneself is always implicated in truth claims about others and is exemplary of this 'crisis of representation'. As Alcoff (1991:10) says "In speaking for myself, I (momentarily) create my self-just as much as when I speak for others I create their selves". In turn, there is a need to pay close attention to the context of speech acts in relation to power, privilege, and one's social location. While queer Asians come to show up for themselves in these communities, they confer knowledge about themselves and others that are generative but will always fail to capture the significant differences that exist among queer Asians. In this light, the community leader is a contested subject; the knowledge that is produced when they speak may only resonate with certain portions of the community membership. The format of GAT and its newsletter illuminates these politics of difference that arise when gathering underneath this identity category. Throughout GAT's newsletter, it is evident that there are many different opinions of old and new members that form a disparate discourse on the organization and related topics such as white members, political versus social events, and the necessity for more cohesion.

Throughout the newsletter, leaders have a prominent voice to share their perspectives that may be interpreted as representative of their constituents although there are always dissenting voices. This creates contradictions in the discourse that falls underneath this umbrella of queer Asian and illuminates the necessity to account for different desires and experiences. This is not to flatten out the discourse produced by queer Asians as all politically significant but rather it resists telling a story that GAT was only dictated by a politics of authenticity. While identity politics are critiqued for their disciplinary nature, queer Asian organizations such as GAT and NHQ should be understood for their contradictions rather than a unified front of queer of colour resistance. I turn to Jasbir Puar's (2007: 23) provocation that aims to defuse the queer liberal binaries of assimilation and transgression, in noting when queer of colour formations and theorizing are held up as always transgressive and subversive this overlooks the conservative proclivities that do exist. I draw out this discussion not as a mean to dismiss community building and community leaders but rather to recognize the necessity for different modes of listening that do not over invest in identity and the speaking subject as a source of knowledge. The problem of the community leader also sheds insight into who figures most comfortably as a queer Asian subject. While many may identify with this identity category there are particular queer Asian subjects that may be rendered as marginal and at times impossible.

Turning to the origins of GAT is useful draw attention to how queer Asian was (im)mobilized within GAT in its early years. In the fall of 1979, following the attendance of a national gay rights march in Washington, Richard Fung, along with Gerald Chan, Nito Marquez, and Tony Souza convened for the first meeting of Gay Asians of Toronto. Richard Fung (CelebrAsian 1983: 7) states in the first issue of CelebrAsian: "The first planning committee for Gay Asians consisted of Gerald and myself, Nito Marquez from the Phillipines, and Tony Souza from India, one of the friends I went with to Washington. Our attempts to contact Asian Lesbians for the planning were not, unfortunately successful". This absence of Asian lesbians continues in the early stages of GAT and in its newsletter until Issue five where Mary Woo Sims is interviewed (1989: 21–31) and is noted as the first 'inclusion' of Asian Lesbians. In her interview (CelebrAsian 1989: 21–31) she makes note of this absence of other Asian Lesbians in the gay scene in terms of the bars and says she wants to be more involved with GAT as she knows there are very few lesbians involved. It is useful to turn to Je Yeun Lee (1996) essay "Why Suzie Wong is not a Lesbian" as a way to reflect on how these spaces render certain subjects impossible. Through Lee's interviews with Asian Lesbians, she notes the ways an orientalist and sexist discourse has contributed to an invisibility of Asian Lesbians as they are always rendered as hypersexual for the pleasure of white men. Even though GAT aims to 'include' Lesbians, the structures of the organization continued to be male dominated and at times rendered the Asian lesbian as still unimaginable. In turn, we see the formation of Asian Lesbians of Toronto (ALOT) that came out of the 1988 Unity Among Asians Conference that was sponsored by GAT and Khush, Toronto's Gay South Asian organization. This conference and the subsequent discourse reveal the ways this identity category was relied upon in strategic means that acknowledged difference through consciousness raising and produced a communal critique of racism, sexism, and homophobia. While the title of the conference calls for unity, this was not simply a call for a gathering on identity but a means to work through difference. One of the conference participants spoke about the conference goal of trying to get different people to work with another: "There was certainly some of that in the official conference events with workshops dealing with ethnic prejudice among different Asian peoples, on men and women working together on how non-Asians can work within Asian groups" (CelebrAsian 1989: 4). While this conference mobilized underneath the term unity, the discussions and the discourse following the conference reveal how community was mobilized in strategic ways that did not expect fixed identities. Even with these meaningful forms of gathering on the basis of this identity category, the formation of distinct organizations such as ALOT illuminates the ways that difference while spoken of, still remained fraught. In a review of the conference, a short article entitled "Asian Lesbian Experience", Tamai Kobayashi (CelebrAsian, 1989: 9) speaks of the problems of sexism:

> The question of sexism within the Gay Asian communities and the responsibility of educating came up with varying intensity. Some comments sent shock waves through the women and some men and it became clear that the different levels of awareness showed how far men have come on the issue of sexism and male privilege, and how far they will have to go.

The troubling ways that sexism persisted in this space that was aspiring for unity among Asians is one motivation to create a separate organization. The absence and marginalization of Asian Lesbians in queer Asian spaces illuminates how calls for inclusion do very little in terms of undoing the structures of inclusion and exclusion that communities are based on. The creation of ALOT is still based on an identity category, although 'queer women of colour' is not only an identity but a critique of multiple axes of social difference. The gathering of queer women of colour tends between an identity politics but also a means to enacting and imagining a politics that can produce a powerful critique of valuation and devaluation within and across different racial, sexual, and gender collectives. In the initial call out to form this group, the framing is in terms of visibility as the newspaper article states "Visible and vocal. Asian Lesbians announce their existence to larger gay and lesbian communities" (Xtra! 1988: 1). While I have emphasized this discussion on the past, I would note how this notion of visibility is a continued thread in the formation and arrival of contemporary queer Asian communities as NHQ states their goal is to "Increase QPOC visibility". The very use of the term QPOC/QTPOC (Queer People of Colour/Queer and Trans People of Colour) is a conscious effort in expanding beyond queer Asian and is one means of resisting a narrow identity politics.

NHQ has grappled with positioning itself as a queer Asian space but also aims to enact a queer of colour politics that resists the enclosures of queer and Asian. Seen most recently at their event entitled "Un/divided (2019)", NHQ presented a photo series of black and white portraits that splice together two individuals, at times producing cohesion but in other cases revealing the stark differences that gather underneath the categories of queer Asian/queer people of colour. Amongst these images we see multiple forms of gender expression and people who do not fit the common image of the light skinned East Asian who has historically and continually shores up as 'the' queer Asian. This photography project forcefully displays the hopes of making sense of the differences among queer people of colour while also acknowledging shared experiences. "Un/divided" exemplifies the ways that contemporary queer Asian spaces continue to invest in identity but in ways that resist how identities and communities have often required a denial of difference.

2 Acts and Gestures of Queer Asian Joy

As noted in the beginning of this chapter the very first GAT newsletter had a photograph of a celebration, which was the end of their annual show entitled "CelebrAsian", one of the many times where queer Asians gathered around performance and communal celebration. These parties and this queer Asian joy are a vital continuity between GAT and NHQ. I suggest that these spaces of communal celebration are significant for their performances and enactment of a queer Asian diasporic aesthetic.

My very first time at NHQ was marked by the performance of Ms. Nookie Galore (also known as Patrick Salvani) who has come to be a queer Asian icon through his unique drag performances and significant contributions to the community. Within NHQ's line up of performances, Ms. Nookie Galore presents herself as a standout with production-like numbers that resist any conventional drag aesthetic. In Diasporic Intimacies: Queer Filipinos and Canadian Imaginaries edited by, Robert Diaz, Marissa Largo, and Fritz Pino, Patrick Salvani (2017: 199) says that "I am not your average gender queer pansexual hairy Asian Filipinx panda queen who parties like a white girl and tells scary stories". In his drag vignettes he mines through his own archives of loss, grief, and fear that bear his intimate connections to his grandmother, friends, and larger Filipinx community that illuminate how his subject position shapes his own artistic practices. I turn to Salvani and his performances as Ms. Nookie Galore for the ways they illuminate the necessity for acts that create spaces and moments of queer Asian communal joy. I turn to Queer performance studies scholar, José Esteban Muñoz (2009: 71–72) and his reflection that "although we cannot simply conserve a person or a performance through documentation, we can perhaps begin to summon up, through the auspices of memory, the acts and gestures that meant so much to us". Based on my memories and what I recall from my first experience with NHQ I highlight Ms. Nookie Galore's gestures that I cherish so much.

On September 7th, 2018, just after one week of moving to Toronto I entered NHQ for their 'House Special' event. The space glowed a vibrant red all night. The neon sign, with the words 'New Ho Queen' peaked above all the heads, acting as our north star all night, while the many red lanterns formed the constellation of glowing red lights. Everyone's skin radiated red, the room was hot, and bodies moved to the music. The whole space was crafted to transport us to a queer elsewhere, it was a queer Asia right here in Toronto, persistent on its status as the orient. I hear the words Asia ring in my ears not only because of the constant signifiers on the walls and on bodies, but primarily through Ms. Nookie Galore's performance. I return to Salvani's (2017: 199) own description of his drag to provide context and the way he describes his relationship to horror:

> I grew up in the Philippines in a place where sometimes there's no electricity at night. Fear became familial and scary stories felt comforting. My Grandma loved telling me scary stories and my mom loved watching horror movies with me. When my grandma died, and I moved across the country from my family, I was comforted by writing horror stories (and cooking lots of Filipino foods). Horror stories provide an alternative way of understanding and relating to loss, family, migration, politics, and community.

While I take the space to interpret Salvani's performance, I believe it is significant to highlight how Salvani comes to articulate himself as an artist and a Queer Filipinx immigrant. Mrs. Nookie Galore, with her full beard, comes to the stage with a long gown and a skeleton in her hands, already distinguishing herself from the typical expectations for a drag performance. Interspersed throughout the performance is a jarring voice that interrupts the flow of the music and resists any smooth transitions between songs. The voices yells "Asia". Its repetition is constant and haunts the whole piece and the room itself. The music is a collection of familiar tunes that the audience sings along to but then are cut off as the voice returns, saying once again, "Asia". The pleasure the audience derives from singing along is short-circuited. We are forced into other forms of looking and observing that demand we grapple with Ms. Nookie Galore's attachment to Asia and its reoccurrence. She uses the word Asia, like NHQ similarly relies on symbols and cultural objects that we have collectively associated with Asia. The formation of this sonic and visual space is a world-making that will always fail to capture "Asia" and all of its cultural and political complexities. Instead of desiring correct forms of representation, NHQ and Ms. Nookie Galore enact a practice of remaking and reusing the culture available to us in order to form a shared sense of belonging and meaning. The performance and its mashup of western pop music that is interspliced with "Asia" is finished off with an epic gesture. Mrs. Nookie Galore pulls out chopsticks that resemble lightsabers as she begins to pull noodles out of her breasts and consumes them. This simple act of eating is racially charged, and while a mundane activity for those who eat with chopsticks there is a significance to spectacularizing this act. As Ju Yon Kim (2015: 10) states "Most racial stereotypes implicate the mundane, which enlivens their flattened portraits with the small details of how people walk, speak, eat or hold their bodies". Galore relies on the ways that these mundane acts are performances of race and through its theatricalization the act is no longer attached to a disciplinary white gaze but is a mode of recognition and means of place making for queer Asians. Not only is the act of eating food publicly and sexually marked by disorder, but the performance in whole is also the epitome of mess. The noodles on the ground and the sonic mash up of songs and voice overs, all exemplify a performative example of Martin Manalansan's (2014) suggestion that mess may be an entry point into queer lives and queer archives. While Manalansan (2014:100) is working from an ethnographic project with queer immigrants, I follow his suggestion that mess does not only produce disgust and shock but can "gesture to moments of vitality, pleasure, and fabulousness". This performance is significant especially in this act of feeding oneself. In a sense this gesture is simply an act of self-nourishment, but accounting for its traces and ephemeral qualities we can consider this moment as a form of communal sustenance.

Mrs. Nookie Galore and her aesthetics and performances provides us a new repertoire, one that may not bear any intimacies to the GAT archive I selected, but enacts a living archive, one that is intertwined with places and people beyond Toronto. Contemporary queer Asian communions are not simply building off the past, but like these diasporic formations, are always drawing from a multiplicity of spaces and histories.

3 Queer Asian Past, Present, and Futures

As I initially posed, NHQ and GAT form in specific contexts that are based on shared desires and impulses for community and recognition that rely on the complicated workings of identity. This desire to be seen and resist invisibility is a particular social and political project that has now been critiqued for its limited vision. It is not to say that demanding visibility is a futile project but rather it is reckoning with the way visibility can stifle the ability to imagine otherwise. The arrivals of GAT and NHQ are sites of visibility that speak back to white queers and while they enact a politics that is attached to particular subjects and objects, they also retain the potential of hope and the building of an elsewhere or as, José Esteban Muñoz (2009) calls a "critical investment in utopia".

I resisted simply retelling a clear-cut description of Toronto and its queer Asian communities that would have provided an absolute assessment of these sites. These objects and sites open up reflections that seem to contradict one another, although I suggest it mirrors how these spaces refuse to be so narrowly defined. Queer Asian is descriptive in many ways but as demonstrated it does not necessarily designate a fixed subject but rather can be an entry point to heterogeneity, gestures of vitality and, powerful critiques of our lived realities. I hoped to account for the messiness of these queer Asian collectives and how even when they seem to fail to be transgressive, they may enact an otherwise, an elsewhere that is never quite fully knowable.

Even with this optimistic reading, I recognize that NHQ arrives at a particular political and social moment where a gathering based on identity easily works along with this current affirmative moment of diversity and multiculturalism. On the other hand, GAT arrived at a particular moment, right before the AIDS epidemic and played a central role in raising funds, creating awareness, and providing direct support services that accounted for the specific needs of gay men of colour. For example, John Paul Catungal's (2018) work illuminates the significant labour in forming queer of colour HIV/AIDS services in Toronto. While GAT and NHQ are only separated by 30 years, they none the less arrive at specific political moments. I turn to Black studies scholar Rinaldo Walcott's (2009:11) reflection on gay rights and his distinction that "Stonewall was queer sexual liberation, alongside heterosexual liberation, but HIV/AIDS was citizen-making". GAT thus appears at this moment of sickness and death where a particular queer subject appears as a rights-seeking subject.

In contrast, NHQ does not bear the same relation to death and sickness in this post AIDS moment and now post PrEP moment but rather, its formation and success is quite reflective of this particular homonormative moment. While I have resisted a narrative of linear progress through reflecting on the continuities, shared intimacies, and lingering of the past, I recognize the ways that contemporary queer Asian gatherings are implicated and reflect this current neoliberal moment. NHQ goals are primarily social in terms of their parties and departs from GAT's more politically inflected goals. That is not to say that NHQ is an apolitical site but rather that its formation and shape it takes is a response to a different set of political conditions with its own temporally unique issues to contend with. To present GAT as solely a site of queer of colour resistance and political organizing that is said to be lost in this contemporary moment would only reinstate binary logics; the past as radical and the present as hopelessly lost to the hegemony of neoliberalism. None the less, the turn to the past opens up important reflections of our present, as we continue to enact spaces and communities that work towards a more just world. While my discussion reflected on the immaterial traces and relationality of the past to the present there is a need for queer Asian collectives to meaningfully engage and remember past forms of organizing that have taken place. While I provide no definitive assessment of these sites, I conclude with affirming their intentions and desires. Queer Asians have invested in these sites of joy and celebration through collective gathering, and while we need to think about life after the party we can still relish in the psychic and social residues that linger from the whirlwind of queer communion.

References

Alcoff, Linda (1991) The Problem of Speaking for Others. *Cultural Critique* 20: 5–32.

Catungal, John Paul (2018) We had to Take Space, We Had to Create Space.: Locating Queer of Colour Politics in 1980s Toronto In: Jin Haritaworn, Ghadia Moussa, Syrus Marcuse Ware, and Rio Rodriquez (eds.) *Queer Urban Justice Queer of Colour Formations in Toronto*. Toronto: University of Toronto Press, 45–61.

Fung, Richard. (1995) The Trouble With 'Asians.' In: Monica Dorenkamp and Richard Henke (eds.) *Negotiating Lesbian and Gay Subjects*. New York: Routledge, 123–140.

Kim, Ju Yun (2015) *The Racial Mundane: Asian American Performance and the Embodied Everyday*. New York: New York University Press.

Lee, JeeYeun (1996) Why Suzie Wong Is Not a Lesbian: Asian and Asian American Lesbian and Bisexual Women and Femme/Butch/Gender Identities. In: Brett Beemnyn and Mickey Eliason (eds.) *Queer Studies: A Lesbian, Gay, Bisexual, and Transgender Anthology*. New York: New York University Press, 115–132.

Li, Alan (2018) Power in Community: Queer Asian Activism from the 1980s to the 2000s. In: Jin Haritaworn, Ghadia Moussa, and Syruse Marcuse Ware (eds). *Marvellous Grounds*. Toronto: BTL, 47–60.

Manalansan, Martin (2014) The 'Stuff' of Archives: Mess, Migration, and Queer Lives. *Radical History Review* 2014(120): 94–107.

Muñoz, José Esteban (2009) *Cruising Utopia: The Then and There of Queer Futurity*. New York: New York University Press.

Puar, Jasbir K. (2007) *Terrorist Assemblages: Homonationalism in Queer Times*. Durham: Duke Unviersity Press.

Salvani, Patrick (2017) Dragging Filipinix: A Series of Performative Vignettes. In: Robert Diaz, Marissa Largo, and Fritz Pino (eds.) *Diasporic Intimacies: Queer Filipinos and Canadian Imaginaries*. Evanston: Northwestern University Press, 198–208.

Scott, Joan (1991) The Evidence of Experience. *Critical Inquiry* 17(4): 773–797.

Sedgwick, Eve (2003) *Touching Feeling: Affect, Pedagogy, Performativity*. Durham: Duke University Press.

Walcott, Rinaldo (2009) Queer Returns: Human Rights, The Anglo-Caribbean and Diaspora Politics. *Caribbean Review of Gender Studies* 3: 1–19.

Primary Sources

CelebrAsian (Toronto, ON) 1983 Issue 1.

CelebrAsian (Toronto, ON) 1989 Issue 5.

CelebrAsian (Toronto, ON) 1989 Issue 16.

Xtra! Toronto Gay and Lesbian News, (Toronto, ON), November 11, 1988, issue 112.

CHAPTER 10

Love Intersections: Queer Sensibilities and Relationality in Art and Cultural Production

David Ng and Jen Sungshine

In 2014, the Vancouver School Board went through a process to update their sexual orientation and gender identity policies. One of the main purposes of the update was to expand upon language around discrimination to include transgender and non-binary people. What was supposed to be a routine update, erupted into a public controversy, which spurred large protests and petitions opposing the policy recommendations, organized mostly by the Chinese evangelical Christian community – a community that we were familiar with (David grew up in an evangelical community). Due to these protests, the school board had to conduct a series of community consultations to hear the concerns of the protestors, as well as the supporters of the policy changes.

Around that time, we both worked for Out in Schools, an organization that facilitates anti-oppression film workshops in high schools across British Columbia, Canada, and also sat on the Pride Advisory Board for the Vancouver School Board. As the school board "controversy" became more and more intense, a media fanfare soon followed. We started noticing a troubling trend in the media, where they were very quick to racialize the people protesting the policy. Headlines like "Ethnic Chinese Groups Protest LGBT Programs Again" (2014) and "Vancouver's 100,000 Chinese Christians 'fraught' over gay debate" were common, frustrating us both not only because we are of Chinese and Taiwanese descent, but also because a very similar controversy had erupted in the white suburban bible belt of Langley mere months prior, and none of the media reports ever mentioned the race of the white evangelical Christians who were protesting the policies.

The hypocrisy of this is of course not a new phenomenon – racialized minorities face constant scrutiny of whether or not they are "deserving" of citizenship. While the currency of the Christian religion in Canada allows for a certain threshold of "passing" via the norms that are reinforced by colonial, white supremacist, Christian, Canada, these tepid conditions are produced through the implementation of systemic racism. The ways that the media responded to the Chinese Christian protestors of the policy is indicative of the fallacies of Canadian "multiculturalism"; the sanctions under which racialized communities can access subjecthood, like citizenship, can be taken away very quickly, especially when a scapegoat is needed to articulate the narrative of the "Canadian subject" as "progressive", "accepting" and "inclusive" – and that "The Other" (i.e. immigrants, Black people, people of colour, Indigenous people) are the conservative culprits that hinder the liberal progression of society.

On a deeply personal level, the school board controversy was traumatic for us, and troubling on many levels. As queer people of Chinese/Taiwanese descent, sitting on one side of the public consultation rooms with our queer white "allies" holding rainbow flags, holding up queer affirming placards; while sitting directly across from those who opposed us, were in fact people that "looked" just like us, our families, and the communities we grew up in. Our growing sense of discomfort was further exacerbated by the microaggressions that we encountered from our queer white "allies" who made ignorant remarks and asked us why "Chinese culture" is more conservative and homophobic. Here, the erasure of our intersectional identities became a key reason why we started Love Intersections – as a platform to share identities that are silenced, or invisibilized by dominant discourses.

At the time, David was also working for Theatre for Living (TfL), a grassroots theatre company in Vancouver that employed audience interactive Forum Theatre to collaborate with communities to address different social issues. TfL Artistic Director, David Diamond (2007), suggested that the Rainbow of Desire exercise would be a potential way for these oppositional sides – the parents supporting the policy, and the parents opposed to the policy – to "see" each other, and "humanize" each other, beyond the political disagreement. The philosophy behind the Rainbow of Desire is to use embodied theatrical exercises to make visible and investigate moments of commonality or solidarity between two sides that are in a deadlocked disagreement.

The Rainbow of Desire begins with a disagreement between two people where they reach an impasse, and neither side can agree upon a particular issue. Using different Theatre for Living exercises, the facilitator – called a "joker" in Theatre for Living – then "animates" the fears and desires of each opposing side. The exercises are designed to be embodied: some of these practices include asking participants to make a shape with their bodies of their strongest emotions without speaking, and audiences are sometimes asked to offer a reflection as to what they are viewing from the body shapes. Eventually the stage is populated with people playing/representing the fears and desires of each "side" of the argument. The joker may then facilitate other interactions between the "animated" elements on stage. The Rainbow of Desire is not designed to "change the views" or prove one side wrong, but rather meant to illuminate moments of solidarity – as small as they might appear – with the belief that it is through these moments that lasting social change and relational understanding can occur. Through our discussions with Theatre for Living, we realized that despite what appeared to be a binary opposition between parents on either side of this topic on trans-inclusive policies in schools, there was one commonality between "us" vs "them": both sides loved their children, and both sides wanted their children to be safe. In collaboration with the Vancouver Public Library, we organized a Rainbow of Desire called "Voices of Love: Reaching Across", and invited parents involved in both sides of the policy, and the broader community, to participate in this theatrical dialogue.

The impact of this event was wide reaching. We immediately received numerous emails and messages from evangelical Christians, transgender Christians and non-Christians, parents, youth – all wanting to express how they felt from the event. Many people shared that the event stirred up something inside them, and that it gave them new perspective to their beliefs and attitudes. This notion of relationship building, even with people we view as "opposing" to us, greatly inspired many of the philosophies of community collaboration and art making that grounded the ethos of Love Intersections. "Love" in the branding of "Love Intersections" is a direct reference to the relationality that we wanted to centre in our work as Love Intersections co-founders.

1 Love Intersections Was Born Out of a Desire to Do Things Differently

By the mid 2010s, we began noticing a pattern of "call out" in the community; both naming and shaming – and subsequent excommunication – of people who were "problematic" or had done something problematic. The "calling out" often led to ruptures in the community, and demands that perpetrators be "taken down", and socially cast out of communities – never to be associated with again. This puritanical "social justice" culture was something we had both experienced and wanted to address through Love Intersections. Not because problematic behaviour should be ignored, but that this carceral approach to shaming and isolating people who made mistakes was harmful not just to individuals who are called out, and also to the communities they belong to. Another philosophy from Theatre for Living also inspired us to explore different paths to using arts for social justice; the notion that "problematic people" don't come from outer space – that we grow them from our communities, and that by casting them out, we don't actually deal with the heart of the issues we want to transform. The works of Kai Cheng Thom, Mia Mingus, Syrus Marcus Ware, and the Black Lives Matter movement also influenced our desire to find creative ways in using the arts to make social justice interventions. How do we build communities, instead of building barriers?

Linked to these philosophies of community building is this notion of "calling in". We were inspired by Ngọc Loan Trần's (2013) *Calling IN: A Less Disposable Way of Holding Each Other Accountable*, which speaks to the practices of "calling in" folks in our communities that have caused harm:

> I picture 'calling in' as a practice of pulling folks back in who have strayed from us. It means extending to ourselves the reality that we will and do fuck up, we stray, and there will always be a chance for us to return. Calling in as a practice of loving each other enough to allow each other to make mistakes, a practice of loving ourselves enough to know that what we're trying to do here is a radical unlearning of everything we have been configured to believe is normal.

This inspired us to find different ways to address racism, patriarchy, and other forms of oppression. We wanted to explore approaches that didn't focus on the trauma of oppression (i.e. "oppression porn"), and the sufferings of people of colour. Rather, we wanted to find ways to use arts to celebrate the lives, identities, and cultures of queer black, Indigenous, people of colour.

Love Intersections began as a series of short documentaries on QTBIPOC (Queer, Trans, Black and Indigenous People of Colour), in an effort to make an intervention on the dominant white queer narrative where we did not see ourselves represented. Love Intersections emerged from a genealogy of queer of colour organizing, and also at a time in Vancouver, in Canada, and around the world, where tensions around the issues of race in queer communities were reaching a boiling point. The 2017 Black Lives Matter protest at Toronto Pride, alongside other Black and Indigenous organizing for prison and police abolition, corporate pinkwashing, Palestinian solidarity and BDS movements against Israeli pinkwashing, are key moments in the racial politics that foregrounded the formation of Love Intersections. At the time, we were solely focused on 'implementing intersectionality' in our art making as a way to make interventions on systemic oppressions. This framework was how we began to articulate our approach of using arts to contribute to our collective and intersecting struggles against racism.

2 Philosophy / Ethos

As documentary filmmakers, we knew that we had to do things differently. Documentarians have a history of parachuting into communities, using exploitative practices of extracting stories from people, and editing the stories to their predetermined scripts – often to produce drama, and to satisfy funding requirements, at the expense of their participants. The salacious media coverage of the Chinese community during the Vancouver School Board controversy is another example of the exploitative nature of sharing aspects of a community's story.

To address this, we built in several key guiding principles in our art making. Firstly, doing work by invitation and not deciding without consent, what stories to tell. Theatre for Living's outreach methodology also informed this philosophy; a core ethic that doing art about social issues involves meaningful collaboration and partnership with communities, and where real relationships are being forged. This value means that the filmmaking process requires built-in, and ongoing consent with participants. David's work with Hello Cool World (a social justice communications company) also inspired some of these ethical filmmaking practices that Love Intersections began to develop, including finding ways to have the participants of the films co-direct the final product of the films.

This collaborative filmmaking process means that the participants have full control over how their stories are told. Similarly in the interview process, we always share interview questions prior to the day of filming, and participants can add, reject, modify questions to their liking. Questions are also always open-ended, and as broad as possible, to allow for the participants to drive the interview process. Finally, Love Intersections offers participants final "veto" power – even at the very last stage of the filmmaking process, if the participants decide to pull their participation in the film, we simply will not premiere or share the film. This comes at a huge financial risk for Love Intersections, but it also reflects the trust and confidence that both of us strive to have with the participants. By working closely with participants, the ownership of the work is also weighted to the communities, and thus most of the films Love Intersections has made has had a deep community "buy in" and ultimately, trust.

An example of this was the production of the film "Carla and Hayfa" – a story about a queer Palestinian-Lebanese person and their family. The filming took place shortly after the Israeli bombing of the Gaza strip in 2014, and the original interview structure included questions about the Israeli occupation of Palestine. In reviewing the questions, Hayfa agreed that the issues of the occupation were important to include but suggested that the way to address them was to focus on her family's love. The process of making this film also changed the way that Jen and David made their future films – that through using film to celebrate love, community, and family, we can address systemic issues.

Doing work "by invitation" also means a practice of listening to communities and hearing the needs of communities. The notion of "intersectional" means contending with layers of identity, and how different systems of power and privilege affect different communities. In practice, this means that the issue that is being "centered" constantly requires attention and malleability. If intersectionality requires us to pay attention to how systemic oppression produces different lived experiences for people in different bodies and communities, then as artists, the work we produce should reflect what is happening in the communities we are representing, whether that be our own, or our collaborators.

One of our core founding values was to decentre directorial power, including giving decision-making authorities to all film participants in every stage of the production and post-production process. Another core tenet we believed in was to only do work by invitation and collaboration, so that the communities we work with felt a sense of ownership of the projects. We also believe that the process of art making is more important than the outcome, and we strived to build genuine reciprocal relationships with the communities that we were collaborating with. This model of prioritizing relationships above neoliberal aesthetic value has also allowed for communities that we collaborate with to "own" the work in a meaningful way. Specifically, prioritizing process over product helped us to deepen our relationships with community members, resulting in a more meaningful creative experience that further encourages future collaboration opportunities.

This early development of our filmmaking model revealed to us, that the impact of the work was not only the engagements with the art objects, but that embodying social justice tenets within our art making processes produces discursive shifts in communities that are transformative in ways that are different than our initial inclinations towards 'increasing representation'. In fact, it was at this point where we started to see the limitations of the politics of representation and began to think deeply about the potential for art making to imagine new worlds beyond representation and recognition. We were inspired by the work of activists and artists around us who were interrogating the tokenistic gestures of representation in "diversity and inclusion" initiatives that were becoming increasingly common in not only the art world, but many other sectors of society. What purpose is affirmative action and representation if it does not shift the foundations of white supremacy upon which racism and colonialism is premised? How can our arts practice recalibrate our relationships to one another, to non-humans, and to the earth? These questions emerged for us, leading us to think more deeply about our work on increasing the visibility of marginalized queer BIPOC people, and find new strategies and methodologies for art and cultural production that interrogates racist and colonial logics, beyond affirmative action and representation.

David Lloyd's interrogation of the (racist) trajectory of aesthetic theory offers us an analytical approach to grapple with the limitations of representational multiculturalism politics. He argues that "[r]epresentation regulates the distribution of racial identifications along developmental trajectory: The racialized remain "under representation", on the threshold of humanity, and not yet capable of freedom and civility as aesthetic thought defines those attributes" (Lloyd 2018: 91). His book *Under Representation* explores how aesthetic philosophy – in particular, Kant's critique of aesthetics – is based upon the notion of development and 'progress' (transcendence), and that 'the racial' indicates the threshold of humanity or who is defined as 'human' in this trajectory of development. Referencing Denise Ferreira da Silva's work on the racial, Lloyd argues that the demands for representation are self-defeating, in that logics of exclusion continue to be reinforced by these claims (Da Silva 2007: XXIV; Lloyd, 2018: 8, 91). The demands for representation and affirmative action that do not shift the underpinning foundational values of white supremacy and systemic racism, will inevitably serve to reinforce and reproduce the racist structures that deem Black people and Indigenous people ('The Savage') as under the threshold of humanity.

When we think about these themes of representation and affirmative action and how they do (and do not) transform racial logics; Glen Coulthard's interrogation of Canadian "multiculturalism" and the politics of recognition also foregrounded much of our thinking of art and cultural production with the intent on shifting racist attitudes and behaviours. In his book Red Skin, White Masks, he discusses the limitations of liberal claims for affirmation and accommodation under colonial subjugation. In referencing the Fanon's

Black Skin, White Masks, and the Hegelian notion of recognition of how one becomes a subject through being recognized by another subject (2014: 28), Coulthard discusses the sanctions under which the Indigenous colonized subject is recognized. In Canada, this manifests as the social formation of 'multiculturalism', which Coulthard argues is large-scale recognition (p. 28), which operates to maintain the conditions of the white supremacist and colonial status quo. Coulthard argues that liberal political organizing for accommodation and recognition upholds and reinforces the colonial system, in that it fails to confront the structure of colonialism itself (35). He proposes a fundamental shift in political organizing, away from affirmative recognition, towards upheaving the current system by redeploying Indigenous cultural practices, in solidarity with those with similar ethical commitments (43). To link to Lloyd, and discourses of aesthetics and race, 'recognition' of minorities is sanctioned under parameters imposed by the colonial nation state, and therefore, claims for affirmative recognition (for example, accommodations in the form of contemporary 'diversity and inclusion' policies Canadian arts funding agencies), reinforce the differential, exclusionary structures of white supremacy.

Lloyd's critique of aesthetic theory and its conception of the racial also connects to part of our approach to art and transformation, that engages with Indigenous theories on decolonization. Linda Tuhiwai-Smith (2012) discusses the 'regimes of truth' in her book Decolonizing Methodologies, where she describes how colonial history (in her account of Hegel), produces the human subject: 'Us' (West) vs 'them' (the Other), and that those who are not regarded as human – the racial – are 'prehistoric' (33). Tuhiwai-Smith argues that Western research and knowledge production has long been a colonial tool to subjugate Indigenous people, and that the extractive, transactional nature of colonialism underpins imperial traditions of Western research, that ultimately uphold the colonial status quo. Tuhiwai-Smith and Shawn Wilson's book Research is Ceremony: Indigenous Research Practices describe the 5 Rs of decolonization: respect, relevancy, reciprocity, relationality, and responsibility (Wilson 2008), as guiding principles for decolonization approaches to research methodologies. The 5 Rs reflect the structural and systemic demands of decolonization approaches, which deem colonial ontologies irreconcilable with Indigenous approaches.

This framework recognizes how the claims for representation (and recognition) actually reinforce and reify the colonial system, and instead, demand for a transformation of values, away from colonial white supremacy. The 5Rs suggest that decolonization discourse demands what Karen Barad (2007) calls an "ethico-onto-epistemological" consideration: contending with the entanglements of ethics within knowledge production – between humans, human and non-humans, the land, and with the past and present. The possibilities of ethico-onto-epistemological transformation formed the core of our approach to art making through Love Intersections: using collaborative art making with QTIBIPOCs to shift attitudes and worldviews at an embodied level.

3 Responding to Homonationalism

Discourses on homonationalism have also been deeply influential to our approach to cultural production and social justice. Omisoore Dryden and

Suzanne Lenon's book Disrupting *Queer Inclusion: Canadian Homonationalisms and the Politics of Belonging* (2015), Lisa Duggen's *The New Homonormativity: The Sexual Politics of Neoliberalism* (2015), and Jasbir Puar's Terrorist Assemblages (2018), discuss the different ways that gender and sexuality movements for LGBTQ2S+ 'inclusion' have been subsumed into the fold of the agenda of nationalism and pro-war imperialism. Puar's book traces how the liberal configurations of gender and sexuality rights have been appropriated into nationalist agendas, which reinforce Orientalist racial regimes that mark brown and black bodies conducive for necropolitical control and death. In Disrupting Queer Inclusion, Dryden and Lenon argue that Canadian homonationalism is produced through an assemblage of neoliberalism, capital accumulation, rhetorics of Canadian exceptionalism, which functions to reproduce systemic asymmetries, which upholds settler colonialism (6).

Homonationalism is also a theme that we've explored through several Love Intersections art and community organizing projects. In 2020, Love Intersections was commissioned to produce a video installation for the Queer Arts Festival (curated by Jonny Sopotiuk), on the themes of homonationalism. We titled the piece The Haunting of Huijing, which employs the Chinese myth of the Hulijing 狐狸精 (9 tailed fox) as a metaphor for fear and disruption to homonationalist discourse. The story of the Hulijing revolves around this fox spirit, who takes on a mortal form to seduce and instill fear in humans. The film uses the Hulijing myth as a way to respond to the biopolitical power that homonationalism helps to regulate: the disciplining of queer bodies into what is productive under neoliberal capitalism, and the naturalization of racial regimes of white normativity that support neo-imperialism. What we wanted to explore is the notion that homonationalism functions to stabilize the nation state, and that xenophobia towards QTIBIPOC are grounded in the threat that transgressions to homonationalism poses to the nation state. This 'phobia' is what we wanted to play with and reclaim: if queers who are outside of homonationalism are constructed as dangerous, fearful bodies needing to be controlled and disciplined, how can we reclaim and reimagine that space of foreclosure? Recognizing also that this refusal of the regulatory regimes of homonationalism produces xenophobic feelings of 'fear' towards abjected bodies, The Haunting of Hulijing focuses on the possibilities of that refusal; that the feelings of 'fear' can reflect destabilizations of homonationalism that are generative. In creating the images for the installation, we used inspiration from macabre and horror to create the tension of threats to homonationalism: a transgression of homonationalist values, at a deeper, embodied, spiritual level – and these values, represented by the Hulijing are irreconcilable under the homonationalist nation-state, thus producing discomforts.

We shot the film in three thematic 'worlds': dystopia, apocalypse, and utopia – to elucidate a queer of colour imagination of a world where the necropolitics of homonationalism could be disturbed by racialized bodies that transgress assimilatory enforcement. In *Cruising Utopias*, Jose Esteban Muñoz (2009) discusses the ways that aesthetics fuel political imagination and suggests that the metaphor of 'utopia', Muñoz suggests that our imaginations of utopias and futurities are key strategies for worldmaking (40). He suggests that the temporality of utopia offers strategies for using the past to map a future, and that this imagining of futurity is a way that we can think about the possibilities for transformation (112). He argues that queers live in a temporal bind that is calibrated through state power and therefore upheld by homonationalism. Along similar themes, *The Haunting of Hulijing* plays with this idea of queer of colour imaginations: apocalyptic worlds, where our bodies transgressions of the homonationalist stoke fears of an end of the world.

4 Diasporic Temporalities

In 2019, we produced Yellow Peril: Queer Destiny – an experimental documentary film that follows the story of Vancouver-based drag artist, Maiden China (Kendell Yan), and her explorations of racial, cultural, diasporic, sexual, and gender identity. In the development of this film, we wanted to experiment with imagery that reflected the spiritual, metaphysical, cosmic, interpersonal, relational experiences of our queer and cultural identities. As a filmmaking methodology, we employed the metaphor of the "Five Elements" in Chinese culture to explore the discursive formation of queer Chinese diasporic identity. The "Five Elements" also have many different applications to understanding life, identity, relationships, health (relationships between organs); they're also known as the Five Phases, the Five Agents, the Five Movements, Five Processes, the Five Steps/Stages and the Five Planets; each element is related to a sensory organ, to taste, and to smell. The elements also have numerous approaches to understanding ways of "being"; they also have principles of metaphysics, and temporalities. We invoked these five elements through the cinematography, as a conduit to understanding queer East Asian cultural formations, as not an intellectual delineation, but a way to investigate the embodiment of queer Chinese, diasporic identity.

In designing the production of the film, we were drawn particularly to a theme that Judith Butler explores in Bodies That Matter (2015): "the order of sexual difference is not prior to that of race or class in the constitution of the subject" (89). Butler uses the documentary Paris is Burning to discuss how symbolic regulatory regimes are simultaneously "a racializing set of norms, while also producing racially informed conceptions of sex" (89). This articulation of the formations of race, gender and sexuality offered to us a different imagination of identity and lived experience beyond the notion of the intersection, in that the norms of sexuality are informed by discourses of race and sex. Butler argues that these symbols are phantasmically instituted and sustained (88), suggesting that power as discourse reifies the symbolic by discursive reiterations through performance (93).

Gayatri Gopinath's analysis of the spatial and temporal formations of diasporic identities also offers a broader conception of 'identity' beyond the body and the material. In *Unruly Visions*, Gopinath (2018) traces the interrelationship between space, history, affect and aesthetics, in the emergence of queer of colour and diasporic epistemologies. She argues that diasporic aesthetic practices are a way of imagining alternatives to white settlerism, by reorienting the normative and regulatory spatial and temporal regimes of white heteronormativity and homonationalism, which are underpinned by modernity (61, 101). Gopinath interrogates the notion of geography, space, and region, reflecting how diasporic notions of "the region" also reify linear temporality and modernity, by figuring the region as premodern (29). The racialized diasporic subject straddles multiple spaces, both removed from the 'motherland', yet abjected from the white normativity in their new homes. This notion of hyphenated spaces, obscured identities, and themes of not belonging also reflect what we wanted to explore in Yellow Peril: Queer Destiny.

These theoretical themes from Gopinath and Butler reveal new strategies and tools for contending with identity and lived experience in my arts practice, beyond (how we were conceiving of) an 'intersectional' approach, that opens up an artistic and philosophical language to explore a wider scope of nuance and depth. Inspired by Butler and Gopinath, we attempted to explore new tools to express our experiences of gender and sexuality. The result of this exploration was our employment of "五行" – the Five Elements – as an aesthetic medium, which opened up wider metaphoric imaginations for creating video scenes that reflected the nuances of identity, spirituality, and temporality that we wanted to explore in the film.

Gayatri Gopinath describes curatorial practices (referencing Erica Lehrer and Synthia E. Milton) as "not only as selection, design, and interpretation, but as care-taking – as a kind of intimate, intersubjective, interrelational obligation", including an obligation to deal with the past (p. 4). "Queer scholars have powerfully demonstrated the ways in which queer art, scholarship, and activism, have always evinced a sense of obligation to document, analyze, archive, and value the small, the inconsequential, and the ephemeral, so much of which make up the messy beauty and drama of queer life-worlds" (4). This approach of rethinking and reimagining the concept of temporality in explorations of queer diasporic identity includes a reckoning (and caring) of the past, in order to imagine new futures (133). This notion of temporalizing queer diasporic discourse led us to rethink the notion of temporal linearity that is afforded to dominant subjects (i.e. white, cis-hetereonormative, male) and to contend with how we were conceptualizing 'the past' in our work of imagining queer East Asian futures.

When we were developing the themes that we wanted to explore in the film, we knew that we wanted to include a conversation about ancestry, and the elders that paved the way before us. We were heavily influenced by our dear friend, Chinese-Canadian artist Paul Wong, whose 1990 touring exhibition, "Yellow Peril: Reconsidered" was ahead of its time in featuring Asian Canadians from different artistic backgrounds exploring their heritage and identity. Paul's prolific work as a queer Asian artist in the 80s and 90s, and the barriers he overcame, paved the path for us to do our work today.

In one of the scenes from Yellow Peril: Queer Destiny, we performed an ancestral veneration ceremony at Larwill Park in Vancouver, which was the original gathering site of the anti-Oriental riots in Vancouver in 1907. We originally conceived the ceremony to honour the past, referencing yellow peril Sinophobia in the 20th century, which re-emerged when we made the film in the form of xenophobia around the housing crisis – and again this year in the form of anti-Chinese, coronavirus-related hate crimes. However, when we began editing the film, we realized there were elements of the temporal relationship between ancestry/history, our present work as artists-activists, and our visions of the future – that were critical to articulate in our film on queer diasporic futurity. In Chinese culture, ancestral veneration is a ceremony that pays homage to relatives in the spirit world, with the underlying belief that you carry your ancestors with you, and that they inform your family and life today. As we crafted the film together, we used the ceremony at Larwill Park as a metaphor of collapsing the temporal boundaries of past, present, and future by reflecting the shared histories of queer people in the Asian diaspora that we hold in present day.

We were also inspired by Saidiya Hartman's *Scenes of Subjection*, in particular, her technique of temporal confusion, where she describes how the performances of black subjugation today reflect the subjugation of the past, and that this 'temporal glitch' reveals the conditions of anti-Blackness that underpin systemic racism, that continues till today (Hartman 1997). Abstracting from Hartman's theorizing of race and time, we further explored temporalizing queer diasporic identity in Yellow Peril; The Celestial Elements (the visual art exhibit that followed the film Yellow Peril: Queer Destiny), where we created an installation called The Wall of Healing: A Race Towards a Cosmic Future. The piece centred around an altar, where we placed objects that referenced medicine, funeral rites (joss paper), cosmology, spirituality, and ancestry. This assemblage intended to create an image of this temporalizing – the collapsing of linear temporal boundaries of diasporic culture, queerness and identity, and thinking about these identity journeys from a spiritual, embodied, and historical perspective. We wanted to articulate this temporal conflation, or as Jose Esteban Muñoz refers to as, "engaging in collective temporal distortion" in order to reimagine the straight, linear, temporality of white cisheteropatriarchy.

This discourse around cultural identity and cultural knowledge reference the 'messiness' of diasporic subjectivity, which produce anxieties within communities of colour. Martin Manalansan refers to this as "messiness of queer migratory lives", that our genealogies are erased or detached from the colonial archives of our new homes, and the fact that our ancestral lineages are often interrupted by trauma is weaponized by the dominant white society to discredit claims for inclusion (Manalansan 2000; Diaz 2016). This feeling of double rejection – not belonging in the 'motherland' and not belonging in the new space, is also a core theme that we explored in Yellow Peril: Queer Destiny (2019), particularly the policing and gatekeeping of culture within racialized cultural spaces. In one scene, Maiden China shares how she has been accused of commodifying or appropriating her own culture; the notion of being "not Chinese enough", as if culture is static, and remains in one place and can only be accessed under certain (imaginary) conditions. In another scene, Maiden China describes a performance she did at a drag competition in Vancouver, where she asked her friend to borrow a lion dancing costume from a local martial arts studio. Their intention was to bring Chinese cultural elements into a queer space (which is predominately white), to disrupt the white normativity in the space. After the performance, someone from the martial arts studio who saw pictures of them with the lion costume, called them out for taking a lion costume for a drag performance – which he was only allowed to perform after practicing martial arts for many years. He felt that their use of the lion costume, without the years of martial arts training, was disrespectful to the tradition.

The editing of this story in the film was a challenging process, because we debated how we were going to hold the complexity of the tensions, while honouring the stories of all the people involved, recognizing that these tensions, produced by the cultural anxieties discussed above, are products of white supremacy. We wanted to edit the scene in a way that did not generate an antagonist, because we believed that all of the stories in this scene were valid. In fact, the complexity and messiness of this story is a way that as artists, we could consider complicating the narrative of Canadian multiculturalism. Robert Diaz (2018) discusses how complex histories of colonized (Filipino/a) bodies are a "corruptive presence on the stages of the seemingly sanitized Canadian multicultural mosaic" (332). This scene that we produced in the film references the generative imaginations of diasporic messiness as a form of disruption to the hegemonic narratives of Canadian immigration. When we screened the film at festivals last year, many questions were asked about this scene from other queer Chinese people who shared stories of similar anxieties they have felt when they tried to reclaim or relearn traditional cultural practices.

5 Futurity

Our story continues to be written, so in lieu of a "conclusion", we end this chapter with an imagination and intention of how we might actualize love and intersectionality in the world. Since founding Love Intersections, our journey has centered around using art and cultural production to shift systemic asymmetries that underpin our ways of thinking and being. How can art – and the process of creation, exhibition, and outreach – reconfigure our relations to one another at an embodied level? How can art practice be used to transform our communities away from colonial, white supremacist logics? How can we strengthen our community bonds and continue to build relationships instead of building barriers? We find ourselves with more questions than questions answered.

In thinking through our non-linear timeline, and looking beyond the knowability of the future, we at Love Intersections hope to continue pushing the boundaries of what it means to be queer artists-of-colour, to take creative risks also means risking your relationships, your spoons, your paycheque.

So you can see, that all of these threads come together for us – relationality, responsibility, queer kinship and story – has only deepened our responsibilities as artists and activists. In today's political climate, we must think deeply about relationships – and invest and imagine ourselves in relationship to one another, just as we are tasked with imagining and investing in a just and equitable future. Because what stands in opposition to hate? Relationships. Thoughtful, tender, co-constitutive and labourious relationships – that are ongoing, fleshy, and complex. When we are in relationships with each other, we are building our communities, and nourishing more queer kinships to grow, for young people and elders to find a sense of safety and belonging, and for us to see our stories reflected back to us. So, let's eat, let's dream, let's build towards and truly be in relation with each other.

References

Barad, K. (2007) *Meeting the Universe Halfway: Quantum Physics and the Entanglement of Matter and Meaning*. Durham: Duke University Press.

Butler, J. (2015) *Bodies That Matter: On the Discursive Limits of Sex*. New York: Routledge.

CBC News (2014) Real Estate Controversy LGBT Policy. *CBC*, June 16. https://www.cbc.ca/news/canada/british-columbia/transgender-policy-adopted-by-vancouver-school-board-1.2676879.

Coulthard, G. S. (2014) *Red Skin, White Masks: Rejecting the Colonial Politics of Recognition*. Minneapolis: University of Minnesota Press.

Cruz, A., and Manalansan, M. F. (2002) *Queer Globalizations: Citizenship and the Afterlife of Colonialism*. New York: New York University Press.

Da Silva, D. F. (2007) *Toward a Global Idea of Race*. Minneapolis: University of Minnesota Press.

Diamond, D. (2007) *Theatre For Living: The Art and Science of Community-Based Dialogue*. Trafford Publishing.

Diaz, R. (2018) The Ruse of Respectability: Familial Attachments and Queer Filipino Canadian Critique. *Asian Diasporic Visual Cultures and the Americas* 4(1–2): 114–136.

Gopinath, G. (2018) *Unruly Visions: The Aesthetic Practices of Queer Diaspora*. Durham: Duke University Press.

Hartman, S. (2003) *Scenes of Subjection: Terror, Slavery, and Self-Making in Nineteenth-Century America*. New York: Oxford University Press.

Jimmy, E., Andreotti, V., and Stein, S. (2019) *Towards Braiding*. Creative Commons.

Li, X. (2007) *Voices Rising: Asian Canadian Cultural Activism*. Vancouver: UBC Press.

Lloyd, D. (2018) *Under Representation*. New York: Fordham University Press.

Manalansan, M. F. (2000) *Cultural compass: Ethnographic Explorations of Asian America*. Philadelphia: Temple University Press.

Muñoz, José E. (1999) *Disidentifications: Queers of Color and the Performance of Politics*. Minneapolis: University of Minnesota Press.

Puar, J. K. (2018) *Terrorist Assemblages: Homonationalism in Queer Times (Second ed)*. Durham: Duke University Press.

Thom, K. C. (2019) *I Hope We Choose Love*. Vancouver Arsenal Pulp Press.

Todd, D. (2013) Vancouver's 100,000 Chinese Christians 'Fraught' over Gay Debate. *Vancouver Sun*, June 30. https://vancouversun.com/life/vancouvers-100000-chinese-christians-fraught-over-gays/.

Todd, D. (2014) Ethnic Chinese Groups Protest LGBT Programs Again. *Vancouver Sun*, May 29. https://vancouversun.com/news/staff-blogs/ethnic-chinese-once-again-protest-lgbt- programs/.

Trần, Ngọc Loan (2013) Calling IN: A Less Disposable Way of Holding Each Other Accountable. *BGD*, Dec 18. http://www.bgdblog.org/2013/12/calling-less-disposable-way-holding-accountable/.

Tuhiwai-Smith, L. (2012) *Decolonizing Methodologies: Research and Indigenous Peoples*. London: Zed Books.

Wilson, S. (2008) *Research is Ceremony: Indigenous Research Methods*. Black Point, N.S: Fernwood Pub.

CHAPTER 11

Emergent Asian-Canadian Feminisms: Insights from Young Filipina/x Feminist Scholar-Organizers

Monica Batac, Julia Baladad, Psalmae Tesalona, Chloe Rodriguez and France Clare Stohner

> To begin theorizing asian feminist consciousness then, one begins with one's own lived, messy, and contradictory experiences by contributing from one's own standpoints.
>
> JO-ANNE LEE

∴

2019 was a year of excited activity for Filipina/x feminist organizing at an unlikely and unexpected site, McGill University (Tiotià:ke/Montréal, Québec). We celebrate and affirm our joint efforts in co-organizing[1] a feminist conference, PINAY POWER II (PPII) [2]. As young feminists who identify as Filipina/x scholars, we turn to scholarly literatures to find something recognizable and reflective of our own experiences. We try to find ourselves in the bodies of literature, while simultaneously searching for pockets of belonging on campus. This search has brought us together to organize and write.

Initial internet searches helped us find remnants of gatherings[3] occurring in other Canadian universities to bring together Filipino academics and community members. As students, we were unsettled by the felt absence of activities

---

1 Other members of the organizing team include Alexandra De Guzman, Amita Biona, and Monica Manuel; Karla Villanueva Danan, Claire Bautista, Sabrina Gill, and Joanne Chio also supported earlier planning and organizing efforts. More information can be found at pinaypower.ca.

2 The conference title, PINAY POWER II, recognizes the scholarly work of Dr. Melinda Luisa de Jesús who assembled the anthology, *Pinay Power: Peminist Critical Theory: Theorizing the Filipina/American Experience* (2005). She also came as a senior fellow with the Institute for Gender, Sexuality, and Feminist Studies in the weeks leading up to the conference.

3 Such as the 2009 conference at University of Toronto organized by Kritical Kolectibo (Goyette, 2009), which resulted in an anthology, *Filipinos in Canada* (Coloma et al., 2012).

and conversations taking place at McGill. We had missed out, disappointed that we could not find similar spaces or events to develop a sense of scholarly and community belonging.[4] Determined to both locate and contextualize our own emerging Filipina/x feminist praxis, we organized ourselves. Today, we collectively identify with an emerging generation of Filipina/x feminist scholars searching for and creating spaces for diasporic community-building within our academic institutions. In this chapter, we weave our individual experiences with threads from Jo-Anne Lee's articulation of asian-canadian feminisms (acf; 2006), with the affirmation that this feminist theorization is painful, yet healing and generative (Nievera-Lozano, 2013, 2020).

We center the experiences of three Filipina/x undergraduate students at McGill, an elite Canadian academic institution. Through their own lived experience and positionalities, Julia Baladad, Psalmae Tesalona, and Chloe Rodriguez[5] of the PPII team theoretically intervene in our understanding of Asian "Canadian" feminisms. Recognizing the hauntings of McGill's historical ties to colonization, Black enslavement and the ever-pervasiveness of whiteness coded as intellectual prestige (hampton, 2020), the chapter puts in conversation three shared yet distinct subject positions: the Filipina American (Julia), Filipina/x Canadian (Psalmae), and Filipina diasporic (Chloe) student, each finding their place within the Canadian nation-state and at McGill. Their reflections help us to understand the specificities of their experiences, instead of claiming the amorphous yet strategically utilized "Asian" identity. Their stories provide insight in how their conscious Filipina/x feminist identity formation and politics develop and refine through their research, education, and community organizing on campus.

We exist alongside prominent tropes of Filipina transnational and diasporic bodies such as caregivers and balikbayans, sex workers and mail-order brides (Velasco 2020). We insist on examining the experiences of Filipina/x diasporic students. Simultaneously, we acknowledge the inherent tensions in naming our experiences. Jo-Anne Lee (2006: 22) describes such strains as simultaneously "a plea for connection … a rant … a two-step dance of ambiguity and

4 The graduate student organizers (Monica and France) have written elsewhere about their early motivations behind organizing the PPII conference (Batac, 2020, 2022; Batac, Stohner, & Danan, 2022).

5 The three were paid workers through McGill's Work Study program. On paper, these roles were under Monica's supervision. Julia Baladad created a short video that illustrates, from her perspective, the decolonial feminist orientation in our group organizing efforts. This orientation resisted the supposed hierarchical formation of student-supervisor towards a relational, peer supported learning approach. You can view the video at https://www.youtube.com/watch?v=-EoUoqq563Y

contradiction." As diasporic Filipina/x feminists, we too contingently claim acf as it enables us to speak our truths from our own distinct experiences. We come to pen this self-articulation as students, wherein our difficult educational journeys have compelled us to refine our critical self-awareness. Lee encourages us to "write, publish, and circulate this consciousness" (34).

We began to sense our own distinct and emergent form of feminist organizing and community building inherent in our relational approach to working with each other. Held together in our intimate work in navigating McGill and the broader Montréal Filipino community for the PPII gathering, we offer this chapter as an attempt to shed light on this emergent feminism, for which we are coming to understand through this reflexive writing. This writing is also part memory work, as it enables us as "diasporic subjects … to revisit the past and present and work through those pains, individually and collectively" (Kwak 2017: 360).

Prior to PPII, Julia, Psalmae, and Chloe had little to no exposure to Filipina feminist scholarship or activism. While Filipinos are one of the fasting growing communities in Canada, according to the Canadian Association of University Teachers (CAUT), Filipinos represented 0.3 percent of all university teachers in Canada, up from 0.2 percent a decade earlier. The absence of Filipina/x/o scholars in the professoriate, let alone the exposure to Filipina/x feminist scholarship, are thus material concerns. The prevalent underrepresentation of Filipina/x/o students in Canadian universities is a concern "often not taking seriously" (Kwak 2017: 357). We pen these words as an explicit response to the pervasive invisibility of Filipina/x youth labour in scholarly and community organizing in Canada (see McElhinny et al. 2012). We engage with the themes of *in/visibility, disability,* and *diasporic isolation* to illustrate the pedagogical power in empowering diverse Filipina/x diasporic students studying at Canadian academic institutions to name their experiences and write their own stories about embracing feminism.

1 Choosing Visibility: Julia Baladad

> Asian Americans as a whole are finally coming to claim their own, demanding that they be included in the multicultural history of our country … It took forever. Perhaps it is important to ask ourselves why it took so long. We should ask ourselves this question just when we think we are emerging as a viable minority in the fabric of our society … We, the visible minority that is invisible.
>
> MITSUYE YAMADA (2015)

The lived experiences of Asian Americans and Asian Canadians in academia are ones of struggle. We find ourselves operating under overbearing pressures and expectations to overachieve and succeed, because to our classmates, professors, and families, Asian equals smart and effortlessly intelligent. While we learn the histories of the Western world, we are not encouraged to question this canon nor research our own stories of migrations, labour, and traumas. When our own stories are unwelcomed and erased in academia, what then is our place within the classroom? Guided by these difficult and recurrent reflections, I share my story of growth and struggle as an emerging feminist of colour, my coming to terms with my feminism within the Canadian context as an Asian American. I offer insight into my lived experiences in navigating my way through McGill as a racialized woman, and what I learned through organizing the PPII conference. This essay discloses my experiences of in/visibility, belonging, and identity.

I grew up in the predominantly white North suburbs of Chicago as a daughter of Filipino immigrants. Since I never had an explicit conversation about race with my parents, I convinced my childhood self that I was half-Filipino and half-American. This mirrored my experiences of being in either Filipino or white spaces, with no in-between, compelling me to accept this oversimplified identity as truth. I felt too American within my Filipino community ("*Amerikana ka talaga,*" my relatives and neighbors would tell me) while also whitewashing myself in hopes that my white peers would somehow look past my brown body.

Indeed, the early formations of my racial awareness resulted mostly from my experiences in classrooms. Entering school complicated my understanding of my identity, as my classmates and teachers identified me as Asian. "But you don't look like the typical Asian," they would say to me, suddenly making me self-conscious about how my body was being racially categorized by the world. In high school, a teacher continuously confused me and the only other Filipina in the class during attendance, even though she never mixed up the names of our white classmates. Identity never seemed to be a problem for my white peers, yet mine seemed so difficult to grasp.

Despite my brown skin contrasting against the white bodies around me, no one saw me for who I was. To find a sense of belonging, I suppressed the "foreign" parts of myself and self-disciplined my behaviour through an external white lens. I unconsciously conformed to my white classmates' beliefs that Asians are a monolith, that we are self-effacing, smarter than average, docile, quiet and hardworking. As an Asian woman, I needed to be the most qualified person in the room, so I worked hard to perfect my English, enroll in Honours and AP classes, get straight-As, and then reprimanded myself when I did anything less. I used my intelligence to gain respect in the classroom. I carried this mentality into university, unaware that I had deeply internalized a white hegemonic understanding of self.

This is my struggle of invisibility. It is being conditioned to become passive. It is remaining silent against racist and sexist remarks. It is lacking a grounding sense of self. It is feeling uncomfortable and undeserving of claiming and taking up space, preferring to remain in the margins. It is upholding the status quo for my (our) survival. This dull comfort of being unseen offers me some protection, but it has resulted in my own perpetuation of Asian American model minority myth, where we are no longer vulnerable to the violence of racism because of our supposed economic status and success. This struggle and acceptance of invisibility means being complicit in my own discrimination.

I uprooted myself from home to study in Canada, hoping to find some grounding and a sense of belonging in university, a space that prides itself in diversity and inclusivity. I moved to Tiotià:ke/Montréal, nervous and excited to be somewhere new and far away. I joined PPII in my second year of undergrad because I needed a job and it was surprisingly Filipino-related. So I seized the opportunity, simply happy to come across other Filipinos on campus for the first time since I had moved there. I entered the position with little knowledge about Filipina-centric feminisms, feminist organizing, and even Asian diasporic experiences despite the fact that I was living this diasporic experience. My early understandings of feminism and activism excluded my Filipina identity, perceived as separate and irrelevant.

Monica once shared that international students and students of colour are always trying to find "pockets of belonging." Her words deeply resonated with me because they sparked in me a deep, critical examination of my own understanding of self. I sat with my identity in all its intersections and complexities for the first time. I was unsettled to finally see my situation through a different lens: I was a Filipina from the United States studying at a Canadian university, which only had two Filipino professors at the time, and I wasn't even aware if they offered any classes or content on anything from our culture. Most of my friends were white, and even the Asian friends I had were not Filipino. I was not aware of the lack of Asian scholarship in my classes, let alone Filipino/a/x scholarship. I was living the same reality of invisibility in my university. Through the PPII job posting, I discovered the anthology *Pinay Power: Peminist Critical Theory: Theorizing the Filipina/American Experience* (2005), my first encounter with scholarly work by Filipinas about Filipina American feminisms. For the very first time, I saw my own racialized experiences, my struggles with identity and belonging contextualized in feminist discourse.

Suddenly, I found myself on a team of all Filipinas/xs, and it felt like home. Gathering with them after two years away from community and family was grounding and familiar. I had finally found my roots away from home. These women understood and shared my feelings of isolation. They encouraged me to explicitly name my experiences, affirming me through it all. My struggles became easier to carry. Through the Filipinas/xs that I worked with and met at the conference, I began to understand the power of visibility and representation, the power of Filipina/x feminism in my life.

So why did I choose invisibility in the first place? Was it a choice? We tend to forget how seemingly instinctual invisibility is for Asian women. Visibility means challenging our stereotypes and disrupting the status quo of the silent, docile Asian woman. I assumed a lot of hurt and pain would come with visibility because I believed I had to endure it alone. However, PPII taught me to overcome this fear, because visibility, as I have witnessed, invites and demands community. Visibility allows me to learn and embrace my truths, viewing them as strengths and unique gifts rather than parts of me that need to be suppressed for the comfort of others. Visibility helped me see many of my struggles and traumas were shared: providing me the space to process this learning collectively.

My confidence only continued to grow when I began communicating with the Filipina/x feminist speakers—scholars, artists, students and community organizers—as part of my work for the conference. I began meeting Asian women who were not afraid to take up space, or be the loudest in the room. And I was going to welcome them to my campus. This conference became my awakening as I looked to these Filipinas/xs as mirrors, seeing my own potential strength and resiliency within theirs. These feminists were bringing to light issues within the Filipina/x community, such as the need for decolonization, the resurgence of Indigenous knowledges and traditions, the histories of our migrant and immigrant realities, and policies surrounding sex and domestic work. I wondered, "Have these stories always existed? Why am I only learning about all of this now?"

The majority of the conference was held in Leacock 232, a conference room that consistently hosts well-established intellectuals and important conferences, a room where many McGill students, including myself, have their classes. So what did it mean for us to take up the same space in McGill? By intentionally placing ourselves within the same walls in which we felt invisible, we carved out our own space of belonging and self-discovery. Our physical claim to space in the institution was a deliberate act of centering ourselves. In radically re-imagining the academic space by inviting artists, community members and organizers, cultural practitioners, and activists, we made visible diverse and equally valuable ways of learning from and being with one another.

Before PPII, I never had an opportunity to work on a project or initiative that spoke to me, that discussed and reflected my own lived experiences. I found myself prioritizing conference planning work over my own studies. We were still in the Winter semester with finals coming up. Yet I would finish all my schoolwork early to commit more of my time to the conference. I was sending emails to invited panelists during lectures, booking plane and train tickets during lunches with friends, meeting with Monica in between classes, and spending late (sometimes overnight) work sessions with the other undergraduate students to keep ourselves accountable to our work. I did not have the words for my emotions at the time, but I had finally found a community with whom I felt and knew I belonged. My feminist consciousness began to form through this work, but it was one that departed from and expanded beyond white-centric feminisms. In witnessing the radical Filipina/x feminists at the conference, I realized that it was the lack of our presence and our experiences in feminist literature and in classroom agendas that contributed to my struggles of invisibility and belonging. I no longer want to feel absent, and I am no longer content with being unheard, and so through this paper, I begin the work of naming, describing, and retelling my experiences.

Asian American and Asian Canadian feminists have a lot to say. My Filipina/x feminist community taught me to be stop being afraid of using my voice. When I am silent, I silence all the stories that have come before me. Through invisibility, I became fragmented from my identity. In choosing visibility, you invite in a community who accepts you for who you choose to be. PPII was an entry point for me into these teachings and awakenings. As Mitsuye Yamada (2015: 35) writes, "We need to raise our voices a little more, even as they say to us 'This is so uncharacteristic of you.' To finally recognize our own invisibility to finally be on the path toward visibility. Invisibility is not a natural state for anyone."

Through visibility, we are able to rewrite our narratives and carve out the spaces we need for our liberation and belonging. I hope my story inspires you to choose visibility and to choose yourself, for your communities are waiting.

2 Re-membering Kapwa—Feminist Organizing along Decolonial and Disability Justice Frameworks: Psalmae Tesalona

> This is the cruelty of ableism: it robs us from each other.
>
> MIA MINGUS (2012)

I remember my arrival to campus as though it were yesterday. The sun shimmered brightly over the gothic buildings, outshone only by my Filipina mother, proudly beaming her way through the campus tour. I distinctly remember our last embrace on the day she left and the deep breath I took as I attempted to memorize the comfort of her squeeze. Her hug imparted strength in its release, conveying her unspoken fears and quiet assurances that I had yet to understand as a young Filipina who had left home for the first time.

In my first-year Introduction to Feminist Studies course, I learned the academic language to speak about the politics of feminism. The most impactful part of this course was the feeling that I was simply returning to my mother's embrace in every paper on transnational feminism. Before I was taught feminism in formal classrooms, it was modelled to me by my Ates and Titas, my community, and my mom. I remembered feminism demonstrated in my mom's strength, my grandmothers' knowledge sharing through stories, and in witnessing the confidence and perseverance of Filipinx[6] folks navigating diasporic displacement and queerness.

Yet, despite this newfound familiarity of feminism rooted in my Filipina identity, my overall learning experience was isolating. While trying to make sense of my identity as a racialized, immigrant woman, my cognitive and invisible disabilities began manifesting themselves in new ways in my second year of study. The humiliation is all-consuming: being told I'm never able or disabled enough, at the mercy of a world that will not accommodate disabled people. Academia's inhospitality to students with disabilities haunts me in my own paper trail of archived emails containing apologies for my illness and remorseful requests for accommodations. I hold the trauma of being hospitalized for my disability during exam season and the distress of having to take finals on the hospital Wi-Fi when professors were unwilling to reschedule. I am haunted by my own self-doubt as someone profiled by mental health professionals as "high-functioning" and thus stubbornly unfit for treatment or support.

Critical disability scholars describe higher education as a place where the dividing lines of discrimination are reinforced through the stigmatization of any deviations from intellectual or physical perfection.[7] The classroom thus becomes a demanding stage to perform ability, (in)competence, and personhood. Asian American feminist scholars are naming the "killing machine" that is academia (Valverde et. al., 2020), and its effects on the bodies, minds, and

6 Filipinx is used as a term inclusive of Filipinos, Filipinas, and folks who search for a more gender-inclusive and/or non-binary self-identifier.

7 For instance, see Jay Dolmage (2017).

spirits of Asian women. Anxieties around any failure to adhere to the expectations of the model minority myth, paired with imposter syndrome are known to lead to debilitating, stress-induced short and long-term health outcomes. I internalized every failure, every misstep, and every missed opportunity as a reflection of my individual inferiority. My relationship with critical theories was unsettled by the increasing tensions between my neurodivergent mind, my Filipina/x identity, and my yearning to assert that I belonged despite my embodied betrayals. In *Care Work: Dreaming disability justice,* Piepzna-Samarasinha (2018) writes that disabled, mad,[8] crip,[9] racialized people shrink themselves as a response to our perceived nuisance. Feeling like a nuisance to my academic community, I shrank and shrank, refining my ability to pass for a (neuro)typical, Westernized, civilized academic-in-training. I learned to reject the fullness of resistant embodied living for some semblance of belonging until my academic work found its grounding in community work.

This essay is an ode to the PPII conference, a notable landmark in my feminist topography. As my first encounter with community organizing work, this conference remains a foundational experience that inspires my ongoing interrogation of the communities I move in service to and the principles that ground my work. In this paper, I reflect upon the genesis of my praxis, using the precolonial Filipino belief of kapwa, the shared self, as a decolonized feminist organizing framework when it is applied alongside the demands of disability justice. This is how kapwa called me into the work of decolonization, feminist solidarities, and liberatory love.

I met Monica at a McGill University Filipino Asian Students' Association (MUFASA) meeting in October 2018. Missing the comfort of hearing Tagalog and craving the company of other Filipinos, I spontaneously attended MUFASA's first general meeting of the fall term. The meeting was organized exactly as I had expected, with an abundance of Filipino snacks and the rambunctious noise of Filipino joy over the occasional cheesy Tagalog joke. Monica was the first Filipina PhD candidate I had ever met, and at this meeting, she proudly announced that she was planning a Filipina feminism conference.

I joined the PPII planning team in earnest. We were a small yet mighty task force of Pinays working on bringing over 200+ Filipina/xs together in the name of belonging. The mentorship of Monica and France Stohner, a community

8 "Mad" here alludes to the use of "mad" as a self-identifying term used by people who experience mental illness, intellectual disabilities, cognitive disabilities, and more (see Gorman 2013).

9 Similar to "mad," crip as used by Piepzna-Samarasinha (2018) is a reclaimed, self-identifying term used by disabled people.

organizer and Master's graduate in Counselling, was unlike anything I had experienced in an administrative role or internship. Although we were organizing within the formalities of an elite, exclusionary academic institution, we relied on the notion of kapwa as a belief framework that guided us towards alternative, radically inclusive organizing strategies. Filipina sociologist Clemen C. Aquino (2004) regards kapwa as a fundamental aspect to Filipino kinship formations. (Re)learning the principle of kapwa reminded me of Filipino kinship formations and community values that preceded Spanish, Japanese, and American colonization.

A concept of interdependence, the call of kapwa dispels "neoliberal myths of independence" (Mingus 2017) by pointing to our reliance on one another as the key to liberation. Kapwa can be understood as an anti-ableist principle through Mingus' concept of access intimacy, a liberatory tool that challenges hegemonic methods of accessibility organizing that neglects our relational needs. In kapwa, we struggle, (re)build, and navigate this inaccessible world together. Working with a narrow budget and all sorts of logistical constraints, our organizing team committed to providing free admission, the provision of hot meals, childcare, and programming at wheelchair-accessible venues to bring together as many Filipina/xs as possible. As an able-bodied Pinay, I remain reflective and accountable to the fact that there is always more that can, should, and could have been done to make our gathering spaces more accessible.

The love, presence, and mentorship of Filipina/xs from diverse sociopolitical positionalities and complex histories were the heart of our conference. The value of a generationally diverse feminist practice was made clear to me when we met the Filipina Tita-organizers of PINAY Québec, a coalition of Filipina domestic workers, care workers, activists, and community leaders who have been advocating for the rights of migrant women in Québec since the early 1990s. We had the pleasure of meeting with them over several months to support a documentary screening and community gathering at the Immigrant Workers Centre of Montréal. We spent the evening serving guests catered Filipino food, insisting that the Titas stay seated as we managed the bustle of the event. After the gathering, we stayed at the venue a little longer to ask the Titas how long they had been friends, what advice they had for dealing with community organizing burnout, and whether we could stay in touch.

"This is the furthest we've ever been from campus," our student team admitted, unconsciously processing the physical, intellectual, and emotional distances that stood between ourselves—Filipina/xs students—and our community beyond the walls of our university.

The spirit of kapwa breathed life into my feminist practice through the sisterhood that emerged between our undergraduate coalition. The intimacy and dependability of our friendships remains one of my most profound examples of revolutionary love. There was a prefigurative nature to the way we organized ourselves in service to one another and out of the unspoken understanding that we needed each other, more than ever before, now that our Filipina feminist dreams had been awakened. In the words of Mia Mingus (2017), disability justice and access intimacy are simply practices of love. Thus, kapwa is not only an anti-ableist organizing praxis; kapwa is an organizing framework born out of decolonial love. We loved one another through our work. We honoured each other's time, safety, and right to rest. We walked each other home, slept and cooked for one another in shifts, and camped in a fellow sister's one-bedroom apartment during the week of the conference as a demonstration of our commitment to sharing the weight of our fears, exhaustion and joy.

In *Living a Feminist Life,* Sara Ahmed (2017) describes the evolution of our feminist politics as an affective process that allows us to reinhabit our past, our bodies, and our spaces. The labour and love required of PPII helped me reinhabit my body, my mind and my cultural identity. Theories surrounding various facets of my lived experience, previously confined to classroom discussions, were now being applied in practice in my work.

I am but in the early process of reconciling how I hold multiple tensions in this work. I uphold stigmas against disability daily as I unlearn what it means to be a 'good' student. I am a settler-student invested in academic institutions that have yet to account for its colonial legacies, sites inhospitable to disabled and racialized students, and people who cannot afford entry into these privileged spaces of learning. Moving forward, I feel challenged in my commitment to manifest kapwa, decolonial organizing and access intimacy to reclaim the university space as a site of resistance, a place where belonging can be created in, with, and for community. I carry with me these lessons and relationships developed through PPII. For me, the work of establishing a feminist decolonization practice begins by undoing ableism in how we take care of ourselves and one another, and how we build new worlds together.

I hold these difficult lessons in light of my learnings from our imperfect organizing work: work that brought me right back into the arms of my community. The transformative power of kapwa and disability justice lies in knowing that together, we powerfully call forth another way, another world. When the speed at which my mind moves and the identifiers that set me apart provoke antagonism, I remind myself of my fundamental belonging, holding steadfast to the revolutionary calling to embody all that I am in the full. Never alone,

I walk crip, Filipina/x, asian canadian feminist paths with others and following the steps of those before us; we move together, we always have. From love and in kapwa, my journey towards liberation goes on.

3 Alienation and the Asian Diasporic Experience: Chloe Rodriguez

When I first arrived in Canada as an international student, I had little to no intention of reaffirming my Filipina identity. I was caught up in the immediacy of assimilation and adaptation. I disliked being known solely as "the international student from a-country-in-Asia-I-forget-where." I did not sit well with the many nameless assumptions and connotations that come with being "imported." And so I quietly allowed this part of myself to linger on the fringes.

It becomes easy to hide behind certain signifiers. I consciously tighten my grip on the English language, clinging to an unassuming, generic North American inflection. And when I get excited and talk too quickly, when I hear my *th* sounds morph into *d*s, I remind myself: speak softer. I am also light skinned and racialized as East Asian due to my Chinese-Filipino background. People often say,*"But you don't look Filipino to me!"* Their voices are full of bewilderment and self-assurance. I can only shrug. That's their problem. I did not come here to confirm people's assumptions.

"Ha!" I would think to myself, strangely pleased, "Sorry I don't fit in your little box."

But still. It stung to have my identity challenged so often.

I come from an expatriate family, having spent half of my life in the Philippines, the other half scattered across the map. I feel anchored to the Philippines as my homeland, while deeming myself a foreigner at the same time. Then, I came to Tiotià:ke/ Montréal to pursue my undergraduate degree. I liked that I could keep my origins ambiguous. I liked that I could be from anywhere and nowhere all at once. I tried to convince myself that rootlessness was freedom, that detaching myself from a certain identity meant that I could craft my own. I was a blank slate in a new environment, and I could control how others saw me. I wanted to be pleasant. Benign. Inconspicuous.

where are you from?

~~the philippines~~

oh, it's complicated.

I joined the PPII organizing team in the second semester of my first year at McGill. When I learned that a group of Filipina/x scholars and community organizers were hiring students for an upcoming conference, my initial reaction was excitement and a slight sense of disbelief. An entire space within feminism dedicated to the Filipina/x experience? I didn't know we had this kind of tradition, nor did I think it was something we *could* have.

I had worked in a number of work-study positions at McGill, but none of them have come close to the kinds of relationships and dynamics that we built around this conference. PPII was the first time I have ever encountered this notion of an Academic Ate (Surla 2019). Ate is the Tagalog word for older sister. This dynamic within our organizing team destabilized the employer/employee hierarchy and detachment from work that I had always anticipated. It also re-introduced concepts of mentorship, respect, and student activism. Student involvement evolved into intervention, and we were encouraged to question the academic spaces we occupied, rather than simply work within them. This was a novel concept to us undergraduates. We were resigned to the fact that we needed to define our work using the tools and frameworks provided by the Western academic institution. The familiarity imbued in the concept of an Ate, one that reaches beyond nuclear family structures to encompass a far-reaching system of Filipina/x togetherness, enabled us to overturn these expectations. We had work meetings on campus and at each other's homes, reconciling the personas we maintained throughout these different spaces. We exchanged ideas and discussed logistics over home-cooked meals (for which we undergrads are forever grateful) filled with the flavours and auras we had been longing for and missing. The conference represented a living, breathing space; we incorporated our own systems of feminist collaboration and learned a more holistic understanding of labour.

The kinds of discussions and ideas that surrounded the conference intervened in the way that I now view my Canadian university experience. My role as a student makes me complicit in McGill, a colonial site and colonizing institution (paperson 2017). Academically, I have always found myself gravitating toward the humanities—the arts, philosophy, languages, cultural studies, and literature. In theory, these subjects are concerned with hegemony and power structures—and thus by extension—matters of race, class, gender, queerness, colonialism, and diaspora. Paradoxically, the humanities, as I understand it, remain within the scope of Western traditions. Cultural imperialism is strong at this Canadian university. Having this opportunity to pause and reflect on what the conference has taught me has shifted my perception of how I have engaged with these disciplines, ever disciplining.

In the graphic memoir *I Was Their American Dream*, Malaka Gharib (2019) writes about her struggles with colonial mentality and placing whiteness on a pedestal. This resonated deeply with me. As my career at McGill progressed, I grew to recognize that white perspectives have a higher standing in the field of academia. Furthermore, having a higher standing in the field of academia (despite its inaccessibility) is what legitimizes one's voice. The conference introduced me to the language and knowledge systems necessary for decolonization. I asked myself questions like: What is my place here, as a settler on Turtle Island, especially following the conscious decision to leave my homeland? I began to understand how my personal history fit into a larger story of empire and colonialism, and that this is inseparable from my identity as a student. I know that I am still early in the process of undoing my colonial (mis) education. It has taken much time, even after the conference, for this understanding to take root in my mind. I have been complicit in upholding these structures. I continue to enroll in these classes, to seek validation from entities whose concerns that I, at the end of day, find alienating. I am still struggling to navigate this dichotomy of someone who is interested in the humanities but is haunted by the way academia fortifies itself within a tower of condescending coloniality. My efforts to cultivate a critical consciousness seemed to collapse in on itself. I felt as if I had relapsed into the state of the colonial subject. Therein lies the central feeling of guilt. I proclaim to object to neo-colonialism, I want to dismantle Eurocentric standards. So why did I come all the way here? By pursuing this kind of education, have I committed a kind of betrayal? PPII served as the site of intervention for this realization, imploring me to breach this nameless and amorphous space of self-positioning.

Many of the things that I discussed previously all point to this central notion of kapwa. The literal meaning of the word kapwa is "togetherness." It is an Indigenous Filipino cultural concept, to see the world with all its beings as a holistic system where everyone and everything exists interdependently and inter-relatedly.

The conference left me with a gift of a little pocket of belonging here in Montréal. Although I have been racialized in the past, before coming to Canada I had only an abstract understanding of what it meant to be racialized in North America. I did not anticipate the sheer alienation I felt when I first came to McGill. It was difficult to make friends, and I chalked it up to the fact that I was not successful enough at assimilating, at making myself palatable. This realization upset me at first, because colonial mentality convinced me that the quality of my English, the Americanization of my cultural references would be enough. But they did not always work to bridge the gap between my racialized experiences and my white peers. My involvement in this conference enabled me to see this dissonance. Yet more importantly, it also provided the means to recover from it—through building community, which eventually led to a more established sense of self and belonging.

In an April 2020 blog post entitled Passing Glance, Filipina writer Rebecca Mabanglo-Mayor describes her experience coming across an artifact from the Philippines in an anthropological exhibit; a small smoking pipe. Far from home, the object seemed isolated from the dynamic, everyday existence that might have surrounded it. Far from the hands which once held it, far from the stories that used to accompany its back-and-forth motion, smoke once rising high into the air. Upon reading the entry, I felt I might have once shared a strange kinship with this lonely object. However, I now understand that my Filipina identity is not static. My Filipina-ness is more than a designation on a museum plaque, more than a curiosity being represented by the institution in which I take up space. Once I found myself involved with the conference and blessed with the gift of feminist sisterhood, I was able to reconcile my Filipina identity with "the living, breathingness of kapwa." I found my Filipina-ness in the resplendent laughter of my sisters, the soaring fire in their voices, the sanctity of their tears, and the strength in their arms as they extended into a warm embrace.

When I first entered the Canadian university I felt the distance from my cultural context. This gap went beyond geographic markers, expanding to the level of the fundamental self. But this notion of kapwa as a knowledge framework tilted my perspective. Community building itself is an important facet of being Filipina/x. Rather than separate artifacts, we are all single threads which contribute to a larger tapestry. Kapwa is the concept of shared self that is inclusive and interconnected in the most expansive sense.

The conference was a catalyst for many lessons. The conversations surrounding PPII helped me find new ways of being Filipina/x: not new in an absolute sense, but certainly new to me. When I left the Philippines, I thought I was leaving behind a patriarchal, conservative environment, not realizing that these conditions were colonial systems of power. Only in coming here did I discover that these frameworks thrived in the spaces that I had led to believe occupied the high tier of "developed." Our people had an identity that preceded Spanish colonization, preceded American imperialism. I am actually remembering how to be a feminist through sisterhood and through kapwa, to accept multiplicity as a part of our/my identity. As Filipina American scholar, Leny Strobel (2018) explains:

> Understand colonialism and imperialism but know that this is not your full story ... How do you carry the lessons you've been taught by our indigenous Kapwa? Know how the shadows of History can be uncovered, acknowledged, and healed. With this new awareness, you will learn to dis-identify with the Story of patriarchy, supremacy, and capitalism. You will write new stories. You will make different choices.

By reflecting on my personal experiences and our shared histories, I begin to understand how we can work together to build spaces of belonging. I no longer seek shelter in rootlessness, in the subdued safety which comes with existing in a vacuum. There is so much strength in kapwa and in the collective. I hope to make different choices. I hope to write stories of visibility and togetherness. And I hope to do all these things with you all.

4 Bridging Our Stories with Yours

We offer Julia, Psalmae, and Chloe's stories of emergent asian canadian feminisms (acf) as powerful illustrations of the intimate learnings stemming from

FIGURE 11.1 Chloe Rodriguez *Untitled*, 2020. Acrylic paint and pencil on wood. *This piece is dedicated to the powerful Filipina/xs in my life; the community organizers, artists, academics, the female figures I grew up with, my ancestors, and my diasporic chosen family*

their individual and shared experiences organizing PPII. Their stories turn us towards emerging, embodied, and experiential feminisms rooted in kapwa, in community. In describing the challenges with articulating and claiming acf, Lee (2006: 30) writes that it "cannot be simply about the politics of identity; it must also be concerned with struggles regarding material issues that affect differentially asian-canadian women's everyday lives." Naming our varied struggles at McGill, we point to the radical and liberatory possibilities of finding ourselves and our feminisms through intentional relational work and community building efforts that seek to create feminist nows for our thriving within this otherwise alienating and isolating academic space.

By writing about these emerging Filipina/x diasporic feminisms, seeded in the Canadian nation state context, we come to understand the shifts in our own critical consciousness, and further, see our individual struggles as shared. Lee (2006: 44) reminds us that "at a minimum, self-identified asian-canadian feminists must create space to learn, share, and support each other in struggles for justice." Demonstrating the coming-to-self experience within and through the colonial academic space, Julia, Psalmae, and Chloe highlight the difficult, yet meaningful work of committing and working through one's own identity formation while students. As Kim Villagante (2018: 158–159) has shared, "Writing myself into the present and future means understanding that my story matters amid this institutionalized multiculturalism that wants to homogenize our experiences." We invite you to explore your own stories of coming into asian Canadian and Filipina/x diasporic feminisms and find the words and means to make them known too.

References

Ahmed, S. (2017) *Living a feminist life.* Duke University Press.

Aquino, C. (2004) Mula sa Kinaroroonan: "Kapwa, Kapatiran" and "Bayan" in Philippine Social Science. *Asian Journal of Social Science,* 32(1): 105–139.

Batac, M. (2020) Foreword. In: Jacqueline Gallos Aquines (eds). *Home Is In The Body: 2SLGBTQIA+ FilipinX Femme North of the 49th Parallel.* Anak Publishing Worker Cooperative Ltd, VII.

Batac, M. (2022). "Failing" and Finding a Filipina Diasporic Scholarly "Home": A De/Colonizing Autoethnography. *Qualitative Inquiry.*

Batac, M., Stohner, F. C., and Danan, K. V. (2022). From Paperback to Praxis: In Search of Filipina/x Feminisms in the Diaspora. In: G. J. Wilson, J. B. Acuff, and A. M. Kraehe (eds). *Love Letters to This Bridge Called My Back.* University of Arizona Press, The Feminist Wire Series, 195–203.

Coloma, R. S. M., McElhinny, B., Tungohan, E., Catungal, J. P. C., & Davidson, L. M. (eds.) (2012). *Filipinos in Canada: Disturbing Invisibility*. University of Toronto Press.

De Jesús, M. L. (Ed.) (2005) *Pinay Power: Peminist Critical Theory: Theorizing the Filipina/American Experience*. Routledge.

Dolmage, J. (2017) Introduction: The Approach. In *Academic Ableism: Disability and Higher Education*. Ann Arbor: University of Michigan Press, 1–40.

hampton, R. (2020) *Black Racialization and Resistance at an Elite University*. University of Toronto Press.

Gharib, M. (2019) *I was their American Dream: A Graphic Memoir*. Clarkson Potter/ Publishers.

Gorman, R. (2013). Mad nation? Thinking through race, class, and mad identity politics. In B. A. LeFrançois, R. Menzies, & G. Reaume (Eds.), *Mad Matters: A critical reader in Canadian mad studies. Toronto: Canadian Scholars' Press*. (pp. 269–280). Canadian Scholars' Press.

Goyette, B. (2009) Against Post-colonial Invisibility: First Filipino-Canadian Symposium Tries to Bridge Ivory Tower and Community Activism. *McGill Daily*. Accessed at https://www.mcgilldaily.com/2009/11/against_postcolonial_invisibility/.

Kwak, L. (2017) Asian Canada: Undone. In: G. Pon, and R. S. Coloma (eds.) *Asian Canadian Studies Reader*. University of Toronto Press, 352–362.

Lee, J. (2006) Issues in Constituting Asian-canadian Feminisms. In: T. Hellwig and S. Thobani (eds.) *Asian Women: Interconnections*. Toronto: Women's Press. 21–46.

Mabanglo-Mayor, R. M. (2020) *Passing Glance*. Retrieved from: https://rebeccamabanglomayor.com/passing-glance/.

McElhinny, B., Davidson, L. M., Catungal, J. P. C., Tungohan, E., & Coloma, R. S. (2012) Spectres of (in) Visibility: Filipina/o Labour, Culture, and Youth in Canada. In: R. S. M. Coloma, B. McElhinny, E. Tungohan, J. P. C. Catungal, & L. M. Davidson (eds.) *Filipinos in Canada: Disturbing Invisibility*. Toronto: University of Toronto Press, 5–45.

Mingus, M. (2012) *Feeling the Weight: Some Beginning Notes on Disability, Access and Love*. Leaving Evidence. Retrieved from: https://leavingevidence.wordpress.com/2012/05/08/feeling-the-weight-some-beginning-notes-on-disability-access-and-love/.

Mingus, M. (2017). *Access Intimacy, Interdependence and Disability Justice*. Leaving Evidence. Retrieved from: https://leavingevidence.wordpress.com/2017/04/12/access-intimacy-interdependence-and-disability-justice/.

Nievera-Lozano, M. (2013) The Pinay Scholar-Activist Stretches. *Nineteen Sixty Nine: An Ethnic Studies Journal* 2(1), 1–17.

Nievera-Lozano, M. (2020) Pain + Love = Growth: The Labor of Pinayist Pedagogical Praxis. In: K. L. C. Valverde & W. M. Dariotis (eds.) *Fight the Tower: Asian American Women Scholars' Resistance and Renewal in the Academy*. Rutgers University Press, 325–349.

Paperson, L. (2017) *A Third University is Possible*. University of Minnesota Press.

Piepzna-Samarasinha, L. L. (2018) *Care Work: Dreaming Disability Justice*. ProQuest Ebook Central https://ebookcentral-proquest-com.myaccess.library.utoronto.ca.

Pierce, L. M. (2005) Not just My Closet: Exploring Familial, Cultural, and Imperial Skeletons. In; M. L. d. Jesus (eds). *Pinay Power: Theorizing the Filipina/American Experience*. Routledge, 31–44.

Strobel, L. (2018) *Dear Motherland. Medium*. Retrieved from: https://lenystrobel.medium.com/dear-motherland-a9f2faa5d580.

Surla, K. (2019). *The Academic Ate: REAL TALK from Pinay Scholars about Life, Work, and Identity in Academia*. PINAY POWER II: Celebrating Peminisms in the Diaspora, McGill University, Montréal.

Tintiangco-Cubales, A. (2005) Pinayism. In: M. L. de Jesús (ed.) *Pinay Power: Theorizing the Filipina/American Experience*. Routledge, 137–148.

Valverde, K. L. C., Pham, C. M., Yee, M., & Mai, J. (2020). Killing Machine: Exposing the Health Threats to Asian American Women Scholars in Academia. In K. L. C. Valverde & W. M. Dariotis (Eds.), *Fight the Tower: Asian American Women Scholars' Resistance and Renewal in the Academy* (pp. 110–157). Rutgers University Press.

Velasco, G. K. (2020). *Queering the global Filipina body : contested nationalisms in the Filipina/o diaspora*. University of Illinois Press.

Yamada, Mitsuye (2015) Invisibility is an Unnatural Disaster. In: C. Moraga and G. Anzaldúa (eds). *This Bridge Called My Back* (*4th ed.*). Albany: SUNY Press, 30–35.

Villagante, K. (2018). Between Earth and Sky: Interview with Kim Villagante. In R. Diaz, M. Largo, & F. Pino (Eds.), *Diasporic Intimacies: Queer Filipinos and Canadian Imaginaries* (pp. 151–159). Northwestern University Press.

PART 3

Building Solidarities

∴

CHAPTER 12

The Butterfly Effect: Asian Massage Parlour and Sex Workers and Historical Chinese Laundries Fighting By-Laws and Organizing Towards Justice

Coly Chau and Elene Lam

In the wake of sexist, racist, misogynist, whorephobic and xenophobic acts of violence that claimed multiple lives in the Atlanta tragedy in March of 2021, Asian massage parlour workers and sex workers were catapulted into national spotlight, along with calls to end anti-Asian violence. The tragedy and activism transpired under the backdrop of the COVID-19 pandemic which has had devastating impacts on racialized, poor, migrant and disability communities, including massage parlour and sex workers (Lam 2020; Lam et al. 2021). Despite the significant growth of "Stop Asian Hate" movements across Turtle Island—in what we presently know as Canada, as well as the US—there remains a need to apply intersectional lenses that centre the experiences of trans and cis women, gender non-conforming and queer people; women and people with disabilities; women and people with precarious immigration status; and women and people engaged in sex work (Lam forthcoming).

In the last few decades, we can count numerous victims of such violence, along with knowing that countless others remain unnamed and cases unreported across Canada and the US. The reality remains that for those whose labour, identities and lived experiences intersect at massage parlour work, sex work, gendered labour, Asian, migrant, women, transgender and gender non-conforming, they have for long remained targets of multiple forms of violence. This reality extends to Black, Indigenous, racialized, migrant, women, trans, disabled, massage parlour and sex workers (Maynard 2017; Fritsch et al. 2016; Sayers 2018; Butler Burke 2018). There is a need to resist that this sort of violence is new or surprising. Rather Asian and migrant massage parlour and sex workers have always been targeted at various levels.

The violence that Asian and migrant women massage parlour and sex workers contend with exceeds that of these tragic incidents and mainstream portrayals of victimization. For those whose identities and labour meet at this conjuncture, the violence they face daily is institutionalized and systemic, through the functionings of sexist, racist, misogynist, whorephobic, and xenophobic society, state and legal systems. This includes state and societal violence in the form of criminalization, policing, detention, deportations, surveillance, degradation, moralistic subjugation and victimization. Sex work prohibitionists have for long been proponents of this violence, advocating through narratives that detach the agency of migrant women and workers, by painting them as victims of modern "slavery"—in order to evoke a sense of moral panic in support of domestic and global anti-trafficking campaigns (Lepp 2002; Agustín 2007; Kempadoo 2012; Sanghera 2012; Lam 2018). Anti-trafficking campaigns attempt to align themselves to legacies of anti-slavery and abolitionist work, but as scholars note, these are in reality efforts towards historical revisionism, rooted in racism, colonialism and imperialism (Kempadoo 2017; Maynard 2018).

With COVID-19, new racial anxieties around fears of contamination have emerged, further enmeshing Asian massage parlour and sex workers with anti-trafficking campaigns and resulting in further exclusion from accessing social supports (Lam et al. 2021)–these social supports include housing, health services and labour protection (Lam and Gallant, 2018). Emergency orders that shut down workplaces and enforced curfews, prevented many workers from working, meanwhile forcing some workers unable to access government supports and relief to continue working while risking fines and punishment (Lam et al. 2021). Communities already made vulnerable are further harmed by public health concerns around contagion, and by new punitive measures and growing inequities around access of government and social supports.

The violence that Asian and migrant massage parlour and sex worker face is further experienced through the policing of respectability and morality within communities. Long histories of silencing or absence of migrant massage parlour and sex workers have left them at the margins of mainstream feminist or anti-racist movements. Massage parlour and sex workers, along with other migrant, feminist, queer and trans, disabled, Black Indigenous and People of Colour (BIPOC), activists, organizers and allies continue to call for collective action and solidarity to address and end societal, systemic and institutionalized violences. These calls recognize that migration and labour are not harmful. What causes harm are oppressive systems of border control, criminalization, detention, deportations, exploitation of migrant labour, colonialism and imperialism that produces conditions for migration. Recently, there have been strengthened calls against carceral politics and feminisms that employ debates of morality and moral panic to punish migrants, women and workers, rather than address societal and state failings. These appeals recognize that persistent rejection of sex work, victimization and rescue can and do harm Asian and migrant massage parlour and sex workers. The violence faced daily occurs beyond sensationalized headlines, and requires understanding of work, class, race, gender, sexuality and lack of migration status. These invitations for collective action and solidarity are recognitions that there are other ways towards social justice and liberation.

It is important to begin this chapter with the statement that: sex work is work. As many massage parlour and sex workers have collectively vocalized: they are workers, not victims of trafficking. Sex work does not equal trafficking. In this chapter, we provide a glimpse of Asian and migrant women massage parlour and sex workers resisting and organizing towards justice. We centre this organizing by examining how the community resist oppressive and discriminatory municipal by-laws, particularly that which has taken place amid violent guises of anti-trafficking and rescue. We present this alongside similar patterns of state and systemic violence in the municipal by-laws that targeted historical Chinese laundries in North America, and highlight how the laundry workers and businesses mobilized. We write within a Canadian context but also utilize examples from the US, recognizing that Turtle Island existed before the settler colonial and imperial projects, and such projects feed into each other.

This chapter focuses on the work of *Butterfly: Asian and Migrant Sex Worker Network*, a network established in 2014 by sex workers, social workers, professionals from the legal, immigration and health sectors, activists and allies. As the first self-mobilized Asian and migrant sex workers grassroot network in Canada, Butterfly was founded on ensuring that sex workers deserve dignity, respect, safety, protection, basic human rights and justice. Butterfly demands that sex workers, irrespective of their migration status, should be treated like all other workers. Butterfly in its work to seek safety and dignity of sex workers here and there, challenges processes of colonial and imperial impositions through transnational organizing. Such organizing and movements challenge notions of belonging, criminality and victimization, particularly within settler colonial context.

1 Butterfly's Fight against Anti-trafficking Initiatives and Discriminatory By-Laws

Butterfly believes in the power, agency and leadership of the migrant massage parlour and sex workers communities. Instead of rooting in notions of help and rescue, Butterfly has established itself as a platform for migrant massage parlour and sex workers to support to one another, to learn and grow together, and collectively fight for justice. To build community, Butterfly outreaches in the workplaces of massage parlour and sex workers, including by connecting them to one another in person and through social media; establishing networks for feedback and safety at hotels; creating networks for mutual support and aid; and by extensively sharing information and building knowledge around issues the communities is facing. The work of Butterfly is led and informed by the migrant massage parlour and sex workers on the ground.

Between 2013 and 2017, a number of anti-trafficking organizations lobbied the City of Toronto to drastically increase the investigations, surveillance and imposition of punitive by-laws in order to shut down massage parlour and body rub parlours across the city. With their campaigns, the City of Toronto's City Council passed a motion called the *Initiatives to Address Human Trafficking* that approved "the review of licensing by-laws concerning trades and businesses that are known to be destinations for human trafficking," under the goal of "condemning the horrific crime of human trafficking" (City of Toronto 2013). This municipal enactment, developed alongside an array of provincial, federal and global measures that undertook similar tones of moral panic around human trafficking—including the *Protection of Communities and Exploited Persons Act* ushered by the Conservative federal government in 2014, which effectively framed all sex workers as victims, and aimed to abolish sex work through criminalizing clients, third parties and other sex work related activities. Through the *Initiatives to Address Human Trafficking*, the City of Toronto's Municipal Licensing and Standards (MLS), began reviewing and implementing city by-laws, including around zoning provisions; investigative and enforcement resources and tools; and means of fines and punitive approaches. The initiative called for increased collaborative efforts between MLS and Toronto Police Services to address what were deemed as issues of human and sexual trafficking. As a result, many Asian and migrant workers in massage parlours in Toronto began to collectively voice concerns about increases in abuse, excessive investigation and prosecutions by the by-law enforcement officers.

In 2016, holistic centres (which includes massage parlours) and workers were investigated over 4,365 times, which amounted to 19.3 % of all investigation in the city—visits to holistic centres increased by 212% (1,780 visits in 2016) and visits to holistic practitioners increased by 323% (2,585 visits in 2016) since the city council motion (see Butterfly 2018; Lam 2018; Lam & Lepp, 2019). In a survey on interaction with law enforcement, half of the respondents, comprised of Asian workers, said that they had received by-law violation charges in the raids (see Lam & Lepp, 2019). After Butterfly's founding in 2014, members of Butterfly began accompanying and supporting workers at court. In one instance, Butterfly found 15 workers lined up at the court, with fines and charges between the amounts of $100 to 5,000. Very few workers were willing to advocate for themselves and their rights, primarily because many of them could not afford to hire lawyers. But also, the crown told many of the workers they could accept a guilty plea deal with a $500 fine, otherwise face a $5,000 fine. During this time, some of the massage parlour and holistic centre workers and owners also lost their licenses because of the by-law violations. They recounted how by-law enforcement officers would spend up to two hours in investigations, to find and enforce only one minor infraction—feeling that the investigations were moreso tactics for intimidation and bullying.

By-law enforcement and city staff also violated the Access Without Fear policy that the City of Toronto had adapted and the city's commitment towards being a Sanctuary City. During enforcement of by-laws, Canada Border Services Agency (CBSA) were contacted to arrest and detain the non-status workers. Through testimonies provided by women who were detained within police stations, immigration centres and prisons, many workers described continued intimidation and threats, and numerous methods to force workers to admit that they were working without status and to implicate others within their networks. Within immigration detention, workers were subjected to indefinite detentions, no language interpretations, repeated strip searches, solitary confinement and seizing of personal belongings and valuables (see Lam & Lepp 2019).

In addition, despite the reality that massage parlour workers continually face daily violence that include physical and sexual assaults, theft, murder and other threats, through the *Initiatives to Address Human Trafficking*, MLS further enforced by-laws 545–177 (l) and 545–343, which effectively prevented workers from locking doors for personal protection and safety, instead risking financial charges and seizure of business licenses (Lam 2018).

As a result of efforts from anti-trafficking campaigning, many workers faced increased surveillance, policing, punishment, detention and deportations. To push back, the massage parlour and sex worker community began by sharing knowledge and information amongst themselves, including on how to avoid receiving tickets and fines. Asian and migrant workers mobilized, attended various community meetings, and learned that English speaking and white workers shared a very different reality—that they did not experience the same degree of policing and hostility from by-law and police enforcement. Butterfly began working to develop and organize workshops for massage parlour and sex workers to learn about municipal by-laws and their rights as workers. In organizing, more workers were willing to speak out about the injustices they faced, including by meeting with the city councillors and staff to share their experiences and concerns. Despite their collective organizing and vocalizing of concerns, city officials would not listen to them. To build solidarity and coalitions of support, Butterfly reached out to different professionals and organizations, mobilizing academics, lawyers and health professionals, and called on the support of other organizations, including those that address violence against women (VAW), racial justice, migrant labour rights, and human rights, in order to collectively advocate for the rights of Asian and migrant massage parlour and sex workers and justice for communities whose liberation are tied to one another.

In 2019, as a result of continued efforts by anti-trafficking advocates the City of Toronto proposed to remove all licenses for holistic centres (including massage parlours), that would have resulted in over 2,500 workers losing their licenses. On top of the daily threats of abusive and punitive enforcement, business owners and massage parlour workers were now in fear of losing of their businesses, workplaces and not being able to work anymore. To resist this, Butterfly and its coalition of support mobilized and packed city hall with over 300 massage parlour and sex workers and their allies—a monumental number. As a collective, they deputed at city hall, speaking from their lived experiences and asserting their rights. They took up space during the entire meeting to halt the city from shutting down holistic centres and severing the livelihoods of thousands of workers. In addition, Butterfly utilized petitions, news and media outlets, and even drew attention to their concerns and built solidarity through art and community events. In May 2019 the interactive multi-media solidarity art show *Power in Our Hand* took place at Tea Base in Toronto, displaying photographs of massage parlour workers and their hands to fight back against encroaching municipal by-laws. As a result of these efforts, massage parlour and sex workers successfully advocated to stop by-law enforcement officers and city staff from calling the CBSA, as well as, ensuring that the city would stop enforcing the by-law that prohibited locked doors at massage parlours.

2 Historical Chinese Laundry Workers Organizing

In the late 19th and early 20th century, Chinese laundries became crucial means of livelihood for early Chinese migrants in Canada and the US. The nature of the work enabled independence, self-employment and entry due to its low capital costs, employability with limited language or technical skills, and access to cultural credit and supports, resulting in laundries emerging as viable labour for the "bachelor societies" (Wang 2004; Thach 2015). While immigration controls at the federal level dictated entry into the nation, through provincial decree of powers, municipalities played a central role in enact restrictive legislations to control Chinese communities through their labour and businesses (Mosher 1998). Municipalities could swiftly and adeptly enact by-laws, particularly by following patterns in other provincial or state legislations. The history of municipal regulation of Chinese laundries reveal contested sites in which gender, race, status, citizenship and morality were constructed and policed. Through framings of public health and safety, municipalities were able to discriminately utilize municipal by-laws, surveillance, enforcement, criminalization and threats of detention on Chinese men labourers and businesses (Shah 2001; Anderson 1991; McLaren 1999).

One of the most notable ways in which municipalities dictated Chinese workers and businesses was through enforcing discriminatory licensing and registration fees. In 1878, B.C. introduced a license specific to Chinese laundries, failure to be licensed resulted in fines, but also seizure of businesses (Roy 1989). In the 1880's in San Francisco, an array of licensing laws and regulations were introduced to bring about large-scale investigations in Chinatown, and in 1885, resulted in the indictment, arrests and detention of 150 Chinese men for their refusal to adhere to the license (Shah 2001; Thach 2015). Despite passing inspections, the owner of Yick Wo was fined 10 dollars and imprisoned (Thach 2015; Shah 2001). The Tung Hing Tong, a Chinese laundry guild, organized over 200 Chinese men to protest and raised money to hire attorneys to support Yick Wo and fight restrictions in San Francisco (Shah 2001; Thach 2015). In 1886, the supreme court ruled in favour of Yick Wo, citing how the laws encouraged "hurtful and unfair discrimination" and was "administered by public authority with an evil eye and an unequal hand" (Thach 2015:43).

It has also been noted that licenses were often refused by authorities for an array of reasons, despite receiving recommendations from health officers or fire wardens (Roy 1989). In Canada and the US, white laundry owners were able to influence additional discriminatory anti-Chinese ordinances and laws, as well as advocate for increasing of fines and jailtime for Chinese violations (Roy 1989; Thach 2015). As Roy (1989) writes, a 50-cent licensing fee for Chinese workers was passed, that upheld the competitive advantage of white laundries. Chinese workers and businesses were also restricted through movement and locations of operations. In 1893, McGuigan's by-law in Vancouver would limit where Chinese laundries could operate (Anderson 1991). In 1913, a Hamilton by-law required that all Chinese men renew their licenses yearly with the city, and were refused options to relocate, effectively tying them to one location (Mosher 1998).

Overall, numerous examples reveal how different ordinances and by-laws were introduced to negatively impact Chinese laundry businesses and workers, effectively relegating businesses and workers to the mercy of the municipalities. In 1873 San Francisco, introduced a $15 worker fine and up to $60 per year fine for businesses not utilizing horse drawn delivery vehicles and in the 1880's, the city further introduced building ordinances—both of which were meant to disproportionately affect Chinese laundries (Thach 2015; Shah 2001). In Toronto, in the early 1900's, new snow removal by-laws that had penalties of $1 fines and 10 days in jail, resulted in 40 per cent of charges being laid on Chinese businesses (Mosher 1998). Cities across Canada and the US were persistent in applying by-laws and ordinances that limited Chinese laundry businesses and workers. In reading scholarly work that examined historical Chinese laundries, we found that from the early 1900's to the mid 1930's, cities were continuously applying prohibitions that disproportionately affected working conditions of Chinese laundry workers—through Sunday Observances in Vancouver and San Francisco, and the Lord's Day Act in Toronto that prevented working on Sunday (Anderson 1991; Mosher 1998; Shah 2001). In 1918, 12 Chinese men were arrested in Vancouver for working on Sunday (Nicol 2019). Later on, cities began implementing operating hours that further prevented Chinese laundries from working overnight, reducing working hours. As many scholars noted, this was heavily and disproportionately targeted to Chinese laundries, and was done while white laundries were able to adapt technological advances and have a competitive advantage. In 1935, laws that reduced working hours were introduced through the Factories Act in British Columbia (Roy, 1989) and the Oakland Laundry Ordinances in California. The Oakland Laundry Ordinances resulted in 38 Chinese men being arrested (Thach 2015). Once again, the Tong Hing Tung organized, fundraised for legal representation, and protested the ordinances in Oakland. Aside from the Tung Hing Tong, other organizing groups emerged, including the Chinese Hand Laundry Alliance established in 1900's in New York with similar goals of mobilization (Thach 2015).

Furthermore, around this time, Chinese people were prevented from participating in municipal elections that would enable them to democratically elect municipal representation—and disenfranchisement would extend well throughout the *Chinese Immigration Act* and *Chinese Exclusion Acts*. Despite this, Mar (2010) and Nicol (2019) note how Chinese workers and communities in Canada were quick to utilize bilingual brokers and empathetic lawyers to help negotiate with the state and address injustices. Their successes in mobilization resulted in cities, such as Vancouver, to seek more powers through the province to control Chinese populations (Nicol 2019). The effectiveness and success from Chinese laundries and worker mobilization to fight against restrictive by-laws reveal a long history of resistance.

3 Reflections on the Past, Present and Future

We place these narratives of Asian and migrant massage parlour and sex workers and historical Chinese laundries alongside each other, because we see history repeating itself. They expose the deeply embedded sexism, racism, whorephobia, xenophobia, discrimination of societal, state and legal systems.

The fact that laundries were a highly racialized, gendered and feminized type of labour, allow for reflections on how municipalities continue to control, punish and criminalize massage and sex work precisely because of the intersections of their identities and labour. Furthermore, the ways in which Chinese men migrants were often described as sojourners and how contemporary Asian migrant massage parlour and sex workers often are depicted through narratives of trafficking, are rooted back in constructed legacies of "yellow slavery," and contemporary conversations around victimhood of modern "slavery" (See Lam et al. 2022).

Agency remains central in understanding experiences of Asian migrant women massage parlour and sex workers. As laundries were viable options for many early Chinese migrant men, massage parlour and sex work similarly enable access and options for employment. Lam et al. (2021) and Shih (2021) note that massage work tends to be a viable option for migrant and low-wage workers, and many migrant Asian workers find it preferable to other forms of physically and emotionally demanding jobs—such as those within nail salons, restaurant and domestic care work. Agency further forces us to examine broader state and societal barriers rather than apply lenses that criminalize, victimize and punish workers. As Agustín (2007) reminds us, "agency does not mean denying structural conditions, nor does it make them over responsible for their fate, but it does consider their own perceptions and desires" (p.41). Instead of being a passive agent waiting to be rescued, Asian migrant massage parlour and sex workers have used and continue to use different ways to resist the oppressions they face (Lam 2016), which shows how their individual survival strategies and resistances express unessentialized notions of agency.

The similarities between historical Chinese laundries and Asian and migrant massage parlour and sex workers draw attention to how municipal by-laws were and continue to be a critical method for the state to control gender, race, sex, migration and labour. As Shah (2001) writes, in the 19th century, public health became one of the most agile and expansive regulatory mechanisms, behind policing and taxing mechanisms. To this day, mechanisms through public health remain crucial, especially in times of COVID-19. We continue to see how different departments, levels of governments, law enforcement and border control can work together to enact discrimination, surveil, punish, detain and even deport workers. There are ongoing legacies in which municipalities side with the advocacy of anti-trafficking campaigns and even historical white laundry competitor businesses, rather than the migrant workers themselves. Law enforcement and policing continue to harm rather than protect migrant workers. As Lam et al. (2021: 2) write, "for many migrant workers, police represent the violence of the criminal legal system, not the liberation from traffickers and exploitation espoused by law enforcement." Municipal by-laws and regulations have significant impact in undermining the well-being, health and safety of massage parlour and sex workers (Lam 2016).

The past reveals a long legacy of resistance. Today, there remains a dire and continued need for collective action and solidarity—to continue mobilizing, organizing and resisting oppressive anti-trafficking rescue. Butterfly understands that liberation means to build coalitions and work with allies from different movements, including sex workers rights, labour rights, migrant rights and justice, racial justice movements, queer and trans liberation, and disability justice, locally and globally (See Lam and Gallant 2018). To do so also means to mobilize and build capacity to fight anti-trafficking discourses and measures, and its oppressive impacts on the community. As noted in this chapter, Asian and migrant massage parlour and sex worker's lived experiences, voices, leadership and agency must be centred. Municipalities and all levels of government, feminist and anti-racist movements and non-governmental organizations need to listen to workers, in order to stop harming the community. Mobilization is an ongoing process and central to *Butterfly*'s work—fighting by-laws is one step closer to justice!

References

Agustín, Laura María (2007) *Sex at the Margins: Migration, Labour Markets and the Rescue Industry*. London: Zed.

Anderson, Kay J. (1991) *Vancouver's Chinatown: Racial Discourse in Canada, 1875–1980*. McGill-Queen's University Press.

Butler Burke, Nora (2018) Double Punishment: Immigration Penality and Migrant Trans Women Who Sell Sex. In: Elya M. Durisin, Emily van der Meulen, and Chris Bruckert (eds.) *Red Light Labour: Sex Work Regulation, Agency and Resistance*. Vancouver, BC: UBC Press.

Butterfly (2018) *Petition: Stop Abuse and Harassment by Bylaw Enforcement & Police Officers*. Toronto: Butterfly.

City of Toronto (2013) Staff Report: Initiatives to Address Human Trafficking. <toronto.ca/legdocs/mmis/2013/ex/bgrd/backgroundfile-63985.pdf>.

Fritsch, Kelly, Heynen, Robert, Ross, Amy Nicole and van der Meulen, Emily (2016) Disability and Sex Work: Developing Affinities Through Decriminalization. *Disability & Society* 31 (1): 84–99.

Kempadoo, Kamala (2012) Abolitionism, Criminal Justice, and Transnational Feminism: Twenty-first-century perspectives on human trafficking. In: Kamala

Kempadoo (ed.) *Trafficking and Prostitution Reconsidered: New Perspectives on Migration, Sex Work, and Human Rights.* New York: Routledge.

Kempadoo, Kamala (2017) 'Bound Coolies' and Other Indentured Workers in the Caribbean: Implications for Debates about Human Trafficking and Modern Slavery. *Anti-Trafficking Review* 9: 48–63.

Lam, Elene (2016) Inspection, Policing, and Racism: How Municipal By-laws Endanger the Lives of Chinese Sex Workers in Toronto. *Canadian Review of Social Policy* 75: 87–112.

Lam, Elene (2018) *Behind the Rescue: How Anti-Trafficking Investigations and Policies Harm Migrant Sex Workers.* Toronto: Butterfly Print.

Lam, Elene (2018) *Survey of Toronto Holistic Practitioners' Experiences with Bylaw Enforcement and Police.* Toronto: Butterfly.

Lam, Elene (2020) Migrant Sex Workers Left behind during COVID-19 Pandemic. *Canadian Journal of Public Health* 111(4): 482–483.

Lam, Elene and Gallant, Chanelle (2018) Migrant Sex Workers' Justice: Building Alliances across Movements. In: Elya M. Durisin, Emily van der Meulen, and Chris Bruckert (eds.) *Red Light Labour: Sex Work Regulation, Agency and Resistance.* Vancouver, BC: UBC Press.

Lam, Elene and Lepp, Annalee (2019) Butterfly: Resisting the harms of anti-trafficking policies and fostering peer-based organising in Canada. *Anti-Trafficking Review* 12: 91–107

Lam, Elene, Peng, Jaden Hsin-Yun, and Chau, Coly (2022) Resistance of *Butterfly*: Mobilization of Asian Migrant Sex Workers against Sexism and Racism in Canadian Anti-trafficking Measures. In Kamala Kempadoo and Elena Shih (eds.) *White Supremacy, Racism and the Coloniality of Anti-trafficking.* New York: Routledge.

Lam, Elene, Shih, Elena, Chin, Katherine, and Zen, Kate (2021) The Double-Edged Sword of Health and Safety: COVID-19 and the Policing and Exclusion of Migrant Asian Massage Workers in North America. *Social Sciences* 10(5): 157.

Lepp, Annalee (2002) Trafficking in Women and the Feminization of Migration: The Canadian Context. *Canadian Women Studies*, Spring/Summer: 90–99.

Mar, Lisa Rose (2010) *Brokering Belonging: Chinese in Canada's Exclusion Era, 1885–1945.* Oxford University Press.

Maynard, Robyn (2017) *Policing Black Lives: State Violence in Canada from Slavery to the Present.* Black Point: Fernwood Publishing.

Maynard, Robyn (2018) Do Black Sex Workers' Lives Matter? Whitewashed Anti-Slavery, Racial Justice, and Abolition. In: Elya M. Durisin, Emily van der Meulen, and Chris Bruckert (eds.) *Red Light Labour: Sex Work Regulation, Agency and Resistance.* Vancouver: UBC Press.

McLaren, John (1999) Race and the Criminal Justice System in British Columbia, 1892–1920: Constructing Chinese Crimes. In: G. Blaine Baker and Jim Phillips (eds.) *In Honour of R.C.B. Risk.* Toronto: University of Toronto Press.

Mosher, Clayton James (1998) *Discrimination and Denial: Systemic Racism in Ontario's Legal and Criminal Justice Systems, 1892–1961.* Toronto: University of Toronto Press.

Nicol, Janet Mary (2019) 'Girl Strikers' and the 1918 Vancouver Steam Laundries Dispute. *BC Studies* 203: 53–81.

Roy, Patricia E. (1989) *White Man's Province: British Columbia Politicians and Chinese and Japanese Immigrants, 1858–1914.* Vancouver: UBC Press.

Sanghera, Jyoti (2012) Unpacking the Trafficking Discourse. In: Kamala Kempadoo (ed). *Trafficking and Prostitution Reconsidered: New Perspectives on Migration, Sex Work, and Human Rights.* New York: Routledge.

Sayers, Naomi (2018) Municipal Regulation of Street-Based Prostitution and Impacts on Indigenous Women: A Necessary Discussion. In: Elya M. Durisin, Emily van der Meulen, and Chris Bruckert (eds.) *Red Light Labour: Sex Work Regulation, Agency and Resistance.* Vancouver: UBC Press.

Shah, Nayan (2001) *Contagious Divides: Epidemics and Race in San Francisco's Chinatown.* Berkeley: University of California Press.

Shih, Elena (2021) The Trafficking Deportation Pipeline: Asian Body Work and the Auxiliary Policing of Racialized Poverty. *Feminist Formations* 33(1): 56–73.

Thach, Johnny (2015) *Organizing Against Discrimination: The Chinese Hand Laundrymen Historical Niche and Ethnic Solidarity in America.* CUNY Academic Works.

Wang, Joan S. (2004) Race, Gender, and Laundry Work: The Roles of Chinese Laundrymen and American Women in the United States, 1850–1950. *Journal of American Ethnic History* 24(1): 58–99.

CHAPTER 13

Asian Canadian Workers Organizing: The Making of the Asian Canadian Labour Alliance

Anna Liu

> When union leaders decry 'a worker is a worker is a worker' as their operative mode, as if they are gender or colour blind, they have failed to see the complexities of capitalism where race, and other forms of social constructs are used to divide and weaken the working class.
>
> WINNIE NG (2010: 65)

∴

A historical look at union attitudes and actions toward women and racialized[1] workers sheds light on the challenges that continue to affect Asian workers in the Canadian labour movement. In their early years, with few exceptions, unions vigorously opposed the inclusion of certain workers from joining their ranks, namely workers who were not white, Anglo-Saxon and male.[2] In some instances, unions even sought to shape public policy to restrict specific groups from accessing work altogether. This included advocating for all-white hiring policies, restricting areas of Asian employment, and preventing further Asian immigration into the country directed at Chinese, Japanese and South Asian early settlers (Creese 1989).

Considering this history, unions have made significant strides from their legacy of exclusionary practices. Today, unions invest considerable resources

---

1 Recognizing that race is a social construct, I use the term 'racialized person' or 'racialized group' instead of the more outdated and inaccurate terms 'racial minority,' 'visible minority,' 'person of colour' or 'non-White.'

2 A small number of unions did organize workers across racial lines, including the Industrial Workers of the World. See Daniel Rosenberg, The IWW and Organization of Asian Workers in Early 20th Century America and Jennifer Jung Hee Choi, The Rhetoric of Inclusion: The I.W.W and Asian Workers.

to promoting equity[3] within the labour movement. Anti-racism campaigns, conferences, committees, and policies aimed at educating members and advance the goal of building a movement that includes all workers. Despite these efforts, unions have yet to make significant headway into racialized communities. Racialized workers, including Asians, do not see unions as the go-to solution to their economic and workplace challenges and still struggle to find their voice in a movement that remains dominated by white men. As a result, even though Asian workers represent the largest group of racialized workers in Canada (Statistics Canada 2013), Asian Canadians[4] continue to be underrepresented in labour leadership and in the movement's priorities.

The labour movement is one of the best funded social movements in Canada. It is fully capable of achieving meaningful victories for working people. In this era of neoliberalism and austerity, unions have the resources to help workers – unionized and non-unionized – to fight back. Although ideological tensions still exist between servicing the needs of their members versus advocating for the betterment of all workers, the labour movement has played a pivotal role in driving positive social change.[5] Gains such as the right to maternity leave and access to same-sex benefits, go beyond working conditions. They create broad societal changes that contribute to poverty reduction and improving the quality of life for everyone in Canada. Today, workers find themselves on the defensive as our healthcare system, education, affordable housing, and workers' rights face increasing erosion, disproportionately affecting our society's most vulnerable, many of whom are Asian. As the official voice of the working class, the 'house of labour' must adapt to these evolving needs.

Within this context, the Asian Canadian Labour Alliance (ACLA) was founded primarily by members with roots in the labour movement, to address

---

3 The labour movement in Canada has largely adopted this term to better articulate the outcome desired when engaging in social justice work. A focus on equity recognizes that each person or group has different circumstances and places emphasis on the resources and opportunities necessary to reach an equal outcome. Conversely, equality means each individual or group of people is given the same resources or opportunities, regardless of whether they need them or not.

4 It is important to note that Asian Canadians are not a homogenous group. The term "Asian" encompasses peoples whose origins are identified with South Asian, East Asian, Southeast Asian, and West Asian descent.

5 Unions that are focused largely on servicing the needs of members, concentrating on the improvement of wages, hours, working conditions, etc. exhibit what is considered business unionism. In contrast, unions that are oriented towards the achievement of social justice for all people, advocating for equity and greater levels of democracy display what is known as social movement unionism. These ideological approaches are still debated within the house of labour.

the needs of Asian Canadian workers. For over 20 years, ACLA has served as a conduit, mobilizing union support and solidarity for struggles faced by Asian communities and as others. As a progressive ethno-racial labour organization operating outside the formal structures of unions, ACLA's mission is to build a bridge grounded in anti-oppression principles, ensuring that labour works in unison with racialized communities to overcome the legacy of exclusion and colonialism in Canadian society.

As someone who has been a member of ACLA for over ten years and served on its executive board, I have an interest in documenting the role and impact of this organization. I undertook a study to capture some of ACLA's stories and analyze its contribution to ensure that the autonomous organizing efforts of this small but significant collective are not lost to history. Throughout this paper, I explore issues and tensions between racialized workers and unions. As a union activist, my critique of unions comes from a place of respect and commitment to building a strong, inclusive working-class movement for all.

1 Forming ACLA

The Asian Canadian Labour Alliance (ACLA), established in 2000, is a collective of labour and community activists of Asian descent that occupies a unique position within the labour movement. While recognized as a legitimate advocacy group, ACLA operates independently and is not formally affiliated with any union or central labour body. This autonomy is often seen as a strength, enabling the organization to bring together Asian activists from diverse unions and labour-oriented community groups.

ACLA's mandate is to develop an Asian Canadian labour identity and to foster a union-positive presence in Asian communities. To achieve this, ACLA works both within the labour movement and Asian communities to elevate the profile of Asian Canadian labour issues. It actively encourages Asian workers to participate more fully in the labour movement and promotes the leadership of racialized workers in unions, communities, and government. ACLA's main goal is to challenge racism from an intersectional[6] perspective, fighting for social, economic, and political justice for all workers, regardless of union and/or citizenship status. Membership in the organization is open to anyone

6 Intersectionality coined by Kimberlé Crenshaw is a term used to describe the interconnected nature of social categorizations such as race, class, and gender, regarded as creating overlapping and interdependent systems of discrimination or disadvantage (Oxford Dictionary).

who self-identifies as Asian, whether South Asian, East Asian, Southeast Asian or West Asian.

The inspiration to form an Asian labour organization stemmed from the incredible organizing successes of Asian trade unionists in the United States. After decades of organizing, driven by large demographic shifts in the workforce and union membership, Asian American labour and community activists successfully leveraged America's national central labour body, the American Federation of Labor – Congress of Industrial Organizations (AFL- CIO), to fund a nationwide Asian American labour organization (Hing 1992; Wong 1992). The effort resulted in the creation of the Asian Pacific American Labour Alliance (APALA), a national structure within the AFL-CIO.

In 1992, APALA's founding convention was attended by 500 Asian Pacific American labour activists (APALA n.d.). Four years later, Canadian Asian unionists Gayle Nye and Winnie Ng attended a subsequent convention, where they were amazed by the sheer number of Asian union activists in attendance. Energized by what they experienced they returned to Canada with a vision of starting something similar. Staying in close contact with APALA, conversations began to take shape in British Columbia and Ontario. A network of Asian activists soon began meeting to discuss what an Asian labour organization in Canada could look like (Kishih and Ahn 2002). ACLA was the culmination of these discussions with British Columbia launching the first chapter, followed by Ontario in 2000.

2 Shining a Feminist, Anti-racist Light on Unions

The historical legacy of unions has often involved protecting a specific group of workers at the expense of others. When employers turned to women and racialized workers to offset the higher wages demanded by unionized workers, unions fought fiercely to exclude them, or limited their job mobility when the former failed (Das Gupta 2007; Fletcher and Gapasin 2003; Forrest 1993; White 2007). These exclusionary practices have left lasting imprints on the structures of unions today. For a long time, unions incorrectly assumed that women, immigrants, racialized workers, and young people were unorganizable believing they lacked the interest or militancy to join a union. Additionally, the work performed by these groups is often concentrated in areas deemed too small or 'difficult' to organize.

Theories of representation help explain why unions have often failed to organize certain groups of workers. Seeing themselves as industrial institutions, unions frequently hire white men for organizing and recruitment positions. One study (Yates 2005: 626) found that 95% of union organizers in Ontario and 78% in British Columbia are white, with the majority being men. Consequently, unions tend to focus on organizing workplaces that are predominantly male and white. A gender- and race-blind analysis of who gets organized can obscure this imbalance, as it treats all workers as an homogenous group. However, as the Canadian economy shifts away from resource extraction and manufacturing toward service oriented, public sector, and knowledge-based work, unions have experienced a significant decrease in traditionally unionized, male dominated sectors (Galarneau 2015). The decline in union density has forced many unions to reflect on their organizing priorities and targets. By understanding issues of representation and diversity, union are challenged to rethink the assumption that workers are a monolithic group, prompting a re-examination of industrial conceptions of who constitutes a worker and influencing both who and how unions organize.

Unions are gradually adopting an intersectional understanding of workers, acknowledging the unique privileges and challenges individuals face based on race, gender identity, age, (dis)ability, and citizenship status. Initiatives to redefine key issues, promote employment equity, support separate organizing, expand collective bargaining priorities, and reform leadership practices have all contributed to enhancing representation for traditionally marginalized members and workers. However, the commitment to these changes varies significantly across unions and even within different local, provincial, and national offices of the same union. The extent to which a truly representative approach will take root within unions remains uncertain.

3 Labour Market Diversity

The formation of an Asian labour organization is timely, given the growing number of Asian workers in Canada. As demand for labour and immigration has expanded alongside the economy, the composition of Canada's workforce has become increasingly diverse. Since the 1960s, when Canada reoriented its immigration policy to target educated and skilled immigrants regardless of race or country of origin, the number of racialized[7] people in Canada have grown exponentially. According to the 2011 census nearly one in five people

7 Statistics Canada uses the term 'visible minority' to describe "persons other than Indigenous peoples, who are non-Caucasian in race or non-white in colour." I substitute the term 'visible minority' and use the terms 'racialized' instead to capture not only the visible difference in skin colour, but also the sociopolitical significance of race. Additionally, 'visible minority'

(19.1%) in Canada belongs to a racialized group, with the broad category of Asian making up over 50% of the racialized population. By 2036, it is projected that approximately 31–36% of Canada's workforce will be made up of racialized people (Morency et al. 2017).

There is compelling evidence documenting the ongoing labour market struggles experienced by both immigrant and non-immigrant racialized workers. Canada's labour market is "colour coded" (Block and Galabuzi 2011), with racialized workers underrepresented in the best jobs available even when factors like age, education level and generational status are considered. Racialized workers are more likely to be concentrated in the lower end of the labour market, typically occupying jobs requiring less education and skills (Cheung 2006; Galabuzi 2008; Jackson 2002). Highly skilled immigrants, in particular, encounter a range of structural barriers; despite arriving with professional designations acquired from their home countries, many end up working in lower-level jobs, such as cleaning or food services. This segmentation increases the likelihood of poverty for racialized people compared to their white counterparts.

As it exists, union coverage remains weak among racialized workers. Of the 2,905,100 unionized workers in Canada, only 7% or 203,100 are racialized (Galabuzi 2008). Part of ACLA's mission is to ensure that public policy proposals spearheaded by the labour movement do not overlook the realities of historically marginalized workers.

4 Unions and Anti-racism Initiatives

While the labour movement has witnessed moments of cross racial solidarity over the decades, few, if any, efforts have been sustained or widespread enough to overcome the dominant union culture. Nonetheless, it is important to recognize the anti-racism organizing groundwork laid by earlier union activists.

The Canadian Jewish Labour Committee (JLC) was instrumental in laying the foundation of organized labour's human rights culture and influencing human rights policy development in Canadian Society. Initially formed to help victims of anti-Semitism, the JLC broadened its focus after World War II to include defending Black and other racialized communities from attacks. The JLC lobbied unions to establish human rights committees at the local, provincial, and national level, including the National Standing Committee

is a Eurocentric term since racialized people constitute the vast majority of the world's population.

on Racial Discrimination of the Trades Labour Congress. This was pioneering work at a time when racism was still prevalent in unions, reflecting broader societal sentiments. These committees focused on extensive education for both union members and the general public. Over time, their efforts evolved into lobbying for anti-discrimination legislation, which led to the enactment of the 1944 Ontario Racial Discrimination Act, prohibiting discriminatory signage. Building on this momentum, and in partnership with human rights organizations and ethno-racial community groups, the JCL helped bring about Canada's first Fair Employment Practices Act was implemented in Ontario in 1951, addressing employment discrimination (Lukas and Persad 2004).

However, racial segregation was still prominent in many parts of the country, particularly in Dresden, Ontario. A concerted campaign was initiated by the Black community in Dresden who reached out to many groups including unions to lobby the government to intervene. Along with allies, labour played a central role testing and confirming racial segregation in Dresden which pressured the provincial government to respond. In 1954, Ontario implemented the Fair Accommodation Act, barring discrimination in services being delivered (Lukas and Persad 2004).

The introduction of the Canadian Charter of Rights and Freedoms in 1981 had a profound impact on Canadian society. In this spirit, the Ontario Federation of Labour (OFL) received government funding to launch a public education campaign titled "Racism Hurts Everyone" (Ng 1995). The campaign produced posters, leaflets, and television ads, and an anti-racism coordinator was hired to oversee the initiative. A week-long educational program was also developed to trained activists from affiliated unions to conduct anti-racism workshops (Das Gupta 1998). Many of the trained activists were racialized people, and as an unintended outcome, the campaign helped build a strong network of anti-racism advocates within the ranks of labour (Das Gupta 1998).

Another significant event occurred in 1986, when African Canadian, Caribbean, Chinese and South Asian unionists came together to form the Ontario Coalition of Black Trade Unionists (OCBTU) (Das Gupta 1998, Ng 2010). The OCBTU, later renamed Coalition of Black Trade Unionists (CBTU), functioned as an autonomous body, enabling racialized union activists from different unions to come together, ensuring that the anti-racism agenda remained at the forefront and holding the predominantly white male union leadership accountable for their actions, or lack thereof.[8] In 1993, OCBTU

8 Today, CBTU remains an active force in the labour movement, frequently collaborating with ACLA on many projects and campaigns. It's strong history has paved the way for many groups, including ACLA.

released a report that exposed the glaring absence of racialized people on staff in Canadian unions, with less than half of the unions listed receiving a 'passing grade.' The report proved effective, compelling union leaders to act quickly to demonstrate their commitment to racial equity by hiring more racialized staff.

Greater momentum was achieved when a resolution adopted during the 1992 Canadian Labour Congress (CLC) convention called for the creation of an anti-racism task force to hold nationwide public hearings and document racism affecting union members (Das Gupta 2007). This initiative expanded support for anti-racism measures, as both rank and file members and institutional affiliates made written submissions and presentations to the task force identifying the harms of racism and pledging to tackle systemic racism within unions and society. The strategies and recommendations were compiled into a report which anti-racism activists hailed as a blueprint for change, identifying sixty-two major areas requiring union action. There was much hope placed in this report, and the project's heightened national profile of the project gave the impression that anti-racism within the labour movement had finally reached a critical level.

However, changes arising from the report have been uneven and inadequate, leaving many activists to conclude that the report had limited traction (Ng 2010; Walker 2006). In a study conducted by Kumar and Murray (2006: 92), fewer than 25% of unions have any program or structure dedicated to supporting racialized workers. Only 17.8% of unions can service members in languages other than English or French (Kumar and Murray 2006: 92–93), which is concerning given that Canada's labour force growth heavily relies on immigrant and migrant workers, many of whom do not speak either of the country's official languages.

Only a handful of unions have initiated projects geared towards the influx of Asians in the workforce. The Union of Needletrades Industrial and Textile Employees (UNITE)[9] and later the Hotel and Employees and Restaurant Employees (HERE)[10] were the first unions to introduce English as a Second Language (ESL) courses for their members. Both unions have a highly feminized membership with a significant portion of the members being first generation immigrants with limited or no knowledge of the English language. When the programs began in the early 80s and 90s, many Chinese women workers were already employed in the garment and hotel industries, and the unions negotiated to implement ESL classes during work hours. Instead of teaching traditional ESL, the curriculum was tailored to the workplace context, teaching

9 UNITE was formed in 1995 through the merger of the Amalgamated Clothing and Textile Workers Union and the International Ladies Garment Workers Union.

10 In 2004, UNITE and HERE merged together and became UNITE HERE.

workers job-specific terminology and how to advocate for their rights, especially in the areas of health and safety (Ng, personal communication).

In more recent years, the International Brotherhood of Electrical Workers (IBEW) introduced a health and safety program in Chinese to educate newly certified electricians about legislative protections and health and safety on the job. Chinese workers were were reaching out to the union hall in search of unionized paid work, as employers were exploiting their lack of "Canadian experience" by paying below minimum wage and disregarding hazardous working conditions. To help these workers secure unionized jobs, a weekend training school was established where workers were taught the trade's terminology and the practical application of the local electrical code, providing them the insider knowledge they needed (CLC, n.d.). These programs were designed for non-members and offered at no cost to the participants. Word of this goodwill spread, generating organizing leads, and eventually many of these workers became members of IBEW.

In a different area, the United Steelworkers (USW) partnered with Migrante, a Filipinx community-based advocacy group, to organize migrant workers working under the federal government's Live-in Caregiver Program (LCP). In 2000, 87% of LCP caregivers were Filipinx women (Goli 2009: 11). Although domestic workers are exempt from unionizing, USW launched the Independent Workers Association – Home Workers Section, offering associate membership to all home workers, both migrant and permanent residents. The campaign advocates for improved employment conditions and greater protections for live-in caregivers. By joining, workers gain access to training, community networking, legal counsel, insurance, and discounted dental services (Khosla 2014).

While USW's efforts with home workers should be applauded, the union was simultaneously engaged in a public campaign to prevent Chinese migrant workers from being employed by HD Mining in northern British Columbia. The union claimed that their concerns are not with the Chinese workers themselves butwith HD Mining's use of cheaper migrant labourers unfamiliar with Canadian safety standards instead of hiring locally. However, in a leaflet titled "BC Jobs for BC Workers," USW's message strongly suggests that jobs should be reserved for Canadian workers, echoing labour's shameful history of opposition to Chinese workers during the construction of Canada's Pacific Railway over a century ago.

Despite some notable advances achieved for and by racialized workers, significant issues persist inside the house of labour. Although there are now more racialized people visibly involved in unions, the underlying power dynamics have not shifted. Racialized people may be present on equity committees, but they are less likely to be found in core union roles such as bargaining, pension, and health and safety committees as well as leadership positions (Walker 2006). In this context, unions continue to act as gate-keepers, limiting the influence of racialized workers on union policy and practice. Consequently, self-organizing among racialized workers remains a crucial force for driving progress and holding union leadership accountable.

5 ACLA in the Community

ACLA recognizes the gap between unions and Asian communities and strives to develop stronger labour connections within these communities. This is accomplished by, first, demonstrating that Asian workers are actively involved in the labour movement and, second, by supporting and taking on issues relevant to Asian workers and their communities. ACLA's dual role is to promote a working-class perspective while ensuring that an intersectional analysis is applied, particularly in addressing the needs of racialized workers, especially Asian Canadian working-class communities. For example, when discussing issues such as universal childcare, ACLA raises questions about the specific needs of Asian immigrant women, both as workers and as women who rely on these services.

ACLA's community role was exemplified during the Severe Acute Respiratory Syndrome (SARS) outbreak in Toronto in 2003, and more recently during the COVID-19 pandemic. Both outbreaks triggered widespread public health concerns, and because both viruses originated from China, East Asians and Southeast Asians were stigmatized as potential carriers, resurfacing deep-seeded prejudices that were once commonplace in Canadian society. Unions responded to these crises by advocating for income support, enhanced employment insurance coverage, communicating health and safety precautions to members, and more recently lobbying for paid sick days. While unions focused on the economic and safety aspects, ACLA worked with Asian community leaders to draw attention to the discriminatory dimension of the crisis.

During the SARS outbreak, many members of ACLA were on the frontlines fighting the racism, xenophobia, and panic that gripped Toronto's Chinatowns, levelling near-catastrophic losses for local businesses as patrons stayed away, fearful of contracting SARS. ACLA recognized the SARS epidemic as part of a larger historical pattern of targeting and scapegoating certain communities during times of crisis. In response, ACLA organized solidarity rallies and dinners at affected restaurants to support these struggling businesses.

Nearly two decades later in 2020, the COVID-19 pandemic brought a sharp resurgence of anti-Asian racism and violence. ACLA worked steadily to bring attention to the impact of COVID-19 on racialized workers, particularly those of Chinese descent or those perceived to be of Chinese descent. In conjunction with labour and community partners, ACLA organized a series of webinars that focused on the specific struggles Asian communities faced during the pandemic, explored the conflict of the model minority myth, and how that perpetuates racial divisions, especially anti-Black racism.

ACLA's responses to SARS and COVID-19 demonstrate its ability to fully engage with community priorities. In contrast, unions' institutional obligation to serve the employment needs of their members often sidelines broader community concerns, like fighting racism when competing interests arise. ACLA can therefore act as a valuable bridge between these two spheres.

Another example of ACLA's role as a community connector is its active participation in the response to the 2010 Maclean's article titled "Too Asian: Some frosh don't want to study at an Asian university" which appeared in the magazine's Guide to Canadian Universities. The article was publicly criticized by community groups and various levels of government for its irresponsible journalism, which conveyed xenophobic and anti-Asian sentiments (Coloma 2013). As a member of the response campaign's steering committee, ACLA reached out to unions and labour centrals to garner additional support. Through this outreach, more unions become aware of the issue, leading the Ontario Federation of Labour to write to Maclean's in solidarity with the campaign, demanding an apology for the article.

Most recently, ACLA played a central role in organizing the Toronto Solidarity Rally Against Anti-Asian Racism, held on March 28, 2021. Over 5000 people gathered at Nathan Phillips Square in response to the murder of eight people at an Asian owned businesses in Atlanta, Georgia against the backdrop of COVID-19 related anti-Asian racism and a long history of systemic exclusion experienced by Asian people in Canada. The horrific crime struck a chord, highlighting the violence disproportionately targeting women and seniors across the country through verbal assaults and physical attacks. The rally's message condemned the misogyny and white supremacy at the root of the problem and underscored the need to stand in solidarity with Black and Indigenous peoples. Demonstrators called for defunding the police, investment in communities, decriminalization of sex work, the need for paid sick days, a livable minimum wage, social housing, and status for all (Lee 2021). ACLA reached out to union allies to assist with the event, bringing in additional marshals and helping with logistics and equipment set-up. The solidarity shown by unions was deeply valued and significantly contributed to the rally's success.

6 ACLA's Progress and Challenges

ACLA's outreach activities aim to strengthen the presence of Asian workers in a progressive labour movement, ensuring that the voices, legacy, and struggles of Asian workers are not overlooked. In its early stages, ACLA concentrated on organizing internally within unions, spreading awareness, and recruiting members. This included setting up information tables at conferences, organizing events and educationals, and finding opportunities to speak at union membership meetings and conferences. These activities continue to be central to ACLA's mission. Through these initiatives, ACLA successfully convinced several unions to provide basic stewards' training in multiple languages. Additionally, ACLA persuaded the Canadian Union of Public Employees (CUPE) and the United Food and Commercial Workers (UFCW) union locals, with large numbers of Chinese members facing language barriers, to translate their collective agreements into Chinese.

While union culture has not been radically transformed by its activities, ACLA is highly valued as an important support network for Asian and other racialized workers. With so few active Asian unionists, this support is vital for cultivating new activists and nurturing existing ones who need to recharge from navigating the union terrain. In this space, encouraging exchanges also inspire individuals to seek leadership positions within the labour movement and elsewhere.

ACLA's supportive role extends beyond providing a sense of belonging and encouragement. It also acts as a resource for those who are dealing with issues in the workplace or with their union. These issues vary from not knowing where to seek help; to feeling uncomfortable raising a concern or being unable to get assistance from anywhere else. The network of members offers a listening ear and advice. ACLA has intervened in cases of racial discrimination, writing letters of support, attending meetings and hearings for moral support, and even helping to file human rights complaints. When the issue has involved a union, ACLA has not held back from voicing concerns over a case. Although this may strain relations with some unions and labour centrals, the ability to speak openly about racism and other forms of discrimination is critical to ACLA's autonomy and independence. ACLA's distinct yet close connection within the union sphere allows it to function as a de facto watchdog organization, holding labour accountable when equity principles are purposely ignored.

In Ontario, tensions have intensified for ACLA in recent years whenever union endorsements for political candidates are considered. These endorsements are crucial for candidates as they can often translate into significant resources, such as campaign volunteers and financial contributions. Unions engage in electoral politics because the outcome of elections directly influence public policy, which in turn affects both current and future union members.

While unions frequently speak about equity and improving representation for marginalized members, both within unions and in electoral politics, this commitment is not always reflected in practice. On several occasions, unions have bypassed their own equity guidelines in favour of making "strategic decisions," leading to racialized candidates receiving less support than white candidates with comparable qualifications and connections to the labour movement. Unions have rationalized these "strategic decisions" by arguing they need to support candidates they believe have the best chance of winning in the current political climate.

On at least two occasions, ACLA endorsed an Asian candidate in municipal elections despite unions choosing to endorse white candidates. These endorsements were not intended as a protest against mainstream labour, but were made because the Asian candidates were equally, if not more qualified, and represented the demographics and interests of the communities in which they ran. Additionally, the justifications offered by the unions for supporting the white candidates were unacceptable and contradicted union policies designed to promote the visibility and leadership of equity-seeking groups. ACLA has become increasingly involved in election work to support racialized candidates who are often passed over by unions for self-serving reasons that reinforce the systemic barriers already faced by these groups.

Union decisions that disregard the discriminatory impact of their actions, such as election endorsements and cases like the HD mining dispute discussed earlier, can hinder the relationship building efforts unions are trying to forge with racialized communities. Community coalition work is essential for union survival and success, yet progress in this area remains underdeveloped, especially within the Asian community. A key issue is that the vast majority of labour representatives interfacing with racialized communities are white, and often lack the cultural awareness and communication skills needed to build effective partnerships within these communities. This issue becomes more pronounced when unions with a significant number of racialized members, are primarily led by white leaders who often speak on their behalf. There are still very few Asian union representatives, and most are not in positions of authority where they can speak for their union or influence decisions on the allocation of union resources.

7 Limitations of Capacity and of Resources

ACLA faces unique challenges within the labour and community organizing spheres due to its autonomous status. One of the biggest challenges is limited capacity, as all the work is volunteer-based and undertaken in addition to the members' existing responsibilities. Two ACLA members interviewed for this study, both from the same union, British Columbia Government Employees' Union (BCGEU), used the same metaphor "working off the side of my desk" to describe how they handle their additional responsibilities with ACLA, revealing the struggle between their regular union duties and their commitment to ACLA.[11] Notably, BCGEU has been quite supportive of ACLA, providing paid time off to promote ACLA at events, approving conference attendance, releasing other Asian members to partake in ACLA activities, and providing access to office space, equipment and supplies. This support has been instrumental to developing and sustaining ACLA in British Columbia. However, when union work intensifies, ACLA activities invariably take a back seat.

As volunteers, ACLA members have limited time to devote to ACLA activities, leading to a focus on immediate tasks and issues at the expense of strategic and long-term planning. The lack of year-to-year planning means that ACLA's organizational direction is often reactive, with no well-defined program or strategic plan to guide the group's efforts. Additionally, because ACLA operates outside the formal union structure, its programming is more precarious than union sanctioned equity measures and anti-racism initiatives, as there is little institutional obligation to ensure its success.

ACLA is fortunate to have several well-respected "movers and shakers" within its ranks, whose access to resources and union relationships can initiate and support new ideas. However, the threat of activist burn-out is a serious concern. The labour movement is notorious for overextending activists for unsustainable periods, often leading to physical and mental fatigue (Rooks 2004). The problem is particularly severe for ACLA given the limited pool of Asian activists to draw from. Additionally, ACLA's mandate to address racism within the labour movement exposes the organization and its members to potential backlash, which could have consequences for both the collective and individual members when boundaries are tested. While this boldness is a strength, it can impact the recruitment of new members. Furthermore, ACLA is not immune to the political maneuvering prevalent in the union environment,

11 Gayle Nye, interview with author, February 27, 2014; Lorene Oikawa, interview with author, April 1, 2014.

and its lack of formal institutional structure makes it susceptible to being used to fulfill personal agendas or union manipulation.

In addition to facing capacity constraints, the organization lacks a stable funding stream, instead relying on one-time donations from individuals and unions. ACLA intentionally chooses not to seek out more financial help from unions in order to maintain its independence.[12] In other words, ACLA recognizes that relying too heavily on union funding could compromise its integrity, particularly when taking a stance that might be unpopular among unions. However, without steady funding, it is difficult for ACLA to mount any significant campaign or initiative independently. More importantly, the organization's ability to envision and plan beyond its current capabilities is inhibited by its financial limitations.

Finally, ACLA faces the challenge of representing the wide range of ethnicities and cultural identities encapsulated within the term "Asian." The diversity and multitude of languages spoken can make it difficult to develop a cohesive sense of affiliation among Asian Canadians. "Asians are more likely to identify as Chinese-Canadian, Korean-Canadian or Indo-Canadian",[13] presenting a unique dilemma for ACLA, as it strives to build connections both within and between Asians workers and their communities. As Canada's demographic continues to shift, with some groups having a heavier concentration of recent immigrants, ACLA's ability to communicate across multiple languages will become paramount.

8 What's Next for ACLA?

As a collective, ACLA has successfully carved out a space for Asian Canadian workers within the labour movement. By adopting an independent and autonomous structure, they have the ability to self-determine issues and priorities most important to Asian workers. Conversely, their decision to forgo a formally integrated and sanctioned relationship within the union structure means they lack official status, which can hinder their legitimacy, access, and ability to secure resources. This is a fundamental paradox that will not be easily reconciled.

Tracing the development of ACLA underscores that workers' interests and needs are shaped by race, gender, and class experiences leading to divergent

12 Winnie Ng, interview with author, February 17, 2014.

13 Lorene Oikawa, interview with author, April 1, 2014.

perspectives within the labour movement. Critics of separate organizing might view the creation of ACLA as a divisive strategy, one that fragments the strength of workers into a special interest group, potentially diluting collective power and focus. However, it crucial to understand the intent behind such efforts. There is a distinction between separate organizing aimed at permanent separation and separate organizing as a strategy to achieve greater political influence and equity (Briskin 1999). ACLA is a prime example of workers organizing to amplify their voices within the labour movement and to build connections with other ethno-racial groups underrepresented in unions.

In 2020, ACLA celebrated its 20th anniversary, a milestone that coincided with the resurgence of the Black Lives Matter movement, sparked by the police killings of George Floyd in Minneapolis and Regis Korchinski-Paquet in Toronto. ACLA was an early supporter of Black Lives Matter in Toronto, participating in their actions and organizing roundtable discussions with other Asian-identified organizations to discuss how members of the Asian community can support the movement. That year, ACLA collaborated with labour partners and the Chinese Canadian National Council – Toronto Chapter and Chinese Canadian National Council – Social Justice to examine the connection between anti-Asian racism and the importance of solidarity with Black and Indigenous communities. These conversations are vital, especially as anti-Asian violence has become widespread, with some media and segments of the Asian community wrongly blaming the Black community instead of recognizing these actions as products of white supremacy and colonialism. ACLA aims to be a critical voice in challenging this ideology by promoting working class solidarity with other oppressed communities. This objective was central to the webinars and other ongoing efforts to challenge the prevalence of racism in all its forms.

After two decades of organizing, ACLA's work is more necessary than ever. The rise in anti-Asian racism due to the COVID-19 pandemic serves as a reminder that racism targeting the Asian community is not new – it has merely evolved in the twenty-first century. The alarming increase in violence, hate crimes, and overt racism has sparked a need for national and international dialogue as well as calls to action to counter the surge in Sinophobia. In this context, ACLA remains one of the few organizations dedicated to articulating the experiences of Asian workers during the pandemic. Asian workers, along with other racialized workers, are struggling to survive in a system already stacked against them. Their concentration in precarious work in sectors such as care work, retail, and food service has put them at greater risk of contracting the virus and has also led to disproportionate unemployment rates. Moreover, the increasing levels of racial hostility and the failure of employers to address systemic and individual forms of anti-Asian racism have further compounded the stress and risks on the job. Sadly, these issues are not new, pre-existing long before the pandemic began.

In response, ACLA has been collaborating with community partners and labour allies to address the rise in anti-Asian racism and workplace discrimination. Through educational workshops and webinars, ACLA has been highlighting the need for solidarity and action during this crisis. The heightened awareness of these issues has led to a surge in requests to speak on the topic. Recent events have also inspired more individuals to join ACLA, reinvigorating the British Columbia chapter and expanding the organization's reach and capabilities. Additionally, it is essential to broaden and strengthen relationships with community allies to maintain strong multiracial alliances. This is a key element in combating white supremacist hegemony, both within unions and beyond, and will be central to the projects and campaigns ACLA embarks on.

Looking ahead, it is evident that ACLA plays a necessary role within the labour movement, though it has not yet reached its full potential. As unions grapple with reinventing themselves to appeal to an increasingly feminized and racialized workforce, ACLA fills a critical gap. While the organization's work is modest in scale, it offers a glimpse of what is possible. Expanding the presence of Asian activists will help reshape the labour movement, bringing new perspectives that will contribute to an alternative vision and drive transformative changes in how unions operate.

References

Block, Sheila, and Galabuzi, Grace-Edward (2011) *Canada's Colour Coded Labour Market: The Gap for Racialized Workers*. Toronto: Wellesley Institute and Canadian Centre for Policy Alternatives.

Briksin, Linda (1999) Autonomy, diversity, and integration: union women's separate organizing in North America and Western Europe in the context of restructuring and globalization. *Women Studies International Forum* 22 (5): 543–554.

Cheung, L. (2006) *Racial Status and Employment Outcomes*. Ottawa: Canadian Labour Congress.

Creese, G. (1989) Solidarity or exclusion: Vancouver workers confront the "oriental problem." *BC Studies* 80: 24–51.

Coloma, Roland (2013) Too Asian? On racism, paradox and ethno-nationalism. *Discourse: Studies in the Cultural Politics of Education* 34(4): 579–598.

Das Gupta, T. (1998) Anti-racism and the organized labour movement. In: V. Satzewich (ed.) *Racism and Social Inequality in Canada: Concepts, Controversies and Strategies of* Resistance. Toronto: Thompson Educational Publishing, 315–334.

Das Gupta, T. (2007) Racism in the Labour Movement. In: G. Hunt and D. Rayside (eds.) *Equity, Diversity, and Canadian Labour*. Toronto: University of Toronto Press, 181–207.

Fletcher, B. and Gapasin, F. (2003) The politics of labour and race in the USA. *Socialist Register* 39: 245–264.

Forrest, A. (1993) A view from outside the whale: The treatment of women and unions in industrial relations. In: L. Briskin and P. McDermott (eds.) *Women Challenging Unions: Feminism, Democracy and Militancy*. Toronto: University of Toronto Press, 325–341.

Galabuzi, G. (2008) The economic exclusion of racialized communities: A statistical profile. In: B. Walker (ed.) *The History of Immigration and Racism in Canada*. Toronto: Canadian Scholars' Press Inc, 279–301.

Galarneau, Diane. 2015. "Unionization Rates Falling." (Catalogue no. 11-630-X2015005). Statistics Canada. May 17. <www150.statcan.gc.ca/n1/pub/11-630-x/11-630-x2015005-eng.htm>

Goli, M. (2009) *The Philippine women of Canada's live-in care giver program: Ethical issues and perspectives* (Master's thesis). file:///C:/Users/Anna/Downloads/ETD4519.pdf.

Hing, Alex (1992) Organizing Asian pacific American workers in the AFL-CIO: New opportunities. *Amerasia Journal* 18(1): 141–148.

Jackson, A. (2002) *Is Work Working for Workers of Colour?* Ottawa: Canadian Labour Congress.

Khosla, Prabha. 2014. "Working Women, Working Poor." <https://www.unifor.org/sites/default/files/legacy/documents/document/workingwomenworkingpoor_letter_web.pdf>.

Kishi, R. and Ahn, J. (2002) Part of the movement: Asian Canadian labour alliance. *Our Times* 21(4): 20–27.

Kumar, P. and Murray, G. (2006) Innovations in Canadian unions: Patterns, cases and consequences. In: P. Morency, J.D., Malenfant, E.C., and MacIsaac, S. (eds.) *Immigration and Diversity: Population Projections for Canada and its Regions, 2011 to 2036*, Catalogue no. 91-551-X. Ottawa: Statistics Canada.

Lee, Min Sook. 2021. "End Anti-Asian Hate: Resisting Violence In All Its Forms." *Our Times Magazine*. April 26. <https://ourtimes.ca/article/stop-anti-asian-hate>.

Lukas, Salome. & Persad, Judy Vashti. 2004. *Through the Eyes of Workers of Colour: Linking Struggles for Social Justice*. Toronto: Women Working with Immigrant Women.

Morency, Jean-Dominique, Malenfant, Éric Caron, & MacIsaac, Samuel. 2017. "Immigration and Diversity: Population Projections for Canada and its Regions,

2011 to 2036." (Catalogue no. 91-551-X). Statistics Canada. January 25. <www150.statcan.gc.ca/n1/pub/91-551-x/91-551-x2017001-eng.htm>.

Ng, W. (1995) *In the margins: Challenging racism in the labour movement.* Unpublished master's thesis, Ontario Institute for Studies in Education, University of Toronto.

Ng, W. (2010) *Racing solidarity, remaking labour: Labour renewal from a decolonizing and anti-racism perspective* (Doctoral dissertation). Retrieved from https://tspace.library.utoronto.ca/bitstream/1807/26495/1/Ng_Winnie_W_W_201011_PhD_thesis.pdf. University of Toronto.

Rooks, D. (2004) Sticking it out or packing it in? Organizer retention in the new labor movement. In: R. Milkman and K. Voss (eds.) *Rebuilding Labor: Organizing and Organizers in the New Union Movement.* Ithaca, New York: Cornell University Press.

Statistics Canada. 2013. 2011 *National Household Survey: Data tables based on labour force status, visible minority, immigrant status and period of immigration, highest certificate, diploma or degree, age groups and sex for the population aged 15 years and over, in private households of Canada, provinces, territories, census metropolitan areas and census agglomerations.* (Catalogue no. 99-012-X2011038). www150.statcan.gc.ca/n1/en/catalogue/99-012-X2011038.

Walker, M. (2006) Are we there yet? The struggle for equity in Canadian unions. In: J. Foley and P. Baker (eds.) *Unions, Equity and the Path to Renewal.* Vancouver, Toronto: UBC Press, 84–93.

White, J. (2007) Looking back: A brief history of everything. In: G. Hunt and D. Rayside (eds.) *Equity, Diversity, and Canadian Labour.* Toronto: University of Toronto Press, 25–48.

Wong, K. (1992) Building unions in Asian pacific communities. *Amerasia Journal* 18(1): 149–154.

Yates, C. (2005) Segmented labour, united unions? How unions in Canada cope with increased diversity. *Transfer: European Review of Labour and Research* 11(4): 617–628.

CHAPTER 14

A Love Letter to Asian Canadian Studies: On Ethical Solidarities and Decolonial Futures

Janey Lew

> The publication of the *Asian Canadian Studies Reader* ... makes me want to weep with joy.
>
> LILY CHO (2018: 232)

∴

Asian Canadian studies has emerged from its developmental narrative of vexed arrival into a period that emphasizes promising futurity. Recently, scholars have been considering Indigenous and Asian Canadian relations in their work.[1] In the last few decades, amid longstanding calls to decolonize academic research,[2] those outside of Indigenous studies have also begun to look towards "Indigenizing" as a radical critical move.[3] Moreover, in post-Truth and Reconciliation era Canada, reckoning with Indigeneity has been invoked with increased frequency as a priority for scholars across diverse fields. Asian Canadian studies scholars, who have been asking these questions for some time, could be poised for significant interventions.

In this chapter, I ask: To what extent is decolonial solidarity important to Asian Canadians, or to be more specific, those of us invested in the intellectual

---

1 Among them, Day (2016); Lo (2008); R. Wong (2008); Phung (2015); Lai (2013); Mawani (2010); Izumi (2015); and Oikawa (2017).

2 In particular, see Smith (2013); Mihesuah and Wilson (2004). These calls have only intensified in Canada since the official apology for residential schools and subsequent calls for reconciliation. See, for instance, Battiste et. al. (2002); Haig-Brown (2008); Johnson (2016); and Louie et. al. (2017).

3 For instance, Findlay (2004). As Braz (2015) notes, Findlay's exhortation has been somewhat curiously canonized. Braz is among several critics who have called Findlay into question. Others include Suzack (2004) and Hill (2012).

(and for some activist)[4] project of Asian Canadian studies? Asian Canadian studies has, to some extent, suffered from immobilization from anxiety. Anxiety is one among several buried affects underscoring Asian Canadian studies. Surfacing these buried affects in order to foreground love is important in order enliven the deep coalitional structure of Asian Canadian studies and to propel Asian Canadian action and solidarity. The chapter ends with a close reading of the personal essay "Ganbatte!" (2008) by Lily Yuriko. Through this reading, I suggest raising up Asian Canadian queer and feminist histories, knowledges, and critiques to guide Asian Canadian studies to ethical solidarity with Indigenous sovereignty and resurgence movements.

1 "There Is No There There"

An urge to theorize and situate Asian Canadian subjectivities, literary contributions, historical significance, and institutional legitimacy has been a tendency in the field since the late 1990s to 2000s. A tension exists at the heart of Asian Canadian studies' self-reflexive ground-setting between asserting that there is indeed a *there there* and a hesitancy about foreclosing the quality, nature, boundaries, and forms of exactly *what there is.*[5]

Miki's "Asiancy: Making Space for Asian Canadian Writing" (1998) critically influenced the direction of scholarship in the field. Addressing the canon wars over difference, language, and legitimacy within Canadian. Literature, or "CanLit," in the 1990s, Miki posits Asian Canadian writing as a site of disruptive power and explicitly broaches the topic of race within the study of English-Canadian literatures. Miki's potent meta-critical analysis shaped the work of subsequent generations of scholars. Despite addressing an institutional context decades in the past, "Asiancy" still speaks to Asian Canadian studies' ongoing tensions and institutional situation. Anxiety over institutional scarcity and precarity remains a preoccupation. There continues to be a lack of space and resources for the flourishment and sustainment of interdisciplinary Asian Canadian studies research. Even recently, as Pon et. al. points out,

4 Scholars who have explicitly addressed the activist underpinnings of Asian Canadian studies include Coloma (2013); Li (2007); Lee (2008); and Beauregard (2008).

5 Returning to the site of her family home in Oakland, California to discover it no longer existed, Stein wrote: "what was the use of my having come from Oakland it was not natural to have come from there yes write about it if I like or anything if I like but not there, there is no there there" (1993: 298).

the particular institutional spaces that have formed are limited in number and capacity and are also relatively new (2017: 11–12).

The anxious urge to narrate or repeatedly ground Asian Canadian studies is partially a response to the implication from dominant discourses within and outside the academy that *there is no there there.* Moreover, the backside of this tension, what I call resistance to foreclosure, is equally reactive against being told by those outside of the field (from within whose institutional spaces we are otherwise captivated or situating our work) the significance, value, and particularities of our racialized bodies, experiences, affinities, and intellectual genealogies. Traversing this tension is the additional pressure of an unspoken imperative to not bite (at least not too hard) the hands that feed us.

Asian Canadian studies has defined itself through resistances to containment, semiotic deferrals, "unfinished projects," and capacious encounters.[6] On one hand, Asian Canadian indeterminacy has been generative. On the other hand, as it moves to confront settler colonialism, the field advances in a direction towards voluntary foreclosure. I refer to foreclosure in the sense of relinquishing assets or investments paid into the structures of capital and privilege within settler colonialism. Asian Canadian anxiety is a condition of settler colonialism. Diagnosing settler colonialism, much like diagnosing anxiety, is only the first step to working through it. Remaining tied to the objects of our losses will not lead us through foreclosure. If decolonization is indeed a goal for Asian Canadian studies, we not only need to see ourselves and our complicities within settler colonialism, but we also need to focus our attention on seeing our ways out of it and making moves to surrender from it, to dispossess ourselves as settler subjects. To survive foreclosure, Asian Canadians also need to renegotiate and recover surrender from a capitalist vocabulary that equates it with losses.

Nearly twenty years after Miki's seminal work, reflecting on the climate of Canadian neoliberal racial politics of the 1980s and 90s whose exhausting effects are still felt in Asian Canadian cultural organizing today, Lai compellingly states that the very term Asian Canadian, which arises from a discursive need to articulate coalitions, is "deeply relational" and that the "site of relation [is] always a struggle" (2014: 4–5). These deep, conflicted, affective dimensions of Asian Canadian settler-colonial racialization undergird the ways and means through which we have gone about grounding our scholarship, and they illuminate our sensitivities when it comes to attachment.

6 See Miki (1998); Lee (2007); Beauregard (2008); and Pon et. al. (2017).

2 Where Is the Love?

The slipperiness of Asian Canadian groundedness, our anxieties over living on borrowed grounds, our obediences and resistances to having our grounds determined by dominant white, heteropatriarcal, settler-colonial normativities and being told to stay within those boundaries, complicate our solidarities but do not altogether mask our longings for it. In this love letter to Asian Canadian studies, I attempt to nudge the field away from anxiety and towards love in order to locate a more solid grounding for approaching decolonial and revolutionary solidarities. To do so, I turn to Audre Lorde's notion of the erotic, or "the power of our unexpressed or unrecognized feeling" (1984: 53).

Across a number of recent contributions to Asian Canadian scholarship are expressions of feeling akin to Cho's unabashed "weep with joy" referenced in this chapter's epigraph.[7] In her book review, Cho shares her personal journey in academia and her struggles to find a home base for her work. Doing so, Cho acknowledges and affirms common experiences amongst those of us in Asian Canadian studies who have been interminably seeking a place that does not seem to exist from which to situate our work. In an analogous narrative, Day remarks on the "profound impact" of taking an undergraduate poetics course taught by Fred Wah, an experience that led her to the United States for further graduate work because Asian Canadian studies "was virtually nonexistent" (2015: 198). Day's actions are driven by the unexpressed feeling alluded to in the words "profound impact." Cho recalls her own significant early career experience, that of writing an essay on the novel, *Disappearing Moon Cafe:* "It was the first time in my life as a student where I was given the chance to think and write about things that felt so close to me, and that I cared about so much" (232). Cho's description reveals a sense of barely contained intimacy and longing for intellectual pleasure and power. Across undercurrents of dissonant belonging, restless captivity, anxious foreclosures, and unsettled relationality, roll waves of Asian Canadian love.

In seeking to answer why Indigeneity and decolonization are important to Asian Canadian studies, it is vital to travel through love to get there. Surfacing

---

7 A handful of examples that demonstrate sublimated personal and affective narratives within Asian Canadian analysis: Shen (2011: 113); Kamboureli (2015: 190); Troeung (2015: 193–194); Fung (2017: 88). Poignantly, in the introduction to *Slanting I, Imagining We,* Lai simply states, "Of course this is a personal project" (2014: IX). She goes on to write, "The cultural movements of [the 1980s and 1990s] were saturated with love, joy envy, competition, rage, horror, sorrow, and dismay. These emotions could be crushing, but they could also lead to generative acts of creation and critique" (2014: X).

the erotic as a constitutive force and source of Asian Canadian studies is, above all, how we arrive at answers to anything that truly matters. As Lorde writes, "The erotic is the nurturer or nursemaid of all our deepest knowledge" (56). Not only that, but in seeking to engage in solidarity with other marginalized peoples, particularly with Indigenous communities, acknowledging love is a crucial act for constituting ethical, desire-based research frameworks such as those posited by Unangax̂ (Aleut) scholar Eve Tuck. Love is a necessary touchstone for ethical research in that it attunes us to "complexity, contradiction, and the self-determination of our lived lives" (Tuck 2009: 416). Love tells us where to look, and it tells us to look more closely and lovingly at ourselves, our histories, and our relations.

We need to recover Asian Canadian love from investments sunk into the multicultural settler colonial nation, an object of our affections that has persistently used emotion against us. Asian Canadian racialization depends upon our emotional captivity within a narrative of model citizenship that at once deprives us of feeling while also consuming our love and loyalty. As Ahmed writes, "emotions can attach us to the very conditions of our subordination" (2014: 12). Persistent representations of Asians as aliens or the machines of capital have also not only emphasized Asian unassimilability, but also stripped Asian bodies of the capacity for feeling altogether. The focus on the Asian body as a primary site of estrangement reinforces multicultural biopolitics of control and difference that at once assign abject feelings onto Asian bodies and, at the same time, evacuate our bodies of feeling.

Denials of feeling and insisting on the unintelligibility of feeling are tied to processes of othering, processes that hold others captive from the reaches of intimacy and affection.[8] Nevertheless, as Kim contends, Asian Canadian publics do not necessarily address themselves first and foremost to, or within, Canadian multiculturalism. Rather, Kim posits that Asian Canadian publics "emerge out of a desire for social intimacy ... and are also produced by a desire for collective belonging and emotional recognition" (2016: 6). Emotional attunement, in contrast to emotional denial, is crucial to shifting the grounds for solidarity, for imagining and creating new grounds for transformative praxis. For Asian Canadian studies, critical struggles with love may constitute the basis for organizing and acting in ethical solidarity.

8 Recent work in Asian Canadian literary studies that attends to affect, trauma, and racial melancholia seeks to address this gap on Asian Canadian racial affects. See Nguyen (2013); Troeung (2010); and Lorenzi (2011).

3 Feminist Wonder, Generative Life and Affectionate Solidarity

Solidarity depends upon an animation that comes from relationship and the wonders of intimacy.[9] In this section, I offer a close reading of the essay "Ganbatte!" by Japanese Canadian elder and lesbian anti-racist activist Lily Yuriko that highlights her experiential knowledge and affective intelligence. Putting Yuriko's essay in dialogue with Tanana Athabasca theorist Dian Million's notion of felt theory, I offer some concluding thoughts on the importance of prioritizing Asian Canadian love in our decolonial solidarity practices and consider ways forward for building ethical solidarities in support of Indigenous sovereignty and resurgence.

In "Ganbatte!" Yuriko describes a moment in the 1980s when she "met two Japanese-Canadian lesbians" at an Unlearning Racism workshop:

> I already knew them both in the Japanese-Canadian community. I knew them from the Powell Street Festival, which is an annual Japanese-Canadian festival that happens the first weekend of August in Vancouver and has been going on for almost thirty years. So, I was elated when I met them. And so were they when they met me, because they didn't know there was somebody in the community who was an older Japanese-Canadian lesbian. And we became friends after that and are still the best of friends to this day.
>
> 31

Here, Yuriko joyfully imparts a moment of feminist wonder, inscribed in the repetition of the word *met*. Wonderment is when "the object that appears before the subject is encountered for the first time, or *as if* for the first time … hence a departure from ordinary experience" (Ahmed: 179). Hence, Yuriko's elation is partly due to the thrill of extraordinary contact, or meeting "*as if* for the first time." Additional texture to Yuriko's story comes from the sense of history, intimacy, and embodied knowledge inscribed in the repetition of the phrase *I (already) knew them* and references to the Japanese Canadian community and Powell Street Festival. The repeated words *Japanese Canadian* and *friends* strengthen the sense of "collective belonging and emotional recognition" (Kim 6), attaching intimacy to the wonder of the encounter. This

9 Ahmed articulates feminist wonder as a relationship to the "creative, something that responds to the world with joy and care, as well as with an attention to details that are surprising" (179).

intimacy gives thickness to their mutual elation upon finding one another and provides the basis for their enduring friendship.

Love combines with wonder and makes it thick with complexity in Yuriko's telling of her life story, which tracks her experiences growing up in the "internment town" of Greenwood, BC, the complexities of being "out" as a Japanese-Canadian lesbian in the 1960s, the racism she faced within lesbian spaces, and her struggles to find and sustain social intimacies (30–31). Throughout the piece, Yuriko acknowledges different groups that contributed to her learning as well as some painful ruptures in relationships. The groups form, dissolve, and change throughout Yuriko's life—and as she moves in and out of groups, she changes as well. Her experiences eventually raise her to understand and affirm the value of her own "life experience and wisdom in dealing with social and political injustices" (31). Different points of love and connection not only affirm and nourish Yuriko's survival through her life's struggles, but also enable her to embody and claim these struggles as part of her experiential wisdom and knowledge.

The word *ganbatte* translates from Japanese as "hang in there" or "be strong," denoting encouragement through struggle.[10] Throughout the essay, Yuriko acknowledges her struggles, but relies on her attitude to keep her going, to encourage her to give back into her communities, and to seek new ones with joy and care. Yuriko embodies what Maldonado-Torres calls a "decolonial attitude": one of self-questioning oriented towards "love and understanding," which involves "re-claim[ing] the subjects and peoples that one encounters in the world and who live in precarious conditions" (2017: 439).[11] Yuriko summarizes her decolonial attitude early on in the piece: "I will never be at peace if there are women or children being violated or hungry. I can't live with injustices in any way" (30).

Turning toward Asian Canadian feminist and queer knowledges, histories, and critiques such as those in "Ganbatte!" has the potential to guide us toward decolonial futures. Yuriko's reflections refracted through her intersectional positionality constitute what Kim calls "affective intelligence" (5). Yuriko's affective intelligence and decolonial attitude impel her to agency through moments requiring social flexibility, learning, and boundary-setting across differences. Emotion, embodiment, politics, and knowledge are intimately interwoven, especially in the groups that she takes part in and that, for her,

10 With thanks to Yuriko for her correction of an earlier translation of the word *ganbatte* that appeared in a previous version of this paper.

11 With thanks to Yomaira Figeuroa, who elaborates on Maldonado-Torres's "decolonial attitude" (2015), for introducing me to the concept.

instantiate life-giving, albeit sometimes contentious, world-making activities. In this way, knowledge is produced through contact and has much to do with how we live through our feelings of contact.

Million's "felt theory" (2008) is a parallel example of experiential and embodied knowledge interwoven by affect and contact. Acknowledging the particularities that define felt theory as an Indigenous theory that comes from Indigenous histories and experiential knowledges, how might Asian Canadian studies interact with this concept? How might we cautiously approach Million's felt theory as an invitation to solidarity without colonizing and appropriating it?

Moments in the history of Asian Canadian coalitional organizing and the knowledge gained from these experiences provide some tools. In *Slanting I, Imagining We,* Lai writes about the concentrated efforts of Asian Canadian cultural organizing in the 1980s and 1990s. Through this, she lays out a document of experience as well as theory that contains key lessons for organizing and collective imagining across differences. One lesson is to avoid taking over the conversation in the work of allyship; another is to speak up and support one another when public conversations persistently undermine the creative struggles of underrepresented communities to organize. In short, showing up in solidarity means taking all precautions to ensure that our presences as allies do not exhaust the people that we intend to support by making their work about us.

Entering into solidarity with acknowledgement in the foreground enables us to work from what we know (that is, our own embodied and experiential knowledges of struggle and cultural politics), whilst encouraging us to act relationally as we remain attuned to the limits or excesses of our knowledge. In other words, acknowledgement urges us to seek and test for emotional recognition without guarantees that we will be met with answers. Acknowledgement holds us in wonder, even as it steps us forward with intimacy, and it urges us to inhabit this place of vulnerability in the face of potential conflict, rejection, or error.

In this way, I can read for resonances across Million's articulation of felt theory and Yuriko's narrative of embodied experiential knowledge whilst acknowledging the limitations of those connections. Both Yuriko and Million discuss the problems of patriarchy, but they each write from the specific histories and conditions of patriarchy within Japanese Canadian and First Nations communities. The two respectively contest white feminism for failing to account for racism and colonialism but do so from their distinct experiences of negotiating feminist values with other pressing political needs within their communities. Yuriko, for instance, expresses frustration at white feminists who do not hear the need for anti-racist work within feminism: "We needed to combat racism, so I couldn't afford to exclude men" (32). Million, on the other hand, writes about the delicate balance of foregrounding feminism within Indigenous struggles for self-determination.

In articulating embodied and experiential knowledges, both Yuriko and Million emphasize the ways that knowledges and histories are constitutive of the people who experience them. Yuriko explains, "It is not possible for me, as a woman of colour, who is a member of a small minority group in Canada, to separate myself from my 'roots' which is the essence of who I am and how I am seen in this world" (32). Yuriko's "roots" in some ways parallel Million's notion of subjective histories: "because *we are who we are* because of this history" (2009: 72).

My point is not to read Yuriko and Million's work interchangeably. Rather, it is to bring them into contact to test for wonder and lay a few bricks for intimacy. It is to acknowledge and find emotional resonance in the directions of bricks already laid in Million's writing, when, for instance, she states that she is "working toward a more expansive idea of community ... and an expansive number of alliances with others whose goal is for generative life and not death" (2013: 27). Million leaves a generous opening for potential solidarities. If the criterion for alliance is a shared goal to work towards "generative life," then perhaps there is room for Asian Canadian solidarity with Indigenous futures if we can acknowledge and reciprocate with love. Solidarity requires a loving openness to difference and an ability to not let difference get in the way of sharing. Ahmed describes an "affectionate solidarity" that may be what is needed to accomplish "the work that is done to create a different world" (141). Yet we must also accept that solidarity is a risky and imperfect formation—for that matter, so is love.

References

Ahmed, Sara (2014) *The Cultural Politics of Emotion*. Edinburgh: Edinburgh UP.

Battiste, Marie et al. (2002) Decolonizing Education in Canadian Universities: An Interdisciplinary, International, Indigenous Research Project. *Canadian Journal of Native Education* 26(2): 82–95.

Beauregard, Guy (2008) Asian Canadian Studies: Unfinished Projects. *Canadian Literature* 199: 6–27.

Braz, Albert (2015) Minus Literature: The Curious Canonisation of Len Findlay's 'Always Indigenize!' *British Journal of Canadian Studies* 28(1): 89–107.

Cho, Lily (2018) At Home in the *Asian Canadian Studies Reader*. *Asian Diasporic Visual Cultures and the Americas* 4 (1–2): 231–234.

Coloma, Roland Sintos (2013) 'Too Asian?' On Racism, Paradox and Ethno-Nationalism. *Discourse: Studies in the Cultural Politics of Education* 34(4): 579–598.

Day, Iyko (2015) Transnationalism Within. *Canadian Literature* 227: 198.

Day, Iyko (2016) *Alien Capital: Asian Racialization and the Logic of Settler Colonial Capitalism*. Durham: Duke University Press.

Figueroa, Yomaira (2015) Faithful Witnessing as Practice: Decolonial Readings of Shadows of Your Black Memory and The Brief Wondrous Life of Oscar Wao. *Hypatia: Journal of Feminist Philosophy* 30 (4): 641–656.

Findlay, Len (2004) Always Indigenize! The Radical Humanities in the Postcolonial Canadian University. *ARIEL: A Review of International English Literature* 31(1–2): 307–326.

Fung, Richard (2017) Looking for My Penis: The Eroticized Asian in Gay Video Porn. In: Pon and Coloma (eds.) *Asian Canadian Studies Reader*. Toronto: University of Toronto Press.

Haig-Brown, Celia (2008) Working a Third Space: Indigenous Knowledge in the Post/Colonial University. *Canadian Journal of Native Education* 31(1): 253–267, 319–320.

Hill, Elina (2012) A Critique of the Call to 'Always Indigenize!' *Peninsula: A Journal of Relational Politics* 2(1): 1–24.

Izumi, Masumi (2015) Resituating Displaced/Replaced Subjects in and of Japanese Canadian History. *Canadian Literature* 227: 194–196.

Johnson (Mukwa Musayett), Shelly (2016) Indigenizing Higher Education and the Calls to Action: Awakening to Personal, Political, and Academic Responsibilities. *Canadian Social Work Review* 33(1): 133–139.

Kamboureli, Smaro (2015) Inside/out of the Field: The Asian CanLit Imaginary. *Canadian Literature* 227: 189–191.

Kim, Christine (2016) *The Minor Intimacies of Race: Asian Publics in North America*. Champaign: University of Illinois Press.

Lai, Larissa (2013) Epistemologies of Respect: A Poetics of Asian/Indigenous Relation. In: Smaro Kamboureli and Christl Verduyn (eds.) *Critical Collaborations: Indigeneity: Diaspora, and Ecology in Canadian Literary Studies*. Waterloo: Wilfred Laurier UP.

Lai, Larissa (2014) *Slanting I, Imagining We: Asian Canadian Literary Production in the 1980s and 1990s*. Waterloo: Wilfrid Laurier UP.

Lee, Christopher (2007) The Lateness of Asian Canadian Studies. *Amerasia Journal* 33(2): 1–18.

Lee, Christopher (2008) Enacting the Asian Canadian. *Canadian Literature* 199: 28–44.

Li, Xiaoping (2007) *Voices Rising: Asian Canadian Cultural Activism*. Vancouver: UBC Press.

Lo, Marie (2008) Model Minorities, Models of Resistance: Native Figures in Asian Canadian Literature. *Canadian Literature* 196: 96–112.

Lorde, Audre (1984) *Sister Outsider: Essays and Speeches*. Trumansberg: Crossing Press.

Lorenzi, Lucia (2011) Shiktata Ga Nai: Mapping Japanese Canadian Melancholy in the Field of National and Literary Trauma. *West Coast Line* 45(3): 100–105.

Louie, Dustin William et. al (2017) Applying Indigenizing Principles of Decolonizing Methodologies in University Classrooms. *Canadian Journal of Higher Education* 47(3): 16–33.

Maldonado-Torres, Nelson (2017) Frantz Fanon and the Decolonial Turn in Psychology: From Modern/Colonial Methods to the Decolonial Attitude. *South African Journal of Psychology* 47(4): 432–441.

Mawani, Renisa (2010) *Colonial Proximities: Crossracial Encounters and Juridical Truths in British Columbia, 1871–1921*. Vancouver: UBC Press.

Mihesuah, Devon A., and Angela Cavender Wilson (2004) *Indigenizing the Academy: Transforming Scholarship and Empowering Communities*. Lincoln: University of Nebraska Press.

Miki, Roy (1998) *Broken Entries: Race, Subjectivity, Writing*. Toronto: Mercury Press.

Million, Dian (2009) Felt Theory: An Indigenous Feminist Approach to Affect and History. *Wicazo Sa Review* 24(2): 53–76.

Nguyen, Vinh (2013) Refugee Gratitude: Narrating Success and Intersubjectivity in Kim Thúy's Ru. *Canadian Literature* 219: 17–36.

Oikawa, Mona (2017) Cartographies of Violence: Creating Carceral Spaces and Expelling Japanese Canadians from the Nation. In: Pon G. and R., Coloma (eds.) *Asian Canadian Studies Reader*. Toronto: University of Toronto Press.

Phung, Malissa (2015) Asian-Indigenous Relationalities: Literary Gestures of Respect and Gratitude. *Canadian Literature* 227: 56–72.

Pon, Gordon, and Roland Sintos Coloma, eds (2017) *Asian Canadian Studies Reader*. Toronto: University of Toronto Press.

Pon, Gordon et. al (2017) Asian Canadian Studies Now: Directions and Challenges. In: G. Pon and R. Coloma (eds.) *Asian Canadian Studies Reader*. Toronto: University of Toronto Press.

Shen, Szu (2011) Where Is Taiwan on the Map of Asian Canadian Studies? *West Coast Line* 45(3): 112–117.

Smith, Linda (2013) *Decolonizing Methodologies: Research and Indigenous Peoples*. London: Zed.

Stein, Gertrude (1993) *Everybody's Autobiography*. Cambridge: Exact Change.

Suzack, Cheryl (2004) On the Practical 'Untidiness' of 'Always Indigenizing.' *English Studies in Canada* 30(2): 1–3.

Troeung, Y.-Dang (2010) Forgetting Loss in Madeleine Thien's Certainty. *Canadian Literature* 206: 91–108.

Troeung, Y.-Dang (2015) Alice Munro Country and Refugee Havens. *Canadian Literature* 227: 193–194.

Tuck, Eve (2009) Suspending Damage: A Letter to Communities. *Harvard Educational Review* 79(3): 409–427.

Wong, Rita (2008) Decolonizasian: Reading Asian and First Nations Relations in Literature. *Canadian Literature* 199: 158–180.

Yuriko, Lily. 2008. "Ganbatte!" *West Coast Line* 42(2): 30–33.

CHAPTER 15

Dumpster Fires, Burning Affects

Malissa Phung

> For all these reasons, I have decided to scalp you and burn your village to the ground.
>
> A Tribe Called Red's "Burn Your Village to the Ground" (2014)[1]

∵

When I first started writing "Indigenous and Asian Relation Making" (Phung 2019), it was during the height of what Alicia Elliot (Haudenosaunee) (2017), Jen Sookfong Lee (2017), and countless others have since called a "dumpster fire" threatening to burn down Canadian arts and letters. This was an unending period of political scandals that left writers, editors, journalists, academics, public intellectuals, and cultural organizers situated within and beyond the confines of the Canadian literary establishment fiercely divided over whether

1 This quote is sampled in A Tribe Called Red's song, "Burn Your Village to the Ground" (2014), referencing the infamous historical revisionist scene from a Thanksgiving pageantry play gone wrong in *The Addams Family Values* (1993) film. The quote comes from a derisive anti-colonial monologue that the gothic, pasty-white face painted Wednesday Addams, played by a young sardonic Christina Ricci, performs as Pocahontas, who breaks the paternalistic settler script to lead a biting satirical revenge fantasy sequence from the Native American perspective at a predominantly white summer camp for privileged settler children. Though the anti-colonial messaging is limited for obvious reasons, one being that this ahistorical colonial revenge fantasy is still framed by and for a white settler perspective, it still offers up a satisfying cinematic corrective to the overabundant visual archive of Hollywood cowboys and pioneers killing off Hollywood Indians played by white actors in red face and Indigenous actors. Thus, I have always been intrigued by the seamless way in which this nineties cult classic could conjure up an equal blend of righteous rage and gleefully gratifying comedy in its retelling of what the Thanksgiving holiday has meant for many Indigenous communities in America, particularly the New England tribes that bore the brunt of the first pilgrims' genocidal attacks. The affective register of this scene takes on a more compelling anti-colonial rage in A Tribe Called Red's sampling of Ricci's caustic performance in their signature electronic pow wow dance fusion of hip hop, reggae, dubstep, and Indigenous traditions of vocal chanting and drumming.

to douse the blazing flames to save what was left of the foundation or to let it all burn to the ground.

I am, of course, referring to a series of controversies that rocked the academic study and publishing world of Canadian Literature often referred to as "CanLit." While it has been argued that such fires have actually been hot, glaring embers stoking the woodwork of CanLit for quite some time, depending on whose perspective one inhabits in these institutional spaces, the incident that first ignited this most recent conflagration began on November 14, 2016, when an open letter signed by UBC Accountable, a group of mostly well-known and powerful CanLit writers and industry figures, called for the public support and right to due process of the novelist and former UBC Creative Writing Program Chair Steven Galloway after he had been fired after UBC's internal investigation over serious allegations of sexual harassment and his role in fostering a toxic learning environment by the program's students and other complainants (McGregor, Rak, Wunker 2018). Regardless of whether these allegations could have been proven in a court of law, a moot point when one considers how rape culture is embedded in all levels of the criminal justice system, these powerful signatories effectively undercut and silenced the complainants in the Galloway affair, mostly made up of aspiring writers who had hoped to make it in the industry by following in the footsteps of many of the signatories that they read and admired. As this public debacle emerged at the height of the #MeToo movement in Canada, it inevitably sparked more attention on the oppressive privilege systems of CanLit's creative writing industry, this time at Concordia University's Creative Writing Program (Spry 2018), thus revealing just how sexist, masculinist, and entitled CanLit's publishing world has always been.

On the heels of CanLit's #MeToo crisis, a second flare-up revealed another longstanding fault line of the Canadian literary world that has been repeatedly called out by Indigenous writers: that of cultural appropriation.[2] One month after the UBC Accountable open letter was released, a project spearheaded by Joseph Boyden who used his star status and power as one of Canada's most successful Indigenous writers at the time to encourage his fellow writers to sign the letter, a scathing exposé was published by *APTN National News*, questioning Boyden's vague and shifting Indigenous identity claims, a revelation that had been simmering amongst Indigenous thinkers, writers, journalists, researchers, and academics as his prominence as a national spokesperson on Indigenous issues grew (Barrera 2016). But before those in the Canadian literary

2 This has been a grievance voiced by Indigenous writers since the 1980s and 1990s, the height of the Indigenous Literary Renaissance in Canada. See, for example, Lenore Keeshig-Tobias's (Chippewa) "Stop Stealing Native Stories" (1990).

and academic establishment who had adored and wrote about Boyden's work had any time to fully digest and contribute to the public debates over Boyden's Indigeneity, Hal Niedzviecki, editor of the Writer's Union of Canada's *Write* magazine, was forced to resign after the public uproar over his opinion piece, "Winning the Appropriation Prize," appeared in a special issue featuring only Indigenous writers in Canada for the first time (McGregor, Rak, Wunker 2018). Arguing for the artistic freedom of non-Indigenous writers to appropriate Indigenous voices and cultures in their cultural production, Niedzviecki's tone-deaf essay and subsequent resignation motivated a group of white editors, executives, and established columnists from Canadian mainstream publications aggrieved on Niedzviecki's behalf to start collecting money on Twitter for an "Appropriation Prize" as suggested in his article of gross entitlement (Koul as cited in McGregor, Rak, Wunker 2018). The absolute ignorance, or more likely deliberate disavowal, in this case of not only Canada's but also CanLit's colonial history of displacing and dominating Indigenous peoples, exploiting and disrespecting their natural resources and cultural knowledges, and forcibly suppressing and misappropriating their voices and cultural expressions simply dumped more fuel onto CanLit's already raging dumpster fire.

Merely days after the Boyden and Niedzviecki affair, a final blaze erupted, forming Canlit's fiery trifecta. Rinaldo Walcott, a prominent Black Canadian studies scholar, announced at an academic conference (May 24–27, 2017)—Mikinaakominis/TransCanadas: Literature, Justice, Relation—that he was quitting CanLit. After writing about Black Canadian cultural and literary production for three decades and seeing very little institutional change to promote and centre Black voices beyond the few tokenistic gestures in both the academic and cultural establishment, he declared that

> CanLit fails to transform because it refuses to take seriously that Black literary expression and thus Black life is foundational to it. CanLit still appears surprised every single time by the appearance of Black work in CanLit. Because Black expression is reduced to surprise there has been no sustained and ongoing serious consideration of Black work in CanLit. You can write the same essay over and over again and no one will notice.
>
> As cited in BARRETT 2017

Walcott's searing protest is to be expected considering how persistently white in body and perspective the academic institution of CanLit has continued to be under his tenure. As a junior scholar in this field, I have long stopped bemoaning how overwhelmingly white the academic spaces and mainstream debates over CanLit's status have continued to be: I have simply moved on to do my own thing beyond the shadows of this field. However, I would not want to discount the brilliant body of work on Black literary expression by Black Canadian writers and scholars such as George Elliott Clarke, M. Nourbese Philip, Afua Cooper, Dionne Brand, Wade Compton, David Chariandy, Christina Sharpe, Phanuel Antwi, Andrea Davis, and Karina Vernon. Despite this critical wealth of Black scholarship on Black Canadian life and letters having managed to do its own thing under such racially toxic conditions, do our postsecondary curricula, faculty, and higher administrative bodies still need to privilege more Black voices and perspectives? Absolutely. But do we stand back and watch CanLit burn when these institutional spaces continue to be hostile and systemically racist to the handful of Black scholars that have made it to the professoriate at each institution as Charmaine Nelson describes her experiences at a Canadian university named after a famous Canadian slave owner (2017)?[3] Absolutely not. It would be unethical to watch and do nothing as our Black (and Indigenous) colleagues get caught in the flames.

It may seem like a bit of a stretch, but I am proposing that CanLit's "dumpster fires" of 2016–2018 have reincarnated into the current blazes of 2020. While the former will undoubtedly be obscure to anyone who does not study or follow the trends and developments of the academic and publishing world of CanLit, the current wildfires would escape no one regardless of their race, class, gender, sexuality, religion, ability, age, political affiliation, and citizenship status or lack thereof. The inferno that has left no one unscathed, but perhaps marginalized classes more scathed or dead than others, has been COVID-19, the coronavirus that originated in Wuhan, China in late December of 2019 and gradually spread to the rest of the world, resulting in a global pandemic that necessitated widespread institutional lockdowns and various public health measures that have left an immeasurable impact on our social, economic, and human life as we know it. As this highly infectious virus spread globally, so did

3 A prominent Art History scholar on the Visual Culture of Slavery, Race and Representation, Black Canadian Studies, and African Canadian Art History, Charmaine A. Nelson describes her experience of working up the ranks at McGill University as an uphill battle with varying degrees of racism and microaggressions that are difficult to lodge a formal human rights complaint but still work to derail her academic career or obstruct her tenure and promotion process (2017). Regardless of the significant level of education, income, and status that Black Canadians like her manage to achieve, she contends that "[i]n big and small ways, black people in Canada are sent the message that our bodies do not belong in certain hallowed spaces, like university. What this 'looks like' is a white, female colleague blocking my entry to a key-access staff washroom until I show her my own key. I learned in that moment that the misperception of my identity had the ability to render me foreign in a place where I had worked for over a decade" (2017).

the rise in anti-Chinese and anti-Asian racist attacks as widely documented in social media, newspaper articles, and local police reports around the globe (Qasim 2020). Adding more destructive kindling to this age old Yellow Peril discourse was President Donald Trump's repeated references to COVID-19 as the "Chinese virus," or "Kung Flu," in press conferences and campaign rallies to fan the rage and unite his political base against his critics (Looofbourow 2020; *Guardian* 2020). Since the 2016 US presidential campaign and Trump's tenure as president, populist xenophobic and white supremacist discourses have succeeded in moving beyond the political fringes to claim legitimacy in the mainstream arenas of white settler societies like Canada and the US. Thus, against this political landscape, it is not surprising that a large percentage of Chinese Canadians have experienced anti-Chinese racism related to COVID-19 (Zeidler 2020). In fact, any Asian or even Inuit community member mistaken to be Chinese has also been the target of coronavirus related anti-Chinese discrimination and hate crimes in Canada (Richardson 2020; Price 2020; Lam 2020).

As ceaseless as the fires burned in CanLit's dumpster fires, so have the wildfires of 2020. On May 25, 2020, an African American man named George Floyd died in police custody in Minneapolis, Minnesota. Horrifying video footage emerged of his death as his arresting officer, Derek Chauvin, held him face down on the street in handcuffs, kneeling on Floyd's neck for at least eight minutes and forty-six seconds, even as Floyd and onlookers at the scene desperately called out for help (Hill, Tiefenthäler, Triebert, et al 2020). Floyd's death re-ignited Black Lives Matter (BLM) protests across America to an extent and diversity never seen before. BLM demonstrations have been ongoing since Black lives dying in police encounters has kept happening in America. The US movement to "defund the police" has also spread across the globe, shining a light on the context of police brutality specific to each locale. In Canada in particular, BLM protests have also taken up this call in their unique way by responding intersectionally to several recent deaths of Indigenous and non-white Canadian citizens as a result of excessive force by the police. In the span of three months in 2020 alone, four mental health crises resulting in the use of deadly police force impacted Black, Indigenous, and Muslim communities across Canada. In the case of D'Andre Campbell, Regis Korchinski-Paquet, Chantel Moore (Tla-o-qui-aht First Nation), and Ejaz Choudry, police officers were called to perform a wellness check or assist family members during each individual's mental health crisis, only to resort to the use of deadly force in each situation (Kelley and Syed 2020; Nasser 2020; Brend 2020; *CTV News* 2020). BLM leaders in Canada have since pushed to defund, demilitarize, disarm, and dismantle the police, when such funds typically spent on police services across the country, to the tune of $41 million per day, should be reallocated to alternative approaches and social services to create safer and more secure societies for all (BLM Canada). Consequently, they are calling for "a reinvestment in Black, Indigenous, racialized, impoverished, and other targeted communities" (BLM-Canada).

Most recently, the intersectional mobilization of the BLM movement in Canada has culminated in the tarnishing of key public monuments, paralleling a political tactic of American BLM activists to dislodge public monuments of historical leaders and figures from the national imaginary that were erected in the Jim Crow era to terrorize African Americans and memorialize the white supremacist society of the former Confederate States America. In the Canadian context, three BLM-Toronto activists were arrested on July 18, 2020 for an artistic demonstration of spraying pink paint and colourful messages of resistance on the colonial and white supremacist statues of Sir. John A. Macdonald and King Edward VII Equestrian in Queen's Park and Egerton Ryerson at Ryerson University (Draaisma 2020).[4] About a month later, following an ongoing period of civil unrest and violent clashes between BLM protesters, the police, and armed vigilantes after yet another police shooting in Kenosha, Wisconsin, left Jacob Blake, an African American man paralyzed, a "defund the police" demonstration organized by the Coalition for BIPOC Liberation in Montreal, a coalition of Black and Indigenous activists, ended in the toppling of the statue of Sir. John A. Macdonald at Place du Canada by a separate diverse coalition of young activists (*CBC News* 2020; Oduro 2020). This time, arresting video footage and photographs of a decapitated Macdonald after having fallen to the ground have gone viral on social media and major news circuits, much to the dismay of Liberal and Conservative political leaders, who have condemned

4 There has been increasing public attention placed on Sir. John A. Macdonald's forgotten yet pivotal role in the genocide of Indigenous communities, the hanging of Louis Riel (Métis), the residential school system, the Chinese Head Tax legislation, and the internment of Japanese Canadians. Likewise, the civil acts of disobedience by BLM-Toronto have been calling attention to the history of colonialism that the monuments of King Edward VII and Egerton Ryerson represent but conveniently gloss over. Their political intervention is even more fitting when one considers the Lazarus-like rebranding journey of the actual King Edward VII Equestrian monument before its final resettlement in Toronto's Queen's Park. Whereas Ryerson's legacy as a public education advocate and prominence in education and politics in Ontario in the nineteenth-century has taken a hit as his involvement in creating residential schools has increasingly come to light, the statue of the King Edward VII Equestrian once stood outside the ancient Mughal Red Fort of Delhi, India to commemorate his imperial reign but was removed and put into storage after India gained independence from Britain, only to be salvaged and purchased from the "graveyard of the British empire" as a gift to Toronto by a Canadian businessman for $10,000 (*The Victorian Web*; Bunch 2016).

the act as a destructive and unlawful act of vandalizing and defacing "our past" and "our history" (Gilmore 2020).

However, this striking symbolic act of civil disobedience did not emerge out of the blue. It has been a Canadian tradition to deface this statue of Canada's first Prime Minister. The Macdonald monument at Place du Canada has been a repeated target of social activists across the ages: Quebec separatists defaced the statue repeatedly in the 1960s; and this was not the first time Macdonald lost his head as he was also decapitated on the anniversary of the hanging of Louis Riel in 1992, only to be defaced repeatedly in the last few years by anti-colonial and anti-racist activists like the #MacdonaldMustFall group (Peritz 2018; *Global News* 2019). If government officials are going to keep restoring and replacing the Macdonald statue as a symbol of "our past" and "our history," are they finally going to include the truth behind what our first Prime Minister engineered in the nation building project of a white supremacist settler colonial Canada? In response to the public debates on social media and the mainstream news circuits over whether the toppling of the Macdonald monument was justified or not, Gregory Scofield (Métis) posted a poignant Facebook response to the unfolding controversy:

> the image of Macdonald's decapitated head is a powerful image for many First Nations and Métis across this country. Without going into elaborate detail, Macdonald was one of the greatest Canadian architects of genocide. He literally starved Indigenous people to death, both physically and spiritually. The greatest land theft and mass murder happened during his years as Canada's first Prime Minister. The fact that it has taken 153 years to topple his statue and indeed decapitate his bronze head, the same likeness of the one that devised so many racist and genocidal policies, is nothing short of a miracle. 153 years of colonial theft. 153 years of Canadian genocide. The statue of Macdonald was erected in 1895, the same and final year he left office. A statue to celebrate what he gave to Canada, and what he did for "our" country. Indigenous people, Chinese Canadians, Japanese Canadians, Canadians of Colour and, of course, my own people—the Métis—have had to walk by his image for 125 years like the thousands of other racist, slave-owing, Indian-killing, internment-supporting, head-tax billing presidents and prime ministers across Turtle Island. The toppling of statues is not a victory. The statues are merely bronze and stone. The heads no longer hold power. The hands can no longer sign people into extinction. And yet the toppling of these statues is, like the statutes [sic] themselves, symbolic of how this country came to be. There is a new narrative being told. Let the old statues and images

> be taken to museums the way Indigenous bones have been held in these institutions for years. Let the images and statues serve as a reminder—to the young and to all of us survivors—as a history lesson in how to tell a truthful story. In how to tell a real story. A story that, after 125 years, is finally being told.
>
> 2020

If the statue is to be restored and re-erected for the umpteenth time, what if it came with a commemorative plaque that finally told the truthful story behind Macdonald's legacy that Scofield's Facebook post so incisively reveals? Would critics finally take ownership of these unsavoury and widely forgotten or disavowed historical details of the nation's history as part of their past and history as well? If so, then why hasn't this history lesson been a part of the efforts to commemorate such historical figures in the first place?

While the CanLit dumpster fires and 2020 wildfires may paint an intractably divisive portrait of our uncertain times, to my mind, they also reveal just how inextricably linked we may be. It is worth comparing these firestorms for the structural inequalities that they insightfully reveal. On the one hand, CanLit's dumpster fires exposed its institutions as offering a promising ideal for inclusivity and diversity as long as the white, male, elite power hierarchy remained intact. Similarly, the wildfires of 2020 made visible that a person's right to adequate health care, survival, and due process is guaranteed as long as one was white, male, healthy, young, able-bodied, and neurotypical. Of course, these systemic oppressions are hardly new phenomena. But what does seem new is the relentless way in which our contemporary moment cannot help but remain fixated on the engulfing flames that they continue to spark in our political imaginary. If it's all a raging dumpster fire, do we raze it all to the ground? Or do we treat it as an urgent call for action for the ways in which the metaphor so usefully lays bare our shared vulnerabilities, sparking our energy to mobilize for concrete change?

To recapitulate, what might the CanLit dumpster fires have to do with the wildfires of 2020 or even this present collection of essays entitled, *Asian Canada Is Burning*? What is it about the metaphor of a raging fire that has become such an apt, affective metaphor for our political era? If Asian Canada is burning, is it burning itself down for the same reasons that CanLit has been burning since the voices that CanLit has excluded and marginalized is shining a glaring light on its abuses and broken promises? Or is Asian Canada burning to set ablaze other oppressive structures and institutions like CanLit to make space for something new? Is it burning down what the editors of *Refuse: CanLit in Ruins* (2018) aspired their collection to do — to *re*fuse, to say no, to blow up and dismantle the colonial, misogynistic, classist, and white supremacist foundations upon which the institution of CanLit was built upon (McGregor, Rak, and Wunker 2017)? Or is it a burning of re*fuse*, "garbage, waste, detritus," nothing worth holding onto (McGregor, Rak, and Wunker 2017)? Or is it to burn, to "re/fuse: to reignite. To think about the fuse. To fuse together. To think about what could be better as we look at CanLit in ruins" (McGregor, Rak, and Wunker 2017)?

If "CanLit reflected the nation to itself, and within itself [... b]ecause the imagination of what Canada and its literature would be was built upon the same foundation [... of intersecting structures of oppression] that the rest of Canada was built on" (McGregor, Rak, and Wunker 2017), then I propose that a burning Asian Canada of the "re/fusing" variety is one not equal to but synonymous with and inextricably linked to Indigenous, Black, and other marginalized communities in Canada. What the CanLit and 2020 dumpster fires make clear is this: never has our collective safety, security, and survival been so dependent upon each other. We cannot argue for a space within and beyond the academy for Asian Canada without also fighting for a space for Indigenous sovereignty, Black Canada, and other intersectional positionalities. We cannot work within the academy without also bearing witness to and mobilizing for change beyond our cultural institutions. The parallel work that happens within and beyond the walls of the ivory tower are equally urgent. This is what the dumpster fires of our age insightfully teach us. Academic and cultural institutions are not created in a vacuum. They are structured by parallel discursive systems that exclude, harm, marginalize, and murder members of our fellow communities. What was happening in CanLit has been echoing beyond the walls of CanLit to varying degrees. COVID-19 and the increasing militarization of our police industrial complex has exposed our shared vulnerabilities. Before we stand back and watch the re*fuse* burn to the ground, we would also do well to remember how Asian Canada was and must always continue to be a coalitional political formation (Lai 2014).[5]

5 To the editors and readers of *Asian Canada Is Burning*, I would invite folks invested in theorizing and mobilizing Asian Canada to consider the historical emergence of Asian Canadian literary and cultural production in the 1980s and 1990s. Larissa Lai attributes this particular formation of Asian Canada to a profoundly relational building process, "built in coalition with broader anti-oppression movements in the arts, involving people who variously articulate the building movements as anti-racist, of colour, Black, First Nations, South Asian, Caribbean, queer, feminist, Japanese Canadian, Chinese Canadian, Korean Canadian, GLBTQ, working class, disability, and more" ("Introduction" 2014).

It is my hope that "Indigenous and Asian Relation Making" (Phung 2019), along with this reflection on the dumpster fires that we have been living through in the latter half of the 2010s, inspires and motivates an ongoing ethic for intersectional and cross-community relation making, a solidarity ethic that privileges the shared histories and circumstances of Indigenous and Asian communities in Canada but is never removed from how deeply connected and interdependent we are on Black and other marginalized communities in Canada for our collective safety, survival, and existence.

References

The Addams Family Values, ed (United States: Barry Sonnenfeld, Paramount, 1993).

Barrera, Jorge (2016) Author Joseph Boyden's Shape-Shifting Indigenous Identity. *APTN National News*. December 23. <aptnnews.ca/national-news/author-joseph-boydens-shape-shifting-indigenous-identity/>.

Barrett, Paul (2017) The Unbearable Whiteness of Canlit. *The Walrus*, July 26. <thewalrus.ca/the-unbearable-whiteness-of-canlit/>.

BLM-Canada. (n.d.) Defund the Police--Demands. <blacklivesmatter.ca/defund-the-police/>.

Brend, Yvette (2020) B.C. Woman Shot Dead During Police Wellness Check Had Just Made Fresh Start to Be with Her Child, Family Says. *CBC News*. June 4. <cbc.ca/news/canada/british-columbia/tofino-port-alberni-woman-26-shot-new-brunswick-wellness-check-chantel-moore-1.5598653>.

Bunch, Adam (2016) Toronto's Royal Statue from the Graveyard of the British Empire. *Yonge Street*. January 20. <https://www.yongestreetmedia.ca/features/KingEdwardVIIQueensPark.aspx>.

CBC News (2020) Activists Topple Statue of Sir John A. Macdonald in Downtown Montreal.August 29. <cbc.ca/news/canada/montreal/defund-police-protest-black-lives-matter-1.5705101>.

CTV News (2020) Officer Involved in Shooting Death of 62-Year-Old Mississauga, Ont. Man Has Declined to Be Interviewed: SIU. July 23. <toronto.ctvnews.ca/officer-involved-in-shooting-death-of-62-year-old-mississauga-ont-man-has-declined-to-be-interviewed-siu-1.5036538>.

Draaisma, Muriel (2020) Police Charge 3 People after Black Lives Matter Protestors Splatter Paint on Statues in Toronto. *CBC News*. July 18. <cbc.ca/news/canada/toronto/statues-defaced-paint-toronto-defund-the-police-1.5654829>.

Elliot, Alicia (2017) CanLit Is a Raging Dumpster Fire. *Open Book*, September 7. <open-book.ca/Columnists/CanLit-is-a-Raging-Dumpster-Fire>.

Gilmore, Rachel (2020) Trudeau 'Deeply Disappointed' After Demonstrators Topple John A. *Macdonald Statue.* August 31. <ctvnews.ca/politics/trudeau-deeply-disappointed-after-demonstrators-topple-john-a-macdonald-statue-1.5086238>.

Global News (2019) Sir John A. Macdonald Statue Vandalized Once Again in Downtown Montreal. March 21. <globalnews.ca/news/5081694/sir-john-a-macdonald-statue-vandalized-once-again-in-downtown-montreal/>.

The Guardian (2020) Donald Trump Calls COVID-19 "Kung Flu" at Tulsa Rally. June 21. <theguardian.com/us-news/2020/jun/20/trump-covid-19-kung-flu-racist-language>

Hill, Evan, Tiefenthäler, Ainara, Triebert, Christiaan, Jordan, Drew, Willis, Haley, and Stein, Robin (2020) How George Floyd Was Killed in Police Custody. *The New York Times.* May 31. <nytimes.com/2020/05/31/us/george-floyd-investigation.html>.

Keeshig-Tobias, Lenore (1990) Stop Stealing Native Stories. *Globe and Mail,* January 26.

Kelley, Mark and Syed, Ronna (2020) Family of Young Black Man Killed in Brampton, Ont., Says He Was Shot by Police After Calling 911 Himself. *CBC News.* June 8. <cbc.ca/news/canada/toronto/fifth-estate-d-andre-campbell-police-shooting-family-1.5602503>.

Lai, Larissa (2014) *Slanting I, Imagining We: Asian Canadian Literary Production in the 1980s and 1990s.* Waterloo: Wilfrid Laurier Press. KOBO eBook.

Lam, Fiona Tinwei (2020) The 'Shadow Pandemic' of Anti-Asian Racism. *The Tyee.* May 7. <thetyee.ca/Analysis/2020/05/07/Shadow-Pandemic-Anti-Asian-Racism/>.

Lee, Jen Sookfong. (n.d.) Open Letters and Closed Doors. *The Humber Literary Review,* <humberliteraryreview.com/jen-sookfong-lee-essay-open-letters-and-closed-doors>.

Loofbourow, Lili (2020) The Real Reason Trump Started Calling the Virus "Chinese." *SLATE.* March 21. <slate.com/news-and-politics/2020/03/trump-calling-coronavirus-chinese-virus.html>.

McGregor, Hannah, Rak, Julie, and Wunker, Erin (2017) Living in the Ruins. In Hannah McGregor, Julie Rak, and Erin Wunker (eds.) *Refuse: CanLit in Ruins.* Toronto: Book*hug, Kobo eBook.

Nasser, Shanifa (2020) Release Evidence in Regis Korchinski-Paquet Death Or Turn It over to Outside Agency, Family Lawyer Says. *CBC News.* June 10. <cbc.ca/news/canada/toronto/regis-korchinski-paquet-toronto-1.5606704>.

Nelson, Charmaine A. (2017) The Canadian Narrative about Slavery Is Wrong. *The Walrus.* July 21. <thewalrus.ca/the-canadian-narrative-about-slavery-is-wrong/>.

Odoru, Kwabena (2020) Montreal City Officials Remove Toppled Statue of Sir John A. Macdonald. *Global News.* August 30. <globalnews.ca/news/7306987/montreal-city-officials-remove-toppled-statue-of-sir-john-a-macdonald/>.

Peritz, Ingrid (2018) Montreal's Sir John A. Macdonald Statue Vandalized with a Vengeance. *Globe and Mail.* August 17. <theglobeandmail.com/canada/article-montreals-sir-john-a-macdonald-statue-vandalized-with-a-vengeance/>.

Phung, Malissa (2019) Indigenous and Asian Relation Making. *Verge* 5(1): 18.

Price, John (2020) Racism Is on the Rise, and Asian Canadians Are Fighting Back. *The Tyee*. May 22. <thetyee.ca/Opinion/2020/05/22/Racism-Rising-Asian-Canadians-Fighting-Back/>.

Qasim, Salaado (2020) How Racism Spread around the World alongside COVID-19. *World Economic Forum*. June 5. <weforum.org/agenda/2020/06/just-like-covid-19-racism-is-spreading-around-the-world/>.

Richardson, Lindsay (2020) Inuit Getting Caught up in Anti-Asian Hate Crimes in Montreal, Advocates Say. *APTN National News*. April 14. <aptnnews.ca/national-news/inuit-getting-caught-up-in-anti-asian-hate-crimes-in-montreal-advocates-say/>.

Scofield, Gregory (2020) A Lot of Folks have been Sharing the Image of the Toppled John A. Macdonald Statue. August 30. <facebook.com/gregorya.scofield/posts/1574250866082316>.

Spry, Mike (2018) No Names, Only Monsters: Toxic Masculinity, Concordia, and CanLit. January 8. <canlitaccountable.com/>.

A Tribe Called Red (2014) Burn Your Village to the Ground. *Soundcloud*. November 25. <soundcloud.com/a-tribe-called-red/burn-your-village-to-the-ground>.

The Victorian Web (n.d.) King Edward VII (1841–1910). <victorianweb.org/sculpture/brock/77.html>.

Zeidler, Maryse (2020) New Poll Reveals Chinese-Canadians' Experiences with Racism. *CBC News*. June 22. https://www.cbc.ca/news/canada/british-columbia/new-poll -reveals- chinese-canadians-experiences-with-racism-1.5621261.

CHAPTER 16

Internationalist Solidarity: Palestinian Liberation, BDS, and the Struggle against Normalization

Boycott, Divest and Sanction Toronto

During a recent trip to Cuba, a few friends and I were visiting a school for the afternoon. We were greeted by Manuel, the director of the school and one of the coaches. As he had greeted us the year before that, his warm smile and endless jokes surpassed the language barriers in our choppy conversation. Though he knew we were travelling from Toronto, the conversation veered towards where we were really from. When the question came to me, I replied, "Palestina." He nodded his head in acknowledgement and understanding, put a fist to his chest and exclaimed, "Arafat!" When the question came to Trevor, he replied, "Vietnam." Manuel's reaction was just as nostalgic, holding a fist in the air, exalting, "Ho Chi Minh!" Despite the out-dated comedy of the exchange, and the political shortcomings of all our high-profile leaders, be it Castro, Ho Chi Minh, or Arafat, we understood that the bonds of a strong leftist political history existed between our people. It doesn't seem so long ago that nations with similar anti-colonial and anti-imperial movements stood in solidarity with one another, merging stories and experiences, refusing to allow the dominant discourse takeover. There was a time when conceding to power meant surrendering not only freedom, but the political values which underlie it. Cuba, Vietnam, and Palestina are thousands of kilometers apart, yet a shared history of liberation movements created a strong bond decades ago that resounds today.

In the early months of the COVID-19 pandemic, marking the 33rd year since the first Intifada, former US president Donald Trump announced the so-called deal of the century that would enshrine the next phase of the everlasting "peace process". His son-in-law and senior advisor, Jared Kushner, authored the document that would frame the coming period of Palestinian struggle for liberation and self-determination. The main points of the "peace plan" are commensurate with the general *a priori* support previous US administrations have offered Israel in relation to its colonial project in Palestine. The difference this time is the flagrant support and permission to annex all of Palestine. In August 2020, the normalization of ties between Israel and the United Arab

Emirates, brokered by the US government, signals a new addition to the list of disappoints and betrayals from neighbors in the region.

While the US is in the lead for its undying support for Israel and absolute disregard for Palestinian human rights, let alone liberation, Canada is not far behind. With organizations like B'nai Brith, the Jew National Fund (JNF) of Canada, the Jewish Defense League (JDL), and Birthright openly supporting the Zionist colonial order and supporting the Israeli military in the suppression of Palestinian existence, Zionism has a stronghold in the Canadian state. Recent bills and legislature outlawing the Boycott, Divestment, and Sanctions (BDS) movement have shown where Canada's alliances lie. With growing global success, BDS has faced multiple obstacles, not least in the arena of grassroots solidarity. The history of this movement is rooted amongst many anti-colonial movements around the world, and particularly other nations in the Global South as well as Indigenous nations in the US and commonwealth countries. Keeping that history hidden and suppressing solidarity among nations and peoples is one of the main goals for the Zionist movement in North America and abroad. As fraught as supporting Palestine can be, Israel and its allies are banking on the power of capital gain and military alliance, luring countries to normalize relations with one of the most atrocious settler colonial regimes. How, then, can we on the Left offer an alternative to rising global fascism? How can we draw on past solidarity movements to inspire our ongoing struggles against the tyranny of power? How do we fight the normalization of the state of Israel and the oppressive infrastructure that keeps it in place? In this piece, I will offer a brief history of the BDS movement, its demands, and its trajectory. The following section will offer a few examples of internationalist Palestine solidarity. Finally, I will end with a discussion of normalization, a renewed internationalist vision of liberation, and the struggle for BDS and a free Palestine.

1 A Brief History of BDS

The struggle for Palestinian liberation is mired by several milestones of injustice. As the far-right response to European anti-Semitism, the development of the Zionist movement in 1850s began the mass migrations of Jews to Palestine, thus beginning the Israeli colonial project. Setting its sight on regional domination after defeating the Ottoman Empire in the First World War, the 1916 Sykes-Picot agreement between Britain and France partitioned Greater Syria (Palestine, Jordan, Lebanon, Syrian, and Iraq) to fall under their spheres of influence. This laid the foundation for the Balfour Declaration of 1917, announcing British support for a Jewish homeland in Palestine. The following decades saw the influx of Jewish colonization and theft of more than half of Palestine under the auspices of the British Empire, leading up the creation of the Israeli State in 1948, otherwise known as the Nakba (great catastrophe). After the six-day war of 1967, whereby Palestine and neighboring Arab countries faced a staggering loss to Western-backed Israeli forces, what was left of Palestine were patches of heavily militarized lands. The beaming pan-Arabism of the decade faded and ushered in another era of Palestinian resistance in the face of Arab and other countries' recognition of the state of Israel.

From its onset, resistance and outrage accompanied the Zionist project and have not ceased. The liberation of Palestine has remained close to many struggles throughout the 20th and 21st centuries. Through the work of organizations such as the Popular Front for the Liberation of Palestine (PFLP) and the General Union of Palestinian Women (GUPW) in the 1960s and 1970s, solidarity relations were fomented globally. During the historical decades of mass uprisings against colonial powers, countries of the Global South were uniting in struggles inspired in part by the philosophy of Marx, Lenin, and Mao.

With the advent of neoliberalism and increasingly Zionist-sympathizing US governments, billions of dollars in annual allowances nourished Israel's colonial project. The ground-breaking signing of the Oslo Accords marked a turning point in the Palestine liberation movement. The accords highlighted the fissure between leftist liberation politics and the politics of acquiescence, demonstrated by the Palestine Liberation Organization (PLO) in the 1990s and onwards. Conceding more land and water theft, dwindling human rights, and an increasing state of infrastructural crisis, the failure of the Oslo Accords and the Palestinian Authority leadership lead to a renewed character of grassroots resistance.

The call for BDS came in 2005, when 170 Palestinian civil society organizations pushed for a Palestinian-led global movement to pressure the Israeli State to comply with international law. Inspired by the anti-apartheid movement in South Africa, which various Palestinian organizations and factions supported throughout the struggle against white supremacy and colonization, the BDS movement has three main demands: 1) the right of return for all Palestinians as outlined in UN resolution 194; 2) ending the occupation and colonization of all Arab lands and dismantling the wall; and, 3) equal rights for Arab-Palestinian citizens of Israel. As explained on bdsmovement.net, boycotts involve withdrawing support from Israel's apartheid regime, complicit Israeli sporting, cultural and academic institutions, and from all Israeli and international companies engaged in the military occupation and violations of Palestinian human rights. Divestments campaigns urge banks, local councils, churches, pension funds, and universities to withdraw investments from the State of Israel and all Israeli and international companies that sustain Israeli apartheid. Sanctions campaigns pressure governments to fulfil their legal obligations to end Israeli apartheid, and not aid or assist its maintenance, by banning business with illegal Israeli settlements, ending military trade and free-trade agreements, as well as suspending Israel's membership in international forums such as UN bodies and FIFA. Adopting and supporting the call for BDS is the main political tactic for activists, institutions, and governments to refuse the normalization of the apartheid Israeli state and to challenge imperialism, colonialism, and Zionism.

2 Internationalist Solidarity: Then and Now

Throughout the 1960s and 1970s, a wave of liberation movements grounded in community activism and global solidarity were burgeoning. Many of these movements found connection with one another through a commitment to political education as well as sharing resources. For example, seeing the Palestinian struggle as one of the main fronts against imperialism in the Middle East, Mao pledged support through military arms and little red books. Many fighters in the Palestine Liberation Organization (PLO) travelled to China for military training. Members of the PLO and the PFLP made linkages with the Japanese Red Army in the 1970s. Other examples include the alliances between Palestinians, the Black Panther Party, and the African National Congress (ANC).

The era of militant leftist resistance seems like a distant memory, now subsumed in a misleading conflation with terrorism and religious fanaticism. The shrinking influence of Left politics on global politics is an intentional outcome of a war against all liberation movements and organizations. The stronghold of the Global North, including surrogates like Israel, has intensified with military and surveillance might that is unmatched. Using similar tactics such as assassination and infiltration to dismantle organizations like the Black Panther Party, namely the Counter Intelligence Program or COINTELPRO, the more radical global Left organizations were disbanded, ushering in a new era of austerity and state repression. In turn, the diversity of tactics of resistance has expanded to the non-violent, cultural, financial, and political pressure of BDS. One tactic among many, BDS is intended for groups and organizations around the world to build the pressure against the Zionist state of Israel to dismantle its apartheid regime. It is no substitute for a local Palestinian movement for liberation and self-determination, nor is it a proponent of a one, two, or no state solution. The pressure that BDS exerts is one that helps reveal the utter injustice inflicted on the Palestinian people and the theft of their lands, and to force an end to apartheid through international support.

The struggle for liberation in Palestine holds the intersection of many power relations. Through a feminist, leftist, anti-imperialist lens, we can see that at the heart of the struggle for Palestine is the colonial theft of a homeland by a foreign occupation. The criminalization of BDS is part of a long and shameful Zionist history of suppressing dissent against the settler colonial existence and practices of Israel. This history is saturated with bloody assaults, incarceration, roadblocks and sieges, theft of water, restricting food, utilities, medicine, and movement, the bantustanization[1] of cities, towns and villages, and military occupation. Given that Israel has never officially outlined its borders, nor does it have a constitution, apartheid policies and laws codify and justify the injustice while international PR campaigns attempt to clean up Israel's image. Greenwashing campaigns have painted Israel as an environmental saviour, "turning the desert green" and perpetuating the myth that Israel is "a land without a people for a people without a land". Canadian Zionist organizations like the Jewish National Fund (JNF) fundraise and donate millions of dollars to (among other ignoble causes) build parks and gardens over demolished villages of slaughtered Palestinians.[2] Zionist homonationalism shines bright through pinkwashing campaigns'[3] attempt to portray Israel as an LGBT haven amongst hostile and homophobic neighboring countries, playing into orientalist politics of western/white liberal progress and overshadowing the harrowing gender based violence that Palestinians of all genders and sexualities face under Israeli apartheid, as refugees, in diaspora, or within historic Palestine.[4] From before its creation, Israel has been suppressing resistance through assassinations and imprisonment of activists and resisters. Held under administrative detention justified through martial law, prisoners are incarcerated without cause, evidence, or trial. They are held without charge and tortured. The settler colonial project inflicted upon Palestinians demonstrates clearly how power

1 Used as an apartheid policy in South Africa, Black South Africans were restricted to sectioned parcels of land known as Bantustans, or Black state or homeland. South African anti-apartheid activists have also described the partitioning of land is Palestine as bantustanization.

2 For more on greenwashing, see <cjpme.org/fs_210> and <whoprofits.org/report/greenwashing-the-naqab-the-israeli-industry-of-solar-energy>.

3 For more on pinkwashing, see <uppingtheanti.org/journal/article/13-coming-out-against-aparheid>, <pinkwatchingisrael.com>, and <bdsmovement.net/pinkwashing>.

4 Historic Palestine is all of Palestine, from the Mediterranean Sea in the west to Jordan in the east, Syria and Lebanon to the north, Egypt to the south west, and the southern tip reaching the Red Sea. Some also refer to it as '48 or '48 Palestine, delineating Palestine prior to the Israeli state.

intersects to create the machinery to maintain ongoing violence in and out of prisons. As Palestinians, we understand too well that *all* prisoners are political prisoners. Israel has made it clear that we are prisoners in our own land, in our own homes, in Gaza, the West Bank, within all of historic Palestine. As we see in Indigenous sovereignty movements across Turtle Island (Canada and the USA), decolonization and abolition is not a metaphor in Palestine. The resistance movement internally and externally has long embraced and practiced a nuanced and insightful politics of alliance and solidarity, one which holds deeply the knowledge of interconnected oppression. Palestine never was and never will be a single-issue cause.

Through BDS, the role of international solidarity is kept alive through a rejuvenated energy of resistance, one that departs from the failures of the "peace process" and encompasses a more thoughtful understanding of Indigenous sovereignty, abolitionism, queer liberation, anti-racism, and de-militarization. BDS activists globally have found new ways to fight the Zionist project and its PR campaigns. In 2020, activists launched the first Palestine Writes Literature Festival, which highlights the intersection between Palestinian art, literature, and politics. In the closing panel, Yafa and Suha Jarrar read a letter written by their mother, Khalida Jarrar, a Palestinian political prisoner held in the Israeli Damon prison. Her letter was smuggled out of prison and read to thousands of viewers online. Her letter highlights the importance of books, literature, and education for incarcerated Palestinians.[5] Evoking the memory of Domitila Chungara, she writes, "We, the Palestinian women prisoners, also say 'let us speak … let us dream … let us be liberated!'" Political prisoners, like Jarrar, are the backbone of the Palestinian resistance and have continued to educate and agitate behind bars. Through work of organizations like Samidoun: Palestinian Prisoner Solidarity Network[6] and news sources like the Electronic Intifada,[7] we can see a clear documentation of the daily injustices facing Palestinians. Every year since 2005, hundreds of campuses and community organizations around the world organize Israeli Apartheid Week (IAW),[8] a week full of actions, demonstrations, workshops, panels, and film screenings with the intent on breaking the Zionist discourse and promoting the boycott of Israeli goods and institutions, divestment from companies that invest in apartheid related companies, and sanctioning Israel's economic activities. Rooted in a

5 Jarrar, Khalida. October 17, 2020. "Khalida Jarrar Smuggles a Letter for Palestine Writes." <palestinewrites.org/news1/khalid-jarrar-smuggles-a-letter-for-palestine-writes>.

6 See <samidoun.net>.

7 See <electronicintifada.net>.

8 See <apartheidweek.org>.

strong history of political alliances, BDS is non-partisan and is not explicitly tied to any particular parties' political agenda. With its three demands, BDS challenges the normalization of the state of Israel by calling into question its apartheid policies and practices and pushing the role of internationalism, both grassroots and institutional.

Fitting the historical trajectory of criminalizing and brutalizing Palestinian resisters, Zionists and their allies have continuously attacked BDS and BDS activists since the 2005 call by refabricating the lazy and politically disingenuous weaponization of anti-Semitism. Conflating anti-apartheid activism with anti-Semitism is one of Zionism's main arsenals to occlude and delegitimize dissent and critique of Israeli apartheid, thereby maintaining the legal guise and ethical legitimacy of an ethnocractic, fascist, settler colonial state.[9] The insistence of the legitimacy of a Jewish homeland for Jews only on colonized land is one of the greatest lies of our times. In July of 2018, this lie was legislated as the Basic Law in Israel. Also known as Israel's nation-state law, the bill blatantly states that only Jews can exercise national self-determination in Israel, downgrades Arabic from a national language, and promotes the development of new Israeli settlements.[10] While Israel legislates apartheid, global media portrays Palestinians as the aggressors. I would argue one of the earliest examples of the heinous appropriation of identity politics and the weaponization of the politics of victimhood was and is exhibited by the Zionist movement's attempt to justify colonizing Palestine. Anti-Zionists of all religions, including Jews, have been integral to solidarity movements for the liberation of Palestine. In an effort to reduce all Jews to Zionists, Israel enacts its own anti-Semitic tendency to speak for all Jews and to tarnish their global image as a generalized, Zionist war-mongering mob. Put to the test, Israel's attempt at moral superiority crumbles in the face of historical fallacies that do not absolve them of apartheid. Thus, it comes as no surprise that Israel's bid for power is not based on political legitimacy. The lure of financial and military gain is more important to Israel's and its parents' (the US and UK) allies than Palestinian liberation. Those of us on the Left must caution against these attempts to normalize and legitimatize Israel and Zionism internationally. We must also remain wary of those who claim Left politics while carving out a special state of exception

---

9 The legislative Assembly of Ontario adopted the IHRA definition of anti-Semitism found here: <ola.org/en/legislative-business/bills/parliament-41/session-1/bill-202. This definition directly threatens BDS activists and the struggle for Palestine, leaving little room to legally challenge Israel>.

10 Nassar, Tamara. July 19, 2018. "Israel Passes Law Entrenching Apartheid." <electronicintifada.net/blogs/tamara-nassar/israel-passes-law-entrenching-apartheid>.

for Israel. Any politics short of anti-Zionism is Zionist. Identity politics can be very confusing, and when employed in the service of a settler colonial state, they are endemic. It is the mandate of BDS activists and our supporters to debunk these myths and show how Zionism engenders and intersects with other power relations, such as imperialism, capitalism, and heteropatriarchy, to accomplish full genocide.

3 The Imperative of Anti-normalization

One of the main struggles facing Palestinians is the struggle against normalizing ties with Israel. In this sense, normalization means declaring a country's relationship with Israel a 'normal' one, a relationship not bound to any historical accountability for settler colonization or the demands of Palestinians for liberation. Countries formalize their political, economic, financial military, social, and cultural ties with Israel. In the era of pan-Arabism and global Left solidarity, making friends with the Israeli enemy was inconceivable. Then Egypt signed. Jordan followed suit. To the unsurprised dismay of the movement for a free Palestine, the year 2020 saw four Arab League nations—The United Arab Emirates, Morocco, Sudan, and Bahrain—favor capital and alliance with Israel over Palestinians. We must, however, remain critical of these US-brokered deals and the pressure and rewards that come with becoming friends with Israel. The vast majority of Moroccans reject this alliance and still view Israel as a regional enemy. In reward for recognizing Israel, Trump recognized Morocco's claim over Western Sahara, Africa's last colony. In the same way the British gave Palestine to the Jews, Trump gave what is not his to give. In his 1979 speech in a Western Sahara refugee camp expressing his solidarity with the Sahrawis, leader of the PFLP, George Habash, stated, "In the Palestinian revolution, we don't just fight against Israel and Zionists, we fight against the Arab regressive forces who are aligned with the Zionist movement."[11] Much like a pandemic, Zionism and the spread of the politics of normalization pose a materially existential threat to Palestinians. They differ in that pandemics are not politically motivated by treasonous infiltrators and are not bound to the same standards of accountability.

The consequences of this normalization include maintaining apartheid structures that uphold Jewish/Israeli superiority over Palestinians in their own

11 Nassar, Tamara. December 15, 2020. "The Intimidation and Rewards of Normalizing with Israel." <electronicintifada.net/blogs/tamara-nassar/intimidation-and-rewards-normalizing-israel>.

land, the siege of Gaza and the repetitive bombings, water, food, and utility shortages, expulsions and displacement, restricting movement, debilitating bodies, and constant death. Normalizing Israel means surrendering freedom and even the most basic of human rights. It means ending the so-called peace process, annexing all Palestinian lands, and subsuming all that's left into the Israeli state. There is nothing 'normal' about how Israel operates, and its violations cannot be swept under the rug. So, when Malaysia continues to show its support of the Palestinian cause and refuses to recognize the state of Israel, it is a reminder that solidarity on an international scale still exists and still counts for a lot.[12] When Black Lives Matter expresses its solidarity with Palestine, we are reminded of the deep roots of our movements for emancipation.[13] Though motivated by starkly different sets of political principles, governmental, institutional, and grassroots demands to destabilize the validity and legitimacy of the state of Israel are wins for the Palestinian cause. BDS and the larger Palestinian liberation movement has laid a strong foundation on campuses, unions, and community organizations and has continued to spread, grow, and flourish despite all odds. A key tenet of the successes of the Palestine liberation movement is its deep ties with other Left struggles. The unity, reciprocity, and coalescence of these joint struggles not only hint at a nostalgic past that seemed full of revolutionary potential, but at a future of possibility and strengthened political goals. Be it in Cuba, Vietnam, or Palestina, governments will come and go, but the people remain and the people will prevail. Though different struggles have different histories, our solidarity is based on a common understanding of justice, one that is indivisible. Quoted by many movement leaders and organizers, such as Martin Luther King Jr., the indivisibility of justice is at the core of solidarity and liberation. In her endorsement for Israeli Apartheid Week 2020, Dr. Angela Davis declared, "If justice is indivisible, it follows that our struggles against injustice must be united."[14] None of us are free until we are all free. No one is free while the state of Israel maintains its apartheid regime in Palestine. Though the repression is strong, it is weaker than our resolve.

---

12 Bowie, Nile. January 24, 2020. "Malaysia in the Middle of Israel-Palestine Conflict." <asiatimes.com/2020/01/malaysia-in-the-middle-of-israel-palestine-conflict>.

13 Peoples Dispatch. June 29, 2020. "Black Lives Matter UK Expresses Solidarity with Palestinians, Rejects Israeli Occupation Plan." <peoplesdispatch.org/2020/06/29/black-lives-matter-uk-expresses-solidarity-with-palestinians-rejects-israeli-occupation-plan>.

14 To read Dr. Davis' full endorsement, visit: <bdsmovement.net/news/angela-davis-calls-unite-anti-racist-struggles-for-israeli-apartheid-week-2020>. See the transcript of Dr. Angela Davis' keynote address at Israeli Apartheid Week 2020 at the University of Toronto, titled "Justice is Indivisible", here: <uoftdivest.com/angela-davis-2020.html>.

Coda

Though a lot has changed between the writing of this article and this Coda, is it clear that many of the core issues facing Palestinians are the same. Palestinians are not new to genocide. Gaza is certainly not new to endless bombings. The few new facts on the ground are no doubt an intensification of a century-long settler colonial project aimed at eradicating the Palestinian people through death and displacement for the purpose of usurping the land for a Jewish supremacist state. The path of normalization paved the way for the Zionist entity's unrelenting genocidal campaign, keeping neighboring states quiet or impotent in the face of this heightened and accelerated blood bath. Imperial allies continue to send weapons, money, and resources. They have helped cover up genocide in the media, helped the Zionist entity with tactics, strategy, and intelligence, and continue to criminalize pro-Palestinian resistance and support. Trump has been re-elected and the rise of the right is still a growing problem.

Though some things will not end overnight, they do change in remarkable ways. The struggle is raging stronger than ever and the world has witnessed an unprecedented global intifada. The multi-pronged liberation struggle and anti-apartheid tactics have mushroomed in very important ways both in Palestine and beyond. However, a dire reality requires more than this. Seeking the end of Israeli colonialism, apartheid, and rule is not only back on the horizon, but at center-stage, and watching it fall will make all of this worth it. We are witnessing the most incredible battle of our time which will have resounding effects for the entire region and the world. Palestine has yet again challenged all settler colonial states and all imperial alliances to reckon with a changing world order. The apex of this struggle is such that it places neutrality into the hot seat and will eventually relegate Zionism to the dustbin of history.

The call for solidarity and resistance is stronger than ever. And while some parts of Asia are burning, it is the duty of those that are not to answer the call. As Ghassan Kanafani wrote,

> Imperialism has laid its body over the world, the head in Eastern Asia, the heart in the Middle East, its arteries reaching Africa and Latin America. Wherever you strike it, you damage it, and you serve the World Revolution…The Palestinian cause is not a cause for Palestinians only, but a cause for every revolutionary, wherever he is, as a cause of the exploited and oppressed masses in our era (Brehony 2017).

With every passing moment, we know we are closer to victory and liberation. It is only a matter of time.

References

Brehony, Louis. (2017) Ghassan Kanafani: Voice of Palestine (1936-1972). *The Palestine Chronicle*. https://www.palestinechronicle.com/ghassan-kanafani-voice-of-palestine-1936-1972/.

CHAPTER 17

Conclusion: Asian Futurism as Living Labour

Ian Liujia Tian

We start *Asian Canada is Burning* with an acute sense of crisis, one that is more about survival than about representative politics. Moving between material and systematic realities and personal stories, chapters in the first part tell us what it means to live in settler Canada as 'Asian'; how do life making activities take place amid violence; what political, economic, and social realities compel and construct belongings, tensions, and happiness. In this part, we collect contributions that spell more in details the histories and lived realties of Asians in Canada as labourers. Chapters in this part provide opportunities for us to think through how experiences of migrations can provide futile ground for politicizing and radicalizing Asians to question Canada's foundational myth of multiculturalism. Several contributors also deploy innovative methods to put into language the complex yet oftentimes tangential stories of Asian migrations in settler Canada.

These global uneven relations provide the background for Part 2 and 3. Chapters in section 2 feature interventions into Asian Canadian studies on issues of gender and sexuality. Deploying film analysis, quantitative interviews, archive and artistic methods, these chapters queer how and what we think as legitimate methods and areas of research, offering crucial directions for Asian Canadian inquiry. Central to this section is problematizing the imagined institutions of patriarchal family. Queerness enters these often heteronormative, gender-binary formations and intersects with racialization and civilizational discourse of 'progress/backwardness'.

While we begin this book with an introduction on solidarity, the last part responds to the questions of complicity as Asian settlers on Indigenous land, and as model minority in a society structured by anti-Black racism. Several contributors in this section are deeply committed to decolonize Asian Canadian inquiry, forging ethical relations with Indigenous peoples. Other chapters present conversations on various issues around sex worker organizing, Palestine and labour unions, and Asians' place within these global struggles. We have followed the imaginations of activists and community organizers to expand our horizon of Asian Canadian studies. While we are holding on to the specific Asian life, we have learnt that to change the social relations that organize our lives means to make new relations.

This said, this book has not sufficiently incorporated issues around environmental studies, other geographies in Canada and the Asian Francophone communities. For example, most of our contributors live in the Great Toronto Area, Vancouver and Montreal. These limits are the editors alone, but also the restrictions of making a book during the COVID-19 pandemic. With all these flaws, we want to acknowledge the deeply troubling times that we are living in, and the impossibility of responding to social issues that exceed what academic criticism can capture.

In making this book, we reflect painstakingly on how to end a book with some sort of hope in the time of crisis. And we want to return to the question of Asian labour. In an opinion piece by Jan Wong, the co-founder of Asian Canadian Women's Alliances, she discussed the discomfort of being looped into the same category as 'Asian' during Asian Heritage Month (Wong J. 2021). The inability for many people to tell 'Asians' apart from each other, for her, speak to the limits of federal push for cultural recognition. In this conclusion, however, we want to stay with the undifferentiated bodies of 'Asians'. In many ways, such sameness exemplifies Marx's abstract labour, a concept to understand how capital treats various kinds of work, or concrete labour, as interchangeable and commensurable in a labour market mediated by money (Marx [1867]1990: 131–7). For us, following Ikyo Day, abstract labor finds its embodiment in Asian labour that also become interchangeable from the side of capitalists (Day I. 2016). For instance, Filipino care workers can be easily replaced by other groups from Southeast Asia, the heterogenous lived experiences and differences of these groups are irrelevant to capitalism, thereby reducing bodies to machinic flesh.

What appears to be a representational mistake for Wong is one that says more about the fundamental global condition we live in: fetishism. The bodies of gendered, sexualized Asian labour, and racialized labour and Indigenous land more broadly, serve as practical function to settler economy and commodity exchange instead of as mere ideological effect of the system. That is, Asian labour is the embodiment of technoscientific fetish of the hyper-productive, mind-controlled human body. They function as the ideal type of human-machine synthesis, or cyborg, as defined in Donna Haraway's seminal work (Haraway 1987). In much of our contemporary capitalist culture, Asia (e.g., Japan, Singapore) symbolizes the technoscientific future of post-Fordist economy, while Asian labour exemplify the fetish for hard-working, faceless clogs in the system of global capitalist production (e.g. Chinese iPhone factories or Indian/Bangladeshi garment factories) (Bui 2020). Gendered labour in Asia become the ground for a liberal, capitalist techno fetish of on-demand, mind-controlled and hyper productive bodies under the commend of capitalist production circus.

These global techno-Orientalist fetishism about Asian labour took hold as early as the 18th century during European colonialism, and continued to North America's demand for railway labuor, sex work and other consequences of global capitalism (Roh, Huang, & Niu 2015). It is, therefore, almost inevitable for us to situate this book in these histories of fantasies to better grasp our contemporary anti-Asian racism. Part of our efforts have been to think through the social, economic, and political realities that take hold over Asian lives in Canada—the commend these realities exercise over our practical imaginations of political limits, futures, and collective happiness.

Asian labour as roboticized, human-machine pushes us to think about the question of humanity, and the claims we make about freedom, liberation and emancipation based on the framework of liberal humanism. While several theorists have perused different lines of inquiry, suggesting illiberal humanism (Chuh 2019), surrogate humanism (Vora & Atanasoski 2019), genres of human (Wynter 2003) and becoming human (Jackson Z. 2020). Our thinking focuses on the techno-fantasy of Asian labour, a fetishism of robot-like humans and human-like robots that are propercised to be our impending futures.

Yet, the very bodies on which this fantasy are built—the masses of Asian labour across the globe—speak very different dreams and desires from the liberal techno progress. Similar to the ways in which Marx describe living labour (e.g., the needs and desires of workers and producers), we find hope in the lived everyday of Asians in settler Canada: our food, sociality, communities, reproduction, desire, proximity and intimacy (Marx, [1867]1990: 648). In this book, we have followed the dreams of Japanese housewives, South Asians in Fiji, Korean missionaries, gay Asians and sex workers; explored the tensions between Asian settlers and Indigenous peoples; and underscored the relations emerge in struggles. In tracing these stories, we can comprehend how the living labour of the mechanized Asian bodies set the condition and limits of racial capitalism's extraction of Asian labour. In making this connection, we have shown the underlying antagonism inherent in the racialization and assimilation of Asians in settler Canada, and perhaps from which new hopes emerge.

If the impossibility of political optimism is not so much the scarcity of theories but the inactivation of histories in its complexities, then this book is nothing but a return to the active creations in Asian Canadian life that are already making the world differently in the here and now. And it is in highlighting the living labour of such innovations and social experiences that we find Tadia's feminist hope in the making—a hope that the future is already being built out of the techno-fantasy of Asian labour (Tadiar 2004: 265). In these practices, we might see how, through our creative daily practices, we claim a different future out of the demise of migrant labour, women, queers and differently abled Asian bodies.

References

Bui, Long (2020) Asian Roboticism. *Perspectives on Global Development* 19: 110–126.

Chuh, Kandice (2019) *The Difference Aesthetics Makes: On the Humanities "After Man".* Durham: Duke University Press.

Day, Ikyo (2016) *Alien Capital: Asian Racialization and the Logic of Settler Colonial Capitalism.* Durham: Duke University Press.

Haraway, Donna (1987) A Manifesto for Cyborgs: Science, Technology, and Socialist Feminism in the 1980s. *Australian Feminist Studies* 2(4):1–42.

Jackson, Zakiyyah (2020) *Becoming Human.* New York: NYU Press.

Marx, Karl. ([1867]1990) *Capital Volume 1.* New York: Penguin.

Roh, David S., Besty Huang, and Greta Niu (2015) *Techno-Orientalism: Imagining Asia in Speculative Fiction, History, and Media.* New Brunswick, N.J.: Rutgers University Press.

Tadiar, Neferti X.M. (2004) *Fantasy Production.* Hong Kong: Hong Kong University Press.

Vora, Kalindi, and Neda Atanasoski (2019) *Surrogate Humanity: Race, Robots, and the Politics of Technological Futures.* Durham: Duke University Press.

Wong, Jan (2021) *Is Asian Identity Even a Thing? Who Cares, Pass the Popcorn for K-drama.* CBC, May 16. https://www.cbc.ca/news/canada/first-person-asian-heritage-month-jan-wong-1.6027548.

Wynter, Sylvia (2003) Unsettling the Coloniality of Being/Power/Truth/Freedom. Towards the Human, After Man, Its overrepresentation- An Argument. *New Centennial Review* 3(3): 257–337.

Index

#MeToo movement 191

abolition 207
accumulation 90, 92
activist 161, 172
affirmative action 115
Agency 148, 155
Ahmed, Sara 29, 135
 stranger 18, 21, 25, 25*n*19, 26
algorithm 86
algorithms 85
anti-Black 42
anti-colonialism 190*n*1, 190*n*1
anti-racist 43
anti-trafficking 148, 149, 150, 151, 152, 155, 156
 human trafficking 150
 Initiatives to Address Human Trafficking 150, 151
 yellow slavery 155
Art for Social Change 111
Asian Lesbians 101, 102
asian-canadian feminisms 126

belonging 17, 18, 20, 21, 22, 23, 24, 26, 58, 59, 61, 62, 63, 64, 65, 66, 67, 68
 (un)belonging 62
Black Lives Matter movement 194, 195, 210
bodies 90, 92, 93, 94, 214, 215, 216
border 94
 border control 148, 155
Boycott, Divestment and Sanctions (BDS) 112, 203, 204, 207, 208, 209, 210
Butterfly
 Asian and Migrant Sex Worker Network 149, 150, 151, 152, 156

Canada Border Services Agency (CBSA) 151, 152
cancel culture 111
capitalism
 capitalist 4, 6, 11, 46, 48, 67, 91, 180, 214, 215
carceral politics and feminisms 148
CelebrAsian 97, 98, 103, 108
Chinatown 17, 21, 22, 27, 28, 29
Chinese Exclusion Act 154
Chinese Immigration Act 4, 154
Chinese laundries 149, 152, 153, 154, 155
Chinese Rescue Home 18, 19, 20, 29
choreography 62, 65, 66
 choreographic narrative 66
Christianity 23, 25, 28
 evangelism 19, 19*n*2, 22, 23
 heathen 24, 25
Church
 Anglican 45, 49, 56
 Catholic Church 45, 49
 Mennonite 45, 49, 57
 Roman Catholic 45, 49
 the United Church of Canada 45, 52
citizenship 17, 18, 22, 23, 24
 as cultural 22, 23
 Canadianization 25, 27
 civilization. *See* discipline
City of Toronto 150, 151, 152
coalition building 195, 198, 198*n*5, 199
collaborative art making 116
collaborative filmmaking 113
colonialism 115, 192, 198, 215
 colonial 4, 6, 8, 9
 genocide 195*n*4, 196
 residential school system 195*n*4
 settler colonialism(s) 3, 7, 8, 9, 10, 45, 46, 48, 49, 50, 52, 53, 55, 117, 180
community engaged art practices 113
conceived space. *See* space: Lefebvre's triad of space
COVID-19 1, 120, 147, 148, 155, 202
cultural appropriation 191, 192
cultural domicide 18, 19, 20, 23, 27, 28
culture 17, 19, 24, 28, 29
 whiteness 19, 21, 22

dance 60, 61, 62, 63, 64, 65, 66, 68, 69
Decolonization 49, 50, 116, 130, 133, 135, 138, 207
 decolonial 2, 51, 88, 126, 131, 135, 178, 181, 183, 184
 decolonizing 45, 46, 51, 55, 116
 postcolonial 52, 53, 54

Diaspora
  diasporic 88, 95, 126, 127, 129, 132, 140*fi*1.1, 141
diasporic messiness 122
diasporic subjectivity 121
disability 60, 61, 62, 63, 65, 66, 68, 127, 132, 133, 135
  difference of 68
  disabilities 1, 62, 132, 133, 147
  educational conceptions of 60, 61
  inclusion of 61
  social model of 61, 62
discipline 22, 23, 26
  cleanliness 20, 25
domestication. *See* discipline
domesticity 17, 19, 19*n*2, 20, 23, 24, 28
  as homemaking 19
  mimicry 26
  spatial 20
  training 22, 23, 24
  white domesticity 20, 22, 23, 26, 27, 29
domicide. *See* cultural domicide
drag 103, 104

exploitation 93, 94

familial. *See* family
family 18, 20, 22, 23, 23*n*11, 23*n*9, 24, 25*n*19
Fanon, Frantz 69
feminist
  feminism(s) 8, 47, 126, 127, 128, 129, 130, 131, 132, 133, 137, 140, 141, 148, 185, 186
Filipina American 126, 127, 129, 139
Filipina diasporic 126, 127
Filipina/x Canadian 126, 127
Filipino Asian Students' Association 133
filmmaking 113, 118
Fung, Richard 97, 98, 99, 100
future 215, 216

histories 4, 7, 10, 17, 51, 88, 97, 98, 105, 120, 122, 128, 130, 134, 140, 148, 176, 182, 184, 185, 186, 199, 210, 213, 215
home. *See* domesticity
homonationalism 116, 117, 118, 119
humanism 215

immigrants
  Asian immigrants 2, 3, 4, 5, 7, 10, 11, 12, 13, 15, 18
  Asian migrants 2, 7, 12, 18, 19
  Chinese immigrants 3, 5, 12
  Eastern European immigrants 5
  European immigrants 4, 10
immigration 1, 4, 6
  deportation 148, 151
  detention 148, 151, 153
in/visibility 127, 128
inclusion 61, 62, 64, 65, 66. *See* belonging
  accessibility as 61, 62, 64, 67*n*3
Indigenous 1, 2, 7, 8, 10, 12, 13, 14, 18
Indigenous-settler relations 10, 11, 13
inequalities 91, 92
intercultural 51, 52, 55
intersectional 114
intersectional oppression 191, 197, 198
intersectionality 114
intimacy 213, 215
Islamophobia 2

Japanese internment 4, 195*n*4, 196

kapwa 133, 134, 135, 138, 139, 140, 141
Komagata Maru 4

labour 1, 4, 5, 8, 9, 10, 11, 89, 90, 91, 92, 93, 94, 159, 160, 160*n*3, 160*n*5, 161, 162, 163, 164, 165, 165*n*8, 166, 167, 168, 169, 170, 171, 172, 173, 174, 175, 176, 177, 213
Lefebvre. *See* space
LGBTQ+ 88, 89, 93
lived space. *See* space: Lefebvre's triad of space
Live-in Caregiver Program (LCP) 48, 167
loss of community. *See* cultural domicide
loss of culture. *See* cultural domicide
Love Intersections 110, 111, 112, 113, 116, 117, 122

massage parlour workers 147, 148, 149, 150, 151, 152, 154, 155, 156
McGill University 125, 127, 133, 143
metonymy 17, 22, 23
migration
  immigration 88, 89, 90, 91, 93, 94
  migrants 1, 4, 7, 8, 12, 89, 90, 91, 93
  migrant women 147, 149, 155
mimicry 17, 19, 20, 22, 26, 27
model minority 42, 43
multicultural 39, 46, 51, 55, 64, 65, 67, 86, 122, 127, 182

multiculturalism 59, 64, 65, 69, 109, 115, 122
municipal by-laws 149, 150, 151, 152, 153, 154, 155, 156

organize
  organizing 159*n*2, 162, 163, 167

Palestine 10, 113, 202, 203, 204, 205, 206, 207, 208, 209, 210, 211
pedagogies 11
perceived space. *See* space: Lefebvre's triad of space
Philippines 59, 59*n*1, 63*n*2, 68
  Filipino 59, 59*n*1, 59*n*1, 64, 68, 70
  Filipinx/Filipin*/Filipin@ 59*n*1
pinay power II 125, 125*n*2, 127
pinkwashing 112, 206
policing 148, 151, 155
political organizing 115
power 89, 91, 93, 94
praxis 9, 126, 133, 135, 182
Protection of Communities and Exploited Persons Act 150
public health 148, 153, 155

queer 6, 9, 10, 88, 89, 90, 91, 92, 93, 94
queer diaspora 119
queer diasporic futurity 120
queer diasporic identity 120
queer kinship 122
queer of colour imaginations 118

racial hierarchies. *See* social order
racialized
  racial 159, 159*n*1, 160, 161, 162, 163, 163*n*7, 164, 164*n*7, 165, 166, 167, 168, 169, 170, 171, 174, 175, 176
racism 154, 160, 161, 164, 165, 166, 168, 169, 170, 172, 174, 175, 176, 177, 196, 213, 215
  anti-Asian racism 194
  anti-Black racism 193, 193*n*3, 196
  anti-Chinese racism 194, 195*n*4, 196
  anti-racism 1, 2, 2*n*1, 4, 7, 8, 10, 11
representation 115

Sanctuary City 151
Saranillio, Dean Itsuji 69
settler colonialism 7, 9, 10
settler state 88, 89, 91, 93, 94
sex workers 147, 148, 149, 150, 151, 152, 154, 155, 156
settlers
  white Christian settlers 51
  white settlers 45, 49, 50, 92
sexism 154
social order 21, 23
social work 43
social worker 42
solidarity 5, 6, 7, 9, 10, 46, 49, 51, 52, 53, 55, 85, 86, 110, 112, 116, 148, 149, 151, 152, 156, 164, 168, 168, 169, 174, 175, 178, 179, 182, 183, 185, 186, 199, 202, 203, 204, 205, 207, 208, 209, 210, 211, 213
space 17, 18, 19, 19*n*2, 20, 21, 26
  Lefebvre's triad of space 20, 21, 22
  See space
surveillance 148, 150, 151, 153
systemic oppression 191
  male privilege 197

theories
  theorizing 5, 9, 100, 120, 125, 129, 198
Thobani, Sunera 69
Titchkosky, Tanya 69, 70
training
  as domestic 20
  economic opportunities 21
  social order. *See* social order
  spiritual 24
  whiteness 21
truth and reconciliation 45, 63, 65, 178
  Truth and Reconciliation Commission of Canada (TRC) 45

union
  unionization 159, 160, 161, 162, 163, 164, 165, 166, 167, 168, 169, 170, 171, 172, 173, 175
universal design for learning (UDL) 61, 62

violence 91, 93, 94

white 45, 47, 48, 52
  white civilization 47
  white identity 45
  white national identity 46
  white norm 48
  white society 47, 121

white supremacist 43, 119, 115, 175, 194, 195, 196, 198
white supremacy 3, 8, 17, 42, 43, 44, 67, 114, 115, 116, 121, 169, 174, 204
whorephobia 154
work
  worker 159, 160*n*3, 162, 163, 165, 166, 167, 169, 170, 171, 172, 174, 175, 214, 215

xenophobia 154

Yellow Peril: Queer Destiny 118, 119, 120, 121

www.ingramcontent.com/pod-product-compliance
Lightning Source LLC
LaVergne TN
LVHW021550230526
839611LV00034B/460